FOR
BLOOD
AND
MONEY

FOR
BLOOD
AND
MONEY

BILLIONAIRES, BIOTECH, AND THE QUEST FOR A BLOCKBUSTER DRUG

NATHAN
VARDI

W. W. NORTON & COMPANY
Celebrating a Century of Independent Publishing

For information about permission to reproduce selections from this book, write to
Permissions, W. W. Norton & Company, Inc., 500 Fifth Avenue, New York, NY 10110

For information about special discounts for bulk purchases, please contact
W. W. Norton Special Sales at specialsales@wwnorton.com or 800-233-4830

Manufacturing by Lake Book Manufacturing
Book design by Beth Steidle
Production manager: Anna Oler

ISBN 978-0-393-54095-6

W. W. Norton & Company, Inc., 500 Fifth Avenue, New York, N.Y. 10110
www.wwnorton.com

W. W. Norton & Company Ltd., 15 Carlisle Street, London W1D 3BS

1 2 3 4 5 6 7 8 9 0

For all the patients who volunteer to participate in clinical trials.

CONTENTS

PART III

PROLOGUE

Sidelines

hmed Hamdy sat in his car staring at the Fry's Electronics store sign. He wasn't sure how long he had been sitting there, but it felt like forever. Paralyzed by shock, Hamdy tried to absorb what had just happened. He had just been blindsided by his boss and fired.

From where he was parked, he could see the headquarters of his former company. Just minutes ago, Hamdy had been escorted out of the building to his car by the head of human resources. She kept watch until Hamdy drove off the corporate parking lot. This morning Hamdy had been the upstart biotechnology company's chief medical officer. The company was filled with the kind of change-the-world enthusiasm that can only be found in Silicon Valley. He had devoted every moment of the last two years to thinking about it, growing it, leading it. Now he felt like a trespasser, even a criminal. He didn't know where he was supposed to go.

In fact, he couldn't bring himself to go anywhere. Bewildered, Hamdy had barely been able to drive, so he had turned into the massive Fry's Electronics parking lot 500 feet away from his old office. Fry's had been founded right here in Sunnyvale, California, and had become a Silicon Valley institution, a kind of techie candy store where budding visionaries would buy their first PC and geek out over processors and routers. It was a symbol of Northern California optimism. An optimism that Hamdy felt quickly fading.

There, in his car, he thought a lot about money. Things would get tight. He would need to sell his corporate stock. He thought about his family. He had no idea what he was going to tell them. Then, Hamdy started thinking about the drug. A profound sense of loss swept over him.

The office park next door, where Hamdy used to work, housed the main offices of Pharmacyclics. Few people had ever heard of the tiny biotechnology company. Those who had heard of it, through the Silicon Valley biotechnology grapevine, knew it to be a weird place. The company was focused on an experimental treatment for blood cancer. They were early in the drug development process and had a long way to go to prove themselves and their new drug. But Hamdy was a true believer. He had been certain that the cancer treatment, his drug, was something special. It was going to work. The drug would have a life-changing impact. It would keep people from dying. It would make him a wealthy man. All of that was taken from him in an instant. Never again, Hamdy thought, would he get another opportunity like this. His emotions were a mix of self-pity, depression, fear, and fury. It was May 2011, and that morning Hamdy had believed he was at the forefront of the battle against cancer. Now he wasn't even a player.

From personal experience, Hamdy understood that developing cancer drugs was like buying a lottery ticket. Most cancer drug researchers were stumbling around in the dark. Occasionally, a variety of factors—including luck—came together to produce a winning treatment. It was a game of overwhelmingly negative odds. The vast majority of novel cancer drugs tested in patients failed.

But Hamdy sensed that new technologies and approaches were about to unleash a biotechnology revolution and that Pharmacyclics' cancer drug would be part of a medical science golden age. Specifically, Hamdy had seen the drug trigger a faint signal in patients with the most common form of adult leukemia. The drug was a small molecule that medical science referred to as a BTK inhibitor. It targeted and infiltrated malignant cells and blocked an enzyme that Hamdy believed helped cancer cells multiply and stay alive. It was just a subtle signal, but for Hamdy it was enough.

The drug was not new. For a time it had been completely neglected and forgotten at the bottom of a test tube where it had been created. There were many great drugs trapped in the pipelines of pharmaceutical companies, waiting for someone to discover them like buried treasure. Even after years of innovation, good drugs languished in the bellies of big conglomerates, bureaucracies too burdened with their own processes and procedures to identify and develop these tiny gems. These drugs could be fished out for pennies on the dollar and developed. And that's what dreams are made of. You just needed the vision to make it happen—and the money. That's how Pharmacyclics, almost by accident, had ended up with its BTK inhibitor.

The money, however, came with strings. Hamdy's anger slowly started to crystallize around a singular man who pulled them.

PART I

CHAPTER 1

The Surfing Scientologist

On Super Bowl Sunday 1997, much of America watched Drew Bledsoe and the New England Patriots play Brett Favre and the Green Bay Packers. As the big game was taking place in New Orleans, a family tragedy that had been playing out about an hour's drive away was concluding.

At age twenty-six, Demian Duggan looked up from his hospital bed and told his father he was ready to die.

"I can feel it here," Demian said. "All I got to do is acquiesce and I'm gone."

Robert Duggan looked at his only son and told him he was there for him. "You have the freedom to do that. I'm right here," Duggan responded.

Originally from Southern California, Demian had packed a lot into his life. A freestyle swimmer on the University of California, Santa Barbara, swim team, he had been assigned a roommate from Croatia, a backstroke specialist. The two swimmers hit it off and spent a summer touring Croatia just as the central European country was emerging from the breakup of communist Yugoslavia. When he returned from the adventure, Demian told his father he was dropping out of school and starting a billboard company in Croatia. Demian had an optimistic American vision for the postcommunist world. He wanted to be like Ted Turner and build a new media empire.

"They're transitioning, they're going to have to promote and advertise, they're going to need a Madison Avenue," Demian exclaimed to his father. "Communism doesn't have a Madison Avenue!"

Duggan could hardly deny his son. He himself had dropped out of UCSB and found stunning business success. Duggan made one demand. He insisted that Demian go to Los Angeles and spend six months at the World Institute of Scientology Enterprises. It offered courses on the business methods of L. Ron Hubbard, the science fiction writer who founded the Church of Scientology. Duggan credited these methods for his own business success.

Demian completed the coursework, moved to Croatia, and built a billboard advertising company with the financial backing of his father. Metropolis Media became a success, putting up ten thousand double-sided outdoor billboards throughout postcommunist Croatia, Slovenia, Serbia, Bosnia, and Macedonia. Demian also fell in love, marrying a Croatian woman whose family helped get the business off the ground.

Unfortunately, a tumor had started growing in Demian's brain. By the time the tumor was the size of a thumb, Demian returned to Southern California. The devastating diagnosis was glioblastoma, a brain cancer with a median survival time of 15 months if treated with surgery and chemotherapy.

Duggan arranged for Demian to have surgery at Santa Barbara Cottage Hospital to remove as much of the tumor as possible. But both Duggan and his son balked at the next standard step of care, follow-up chemotherapy and radiation. Duggan had seen relatives and others go through chemotherapy and was convinced it would only make a bad disease worse. Duggan hated chemotherapy and in this instance he didn't believe it would make much of a difference.

Instead, Duggan connected with a man he had tracked down in Louisiana who had come up with an alternative treatment—a proprietary protein mixture given daily that was far from prescribed medicine. Demian started doing better and returned to Croatia but stopped the alternative treatment because it was too time consuming. He eventually came back to the United States as the cancer overwhelmed him.

Duggan believed that the alternative treatment had worked before it was stopped and took Demian to Baton Rouge, Louisiana, to try again. Within a short period of time, Demian had to check into the hospital.

At the hospital, Duggan took the night shift and continued to administer the protein serum, while his wife, Patricia Duggan, took the day shift.

On the same day the Green Bay Packers rolled to a Super Bowl win, Demian told his father he was spiritually prepared to leave because he knew he was more than just a body. Scientologists believe they are taking a scientific approach to enlightenment, and Demian's words were consistent with the core Scientology belief that the being is immortal and separate from the body.

"I'm a spiritual being and this body is not cutting it," Demian said. He asked his father to do certain things, particularly adopt other children, through which he could live on.

That night, Duggan watched Demian die. Afterward, struck with grief, Duggan went to the Church of Scientology's spiritual headquarters in Clearwater, Florida, to receive counseling. There, he came to terms with the devastating loss and gave himself a pep talk.

"I had twenty-six unbelievable years with him. He's still around. He wants to come back," Duggan thought to himself. "What am I going to do here, sit and mope? I'm going to go on with life and follow his instruction. And I got to get busy doing that."

///////////////

ROBERT W. DUGGAN WAS not destined to lead a biotechnology company. He had no scientific training and no experience in the highly regulated biopharma industry. Zero. The companies in the sector were generally led by gray-haired men, often with MDs or other advanced degrees, who had climbed corporate and academic ladders for decades. Duggan didn't even have a college diploma.

But at the age of fifty-two, what Duggan had was a track record of business success and supreme confidence in himself. He literally believed he could accomplish anything if he put his mind to it.

Duggan had grown up in the area between San Jose, California, and San Francisco that is now known as Silicon Valley. When Duggan was attending Catholic school in the early 1950s, Santa Clara County was mostly an agricultural community dotted with orchards and fruit canneries, but that was starting to change. Duggan's Irish Catholic father was an industrial engineer making $800 a month at Westinghouse Electric Corporation, and his mother was a nurse. They raised their five children in a small house in San Jose, four doors down from the Santa Clara border.

As a child, Duggan found more success on the athletic field than in the classroom. He had a photographic memory and a mesmerizing grasp of numbers, but his grades were just decent and not great. He had a hard time concentrating on schoolwork, often turning to sports out of frustration and to channel his energy. Like many kids, he learned to read by skimming the newspaper's sports section.

At St. Francis High School in Mountain View, California, Duggan played on the basketball team. His family had enough to get by, but if he wanted to buy something extra, he had to earn the money himself. By mowing lawns and selling apricots, the young man scrounged up enough cash to order a surfboard from a Sears Roebuck catalog. He loved taking the surfboard to the beaches around Santa Cruz.

With ocean waves just steps from campus, UCSB was the perfect college for Duggan. He went there in 1962 to learn business economics because he had a vague notion about a future in business. The school part was a frustrating experience. Duggan struggled to relate to coursework he found overly theoretical. With a mischievous side, he once answered a test question on the economic theory of the Lorenz curve by describing Sophia Loren, the bombshell actress. Duggan was far more focused when it came to surfing, playing basketball and badminton, and having a good time. He started dating his future wife, Patricia "Trish" Hagerty, and loved college life outside the classroom.

Inside the classroom, Duggan remained lost until his junior year, when he took a corporate finance class taught by Herbert C. Kay. A popular lecturer on campus, Kay connected with his student and filled him with an enthusiasm for stock market investment analysis. With Kay, Duggan found the course material practical as opposed to the abstract concepts that seemed to dominate his other classes. Kay's corporate finance instruction could help him succeed in the real world. Suddenly, Duggan knew what he wanted to pursue in life.

There was one problem. Like other men on campus, there was a looming event hovering over Duggan the entire time he was in college. The Vietnam War. Duggan wanted no part of it. In 1966, staying in school remained a possible path to deferring army service, but Duggan's college days were coming to an end and his grades were not good enough for him to go to graduate school. To dodge the war and stay out of Southeast Asia, he came up with a creative plan. He dropped out of UCSB in his senior year.

Local draft boards sometimes gave students who hadn't graduated additional time to get their college degrees before being forced to go to Vietnam. After dropping out at UCSB, Duggan enrolled as an undergraduate at the University of California, Los Angeles. The gambit won him two more years of deferments. By the time the Selective Service System came calling again in 1968, Duggan was married with a new baby daughter, effectively keeping him in Los Angeles and out of the war.

While taking classes at UCLA, Duggan moonlighted as a stock speculator. He had teamed up with Kay, and they started trading stocks together. They focused on the shares of small companies that were being issued to investors for the first time through initial public offerings (IPOs). The duo found that investment bankers were often pric-ing IPOs at a discount to ingratiate themselves with customers. Kay mentored Duggan in conducting exhaustive research and visiting the companies he was considering as an investment.

One of Duggan's best trades was buying shares of Ponderosa Steak House. He invested after traveling to the chain's Dayton, Ohio, headquarters and seeing people lined up outside on a snowy night to get into one of its restaurants. "Holy shit!" Duggan said to himself. "This is a really good indicator." The stock soared. Duggan leveraged his bets over many investments and within two years made close to $500,000, equivalent to about $3.4 million in 2022. He never got that college degree.

The early 1970s were heady times for the Duggans. They moved to the Topanga Beach neighborhood and Duggan kept an office in nearby Santa Monica. He would spend his evenings playing Frisbee or base-ball on the beach. Trim and fit with wavy black hair, Duggan even ran the odd marathon. Patricia's sister, Nancy Hagerty, and her husband, Daniel Patterson, a member of the US Olympic volleyball team, often crashed at the beach house. Duggan and Patterson became fast friends. It was a great life.

Demian was born in 1971. That same year, Duggan put up $50,000 for a 50 percent stake in a new macramé business called Sunset Designs. It evolved into a company that sold Jiffy Stitchery needlepoint kits for people to use for home projects. Duggan came up with the corporate strategy after reading a newspaper article about the Federal Trade Com-mission's 1972 action accusing the nation's four biggest cereal compa-nies of monopolizing the cereal market. Ralph Nader, the revolutionary consumer advocate, called the government's case "one of the most important developments in antitrust enforcement in the last decade."

For Duggan, it was the cereal companies that were inspiring. "Wow, isn't that the goal of every business to get to monopoly?" Dug-gan thought. "Isn't that the winner's circle?"

Duggan got the government's complaint and read it. The complaint accused the Kellogg Company and General Mills of using deceptive trade practices like flooding grocery stores with similar products and controlling prime shelf space to block competition. Duggan used the government's complaint as a blueprint for Sunset Designs. "Guys, we need to do these things," he told his partners. Soon, Duggan's company was marketing thirty-three different Jiffy Stitchery Kits, instead of just three. Sunset Designs went on to dominate the market and was sold a few years later for $15 million.

///////////////

AS THE 1970S ROLLED on, Duggan remained restless. For those who encountered him, conversations with the entrepreneur tended not to be linear. He was always brimming with ideas and excitement and would go off on tangents, sometimes leaving people unsure about what they were really discussing. He lost about 80 percent of his net worth in 1974 amid the brutal stock market crash and started to question himself. The thriving Los Angeles counterculture scene gave him and Patricia, herself an artist, opportunities to experiment through pragmatic self-help concepts that appealed to them both. Duggan attended Werner Erhard's EST seminars and was roused. Later, Duggan found his way to the writings of L. Ron Hubbard.

Duggan first read Hubbard's writings on business administration and found them appealing. He also picked up *Dianetics: The Modern Science of Mental Health*, Hubbard's best-selling book. But it was Hubbard's technology of study course that really resonated with Duggan. For a guy who struggled with school and maintaining focus, Hubbard's message that speed-reading and rote memorization were not the way to comprehend a subject made a lot of sense. Hubbard's course promised an approach to learning that could help anyone learn any subject. Duggan took to heart Hubbard's ideas of breaking down complex notions into simple concepts and regularly looking up the definitions of words. Duggan began devoutly consulting dictionaries, convinced misunderstanding a single word could lead to disaster. He would frequently define terms and reference etymology during conversation.

More than anything else, Duggan drew inspiration from an article that was published in 1980 in the *National Enquirer*. "Everybody reads it, but nobody says they read it," Duggan would say of the tabloid newspaper. The article focused on Alfred Barrios, a Los Angeles psychologist who developed self-actualization seminars (and, coincidentally, worked on using hypnosis to heal cancer). Barrios had come up with a list of twenty-four personality characteristics that geniuses have in common and argued in the article that adopting these traits could empower anyone to operate on a genius level, regardless of their education or experience. Hubbard wanted his followers to know these twenty-four qualities and issued an executive directive that republished the article. A member of the Church had recommended the article to Duggan. It implored people seeking greatness to work hard, have the courage to do things others consider impossible, continually accumulate information, and never doubt they would succeed.

Duggan decided he wanted to build a business with his brother-in-law. "We got to do something together, Danny!" Duggan would exclaim to his Olympic athlete brother-in-law, Dan Patterson. They decided to open a Hot Dog on a Stick franchise stand at the outdoor Marina Pacifica mall in Long Beach. One day, Duggan came bursting through the door. "I saw the most amazing thing at the Fox Hills Mall," Duggan bellowed. "People are lining up to eat cookies!" The brothers-in-law pivoted almost immediately.

Duggan concocted a recipe with his sister-in-law, Nancy Hagerty, that kept the cookies soft. They abandoned the hot dogs and focused on a stand called Cookie Munchers Paradise. Duggan had one rule: no coffee. He detested coffee. Always thinking big, Duggan wanted to open thirty-six stores in thirty-six months. He financed the operation and would often barrel in, put on an apron, and get busy. "If people taste these fucking chocolate chip cookies they are going to buy the sucker," Duggan would say. He started standing outside with a sample tray, convincing people to buy cookies. A terrific people person, his over-the-top enthusiasm could be infectious.

After three years, behind the ambitious initial forecast, Duggan and Patterson had opened sixteen locations. Duggan suggested they add a few menu items, like sandwiches, and call their company Paradise Bakery because mall operators at the time were charging bakeries lower rents than cookie stores, which had become popular. Patterson was shocked by how much the name change improved profitability. They sold the chain to Chart House Enterprises for $6 million. Nancy Hagerty divorced Patterson and went on to wholesale similar soft and chewy cookies to McDonald's.

///////////////

BY 1990, DUGGAN HAD made enough of a name for himself through his investing activities that he was invited to serve on the board of trustees of the UCSB Foundation, the main fundraising arm of the university from which he had dropped out. He was also in the Ethernet business through Communication Machinery Corporation, investing in the company and becoming its chairman. It made a computer networking technology used for establishing local area networks. The company ended up being sold to Rockwell Automation for $40 million in stock, giving Duggan a $15 million after-tax payday.

Through his UCSB network, Duggan met Yulun Wang, a UCSB computer engineering PhD. Wang convinced Duggan to back a new company, Computer Motion, that would make robots for outer space. NASA never wanted the robots. But a Santa Barbara surgeon who knew Duggan thought people in his line of work would be interested in them. Yulun and Duggan changed course and Computer Motion started making medical robots. The robots assisted surgeons in moving endoscopes to look and take stable images inside the bodies of patients during minimally invasive procedures.

Duggan became CEO around the time Computer Motion conducted an IPO, which was, all these years into his frenetic business existence, a few months after cancer had claimed Demian.

It was Duggan's foray in the healthcare industry. He started to proselytize his ideas about "patient- and physician-friendly" surgical techniques that he believed Computer Motion was pioneering. The company generated $24 million of annual revenues, and its operations in Strasbourg, France, led President Jacques Chirac to award Duggan the French Republic's Legion of Honor.

Nevertheless, Computer Motion lost money and faced a larger and better competitor, Intuitive Surgical. But Computer Motion had some early patents for its robot system and sued Intuitive Surgical for patent infringement. So to solve the patent litigation, Intuitive Surgical bought Computer Motion in a $150 million deal in 2003. For Duggan, the deal came just in time. The situation was so precarious at Computer Motion that Duggan made sure the company got a $7.3 million loan from Intuitive Surgical so it could stay afloat during the time between signing the deal and closing it.

///////////////

WITH THE SALE OF Computer Motion locked in, Duggan was free to focus on a new project. He remained a board member of Intuitive Surgical, but the Intuitive Surgical executives had essentially taken over the operation of the company. Duggan would eventually sell most of his Intuitive Surgical stock. At age sixty, he had a net worth of about $65 million and ran a small investment advisory firm, Robert W. Duggan & Associates, that had a few dozen clients. Mostly, he invested his own money out of an office in Santa Barbara. He was also well on his way to becoming the biggest and most important financial donor to the Church of Scientology, including funding a program to place *Dianetics* in libraries all over the United States.

Around this time, Duggan turned his attention to a small biotechnology company called Pharmacyclics. The company was based in

Sunnyvale, California, not far from his childhood home. But that was not why it was interesting to Duggan.

For years, Pharmacyclics had been trying to develop motexafin gadolinium, a drug designed to make cancer cells more susceptible to radiation, thereby enhancing the impact of radiation therapy. The company had been testing the drug, also known by its brand name, Xcytrin, specifically in brain cancer.

With his late son, Demian, on his mind, Duggan felt a connection to what Pharmacyclics was trying to accomplish. He started buying Pharmacyclics shares.

As he accumulated Pharmacyclics stock in 2004, Duggan thought it was time to introduce himself to the company's chief executive officer. He decided to give Richard Miller a call.

CHAPTER 2

Man of Science

Richard Miller considered himself to be a man of science. He was exactly the kind of person Bob Duggan wasn't—an MD and Stanford University clinical professor, who was very much a biotechnology insider. Miller was even married to Sandra Horning, a Stanford oncology guru slated to be the next president of the prestigious American Society of Clinical Oncology.

At age fifty-four, Miller was the cofounder and CEO of Pharmacyclics, a small biotechnology company with a stock that had plunged. Out of the blue, he got a call from Bob Duggan, a man he had never heard of before. Duggan said he had been buying Pharmacyclics stock and would like to meet. Miller had desperately been trying to defend Pharmacyclics to a skeptical Wall Street and was looking for new shareholders.

Miller said he would be happy to set up an appointment.

Duggan had done some homework on Miller. Short with a bald head and glasses, Miller had made a big name for himself in Silicon Valley, playing an important role in the development of a groundbreaking cancer therapy. Duggan found him to be self-assured, passionate, and sharp.

At the meeting in Miller's office in Sunnyvale, Duggan told Miller about how his son, Demian, had suffered from a brain tumor and died at age twenty-six. He said he was interested in Pharmacyclics as an investor—and as a person—because the company was targeting brain cancer. He also went through his business background, including Computer Motion, which had just been sold.

Miller was moved by Duggan's story and described the state of Pharmacyclics' clinical trials. The company's big study to test its lead drug candidate, Xcytrin, in patients with different kinds of cancer that spread to the brain had failed miserably, tanking Pharmacyclics' stock. The trial had been a later-stage study that Miller had hoped would lead the US public health regulator responsible for ensuring the safety and efficacy of medicines, the Food and Drug Administration, or FDA, to approve the drug for the US market. Amid the disappointment, Miller had fixated on indications that the drug showed some promise in a subgroup of patients—those whose lung cancer had spread to the brain. This led Pharmacyclics to start enrolling 550 patients in a new late-stage trial that Miller thought could confirm the clinical benefits observed in this patient subgroup.

Duggan liked that Pharmacyclics was going after brain cancer. Pharmacyclics even had an earlier-stage study of Xyctrin in patients with glioblastoma, the specific brain cancer Demian had endured. Miller sized Duggan up and figured he was a good guy. He came away from the meeting thinking that Duggan didn't know any science, but that he was a man driven to find treatments for brain cancer patients because of his deep emotional connection to the legacy and memory of his son. Miller also surmised that Duggan was rich and that Pharmacyclics' stock was attractive to him because it was cheap.

Not too long after their initial meeting, Miller got another call from Duggan, who said he had bought more Pharmacyclics stock and wanted to ask more questions. Duggan talked to Miller from time to time and continued purchasing more Pharmacyclics stock. By September 2004, Duggan had bought nearly a million shares, 5 percent of Pharmacyclics, worth about $10 million at the time, given that the stock hovered around $10 a share. Miller thought he had found an ally.

///////////////////

RICHARD A. MILLER LOVED medicine and baseball. He had grown up playing stickball on the streets of Newark, New Jersey, and played college baseball for Franklin & Marshall College, where he majored in chemistry. With a medical degree already in his back pocket, Miller showed up at Stanford University in Palo Alto, California, and started doing work in the mid-1970s on cancers of the infection-fighting cells of the immune system, the human body's biological defense network.

Stanford had become a research powerhouse in lymphoma, a cancer of the blood. There are different types of lymphoma, but they all start in the white blood cells of the immune system called lymphocytes, usually either B cells or T cells, that become malignant and grow out of control.

Ron Levy, a star at Stanford, brought Miller onto a bleeding-edge research project looking at something called monoclonal antibodies. These are synthetic proteins engineered in the lab from both humans and mice that galvanize the immune system to attack cancer cells and other diseases. Monoclonal antibodies potentially offered a way to treat lymphoma.

Levy and Miller were excited enough that they founded a company to commercialize the technology and later, in 1985, teamed up with others to found Idec Pharmaceuticals. They found it easy to raise money from big venture capitalists on Sand Hill Road, close to Stanford's campus. Their funding was led by Brook Byers, of the distinguished firm Kleiner Perkins Caufield & Byers, who brought in a professional CEO.

Thirteen years later, Idec would produce rituximab, the first monoclonal antibody approved by the FDA for treating cancer, specifically non-Hodgkin's lymphoma. It would be sold under the brand name Rituxan. When Idec originally started up, Levy stayed on at Stanford, but Miller left the university and joined Idec at its founding to run research. Just in case the biotechnology thing didn't work out, Miller kept on practicing medicine part-time at Stanford Medical Center. Miller enjoyed helping patients and would continue the practice of seeing them one afternoon per week for the rest of his career.

One of Miller's cancer patients was Jonathan Sessler. Their relationship had already spanned many years, as Miller had first started treating Sessler while Miller was still an attending physician at Stanford. At the time, Sessler was working toward his Stanford chemistry PhD. Sessler had been diagnosed in college with lymphoma, which had been successfully treated with radiation, but when he first showed up at Miller's clinic, the young doctor had to break the news to Sessler that his cancer had returned. Miller treated Sessler with six months of brutal chemotherapy. It was so bad, Sessler would reflexively start throwing up before his chemo appointments.

As difficult as it was for Sessler, the treatment worked and he became a chemistry professor at the University of Texas at Austin. But his cancer experience left an indelible mark and motivated him to apply his knowledge of chemistry to cancer therapies. Sessler continued to see Miller for follow-up appointments and during his clinic visits would update Miller on his latest work and ideas.

At one appointment, Sessler described his synthesizing of new ring-shaped molecules that could hold heavy metals like gadolinium at their core, potentially making tumor cells more sensitive to radiation. He thought they could be designed to accumulate selectively in cancer cells. The shape of these molecules reminded Sessler of the five-pointed star in the state flag of Texas, so he named them texaphryns. Miller was intrigued. Making radiation therapy more effective would be a game changer for cancer treatment. "Jonathan, we can start a company on this," he said.

In 1991, Miller left Idec and together with Sessler started Pharmacyclics. He raised money from the same venture capitalists who backed Idec, and this time Miller got to run the show as CEO. He was excited and believed in the texaphryn approach and the resulting drug Xcytrin. So did Wall Street. By 2000, Pharmacyclics was a publicly traded company with a stock that changed hands for $80 and a market valuation of more than $1 billion.

But when Xcytrin failed its broad, late-stage trial, the stock tumbled. Then, in December 2005, after Duggan started buying Pharmacyclics stock and first met Miller, Xcytrin failed its second pivotal trial, the late-stage study testing Xcytrin only in patients with brain metastases from lung cancer.

As a lover of baseball, Miller knew what this meant. Xcytrin now had two strikes, and Miller needed someone to throw him a pitch he could hit.

///////////////

J. CRAIG VENTER CAME to South San Francisco, California, the birthplace of biotechnology, to start a revolution he believed would change the industry forever. In 2000, he had famously stood next to Bill Clinton in the East Room of the White House as the US president announced a monumental scientific breakthrough. A maverick geneticist, Venter founded Celera Genomics and, as its president and chief scientific officer, led its quest to sequence the map of the human genome. It was a momentous scientific race that pitted Venter against the Human Genome Project, lavishly funded by the US government. Venter's competition pushed the Human Genome Project to work faster to decode the genetic blueprint of human beings. In the end, Celera and the Human Genome Project came together at the White House to jointly announce they had successfully mapped the human genome.

Venter thought that the map of the human genome could be mined for practical purposes, revealing mysteries that would lead to the development of new medicines and disease cures. Wall Street bought into this idea, and Celera's stock soared to a market valuation of $14 billion. To get into the drug business itself, Celera used its high-flying stock as currency in 2001 to buy a company called Axys Pharmaceuticals for $174 million.

Axys' headquarters and its adjacent 43,500-square-foot chemistry building were based in South San Francisco, the heart of the biotechnology world. The industry had blossomed along the western shore of San Francisco Bay after the foundational biotech company, Genentech, set up shop in the city's industrial area east of Highway 101. Genentech led the way in creating synthetic insulin and was the first biotech company to raise money from venture capitalists and conduct an initial public offering in the stock market; the company's stock pioneered the biotech investing sector. The new market opened an important funding mechanism for smaller companies narrowly focusing on new medicinal breakthroughs, and it gave investors the opportunity to bet on high-risk, high-reward companies developing as little as one or two drugs. If the drugs panned out, investors could make a huge score, but the companies had the opposite of a diversified product portfolio. If their main drug failed, there was nothing to cushion the failure. This differed substantially from pharmaceutical companies, whose stocks were buoyed by a portfolio of different drugs.

Venter traveled from Celera's headquarters in Rockville, Maryland, to South San Francisco to share his fresh vision for biotechnology that would fuse medical science with software and algorithms. He told the fifty-five chemists and biologists at Axys that Celera wanted to make drugs in a new and improved way. The old methods used by the likes of Genentech and big pharma depended too much on messy human creativity, luck, and serendipity. They would be overtaken by the precision and knowledge that could only be found in big scientific data and computer-driven analytics. The idea was to have Celera use insights collected from all its genetic decoding to hone in on specific biological targets and have the chemists at Axys design potential drugs for them. Celera would figure out which experimental drugs would be effective by simulating how they interacted with genes and proteins, bolstering the success rate of in-human drug trials to 1 in 3 instead of 1 in 10.

If Venter was right, Celera could eliminate billions spent on trials that went nowhere. To be approved by the FDA, a drug had to travel through a regulatory thicket of preclinical tests in the lab and in animals. Then, clinical studies had to be conducted in human beings: phase 1 trials that test the drug in a small number of patients, maybe as few as twenty individuals; phase 2 trials that gauge the drug's safety and effectiveness in a larger group of patients; and big phase 3 trials that often compare the drug against other treatments to gain regulatory approval. For a single drug, the cost of all these trials could exceed $1 billion. Venter claimed he could create a more rational and efficient way for developing drugs.

The Axys chemists more or less rolled their eyes. They knew the path to success in drug development was insanely complex and thought Venter's ideas seemed far-fetched. Indeed, nothing much happened after Venter's whirlwind visit. The founder returned to Maryland, and within a year he had left Celera. The Axys chemists simply went back to business as usual, pursuing new research concepts and making compounds in the same way they had done before.

Around 2002, some of those Axys chemists began focusing on the hot new field of tyrosine kinase inhibitors.

There are hundreds of different kinases in the human body, enzymes that play crucial roles in catalyzing cell development, communication, and division. One group of these enzymes, tyrosine kinases, control a lot of the on/off growth decisions within a cell. When these switches get fouled up, cells can begin to grow out of control, sometimes producing tumors.

A tyrosine kinase inhibitor does exactly what it says; it blocks the enzyme from switching anything on or off. It fixes the broken switch.

At Celera, a small group of chemists started thinking about inhibiting an enzyme called Bruton's tyrosine kinase, thinking such an endeavor could contribute to a treatment for rheumatoid arthritis, the painful disorder that makes the joints in the hands and feet ache.

Known by its acronym, BTK, Bruton's tyrosine kinase is a signaling enzyme. It helps B cells develop into fully functioning cells that fight off infection and multiply. But overactive B cells can sometimes trigger the immune system. Instead of protecting the body, the immune system produces inflammatory cells and antibodies that end up attacking healthy body tissue, causing autoimmune conditions like rheumatoid arthritis. The drug developers at Celera viewed rheumatoid arthritis as a lucrative market and thought that blocking BTK could be a way to stop the proliferation of overactive B cells that cause inflammation.

To nail down the biology of BTK, the chemists decided to build covalent warheads, small molecules that irreversibly bind, or stick, to their target. At the time, the drug industry overwhelmingly shunned covalent compounds precisely because of their permanence. Scientists preferred drugs that bind to their targets and let go. Despite this, the group wanted to synthesize covalent compounds, but only as probes to figure out what inhibiting BTK did to the cellular system and to validate the enzyme as a target. These covalent compounds were meant to be tools, not viable drug candidates. With an eye toward developing an actual drug, the group at Celera also synthesized inhibitors that did not stick to BTK.

In the middle of this highly technical work, a young, creative chemist in the group, Zhengying Pan, had an idea for a compound and charged into the office of Paul Sprengeler, a computational chemist. A tall burly man with a mop top of black hair, Pan had come to the United States from China in 1994 after graduating with a chemistry degree from Peking University in Beijing. He got himself a PhD in organic chemistry from Columbia University in New York and headed to Stanford University in 2000 to do postdoctoral research. Two years later, Pan started working at Celera's South San Francisco chemistry building.

Sitting in Sprengeler's office, the two chemists designed Pan's molecules on a computer. They took the two-dimensional structure Pan had drawn on paper and started building in three dimensions. The Celera chemists in South San Francisco specialized in this kind of structure-based design. The whole process took less than two hours.

Working in the lab, Pan generated chemical reactions to synthesize the irreversible compounds he had designed with Sprengeler. Pan created his molecules over several days. Then his group tested one of them in a mouse and showed that the compound successfully hit BTK and blocked it. The testing also showed a lessening of rheumatoid arthritis characteristics in the mouse model.

Pan's problem was that nobody at Celera thought that any of this was particularly important. The nascent BTK program was never on the radar of Celera's top executives. Soon, Celera decided to give up on all the drug development going on at its South San Francisco facility, including the work on BTK. Celera's executives back in Maryland decided to get out of the medicine-making business and shut the place down. For Celera, the idea of mining the human genome map to make drugs was a dead end, another false start among many in the biotechnology business.

Nevertheless, before Celera closed up its South San Francisco outpost, Pan's irreversible BTK inhibitor was given a code name: CRA-032765.

///////////////

DOWN THE ROAD IN Sunnyvale, Richard Miller was still looking for that pitch to hit. He had talked to Pharmacyclics' board about maybe finding new drug candidates, but was unsure what to do next. "Great drugs don't just grow on trees," he thought to himself. Around this time, in March 2006, he got a call from Ken Brameld, a young computational chemist at Celera.

One advantage of continuing to practice medicine and keeping a foot at the Stanford Medical Center was that Miller had been able to network with new generations of doctors and researchers and stay on top of their ideas. Miller always seemed to be hanging around, gossiping with the new attending physicians and swapping ideas with the professors. Young resident physicians would regularly ask Miller for advice on their patients and enjoyed being around him. He was incredibly bright and approachable. Brameld connected with Miller through this network.

Brameld visited Miller at the Pharmacyclics offices in Sunnyvale on a Friday afternoon seeking counsel. He explained to Miller that Celera had decided to give up on the drug development game and ceased all its activities in South San Francisco. Most of the chemists and biologists, including Zhengying Pan, had already been laid off. Much of the chemistry building had gone dark. Just a handful of employees remained to close up shop, and most of them were spending the majority of their time outside of the office, looking for a new job. They had been ordered by headquarters to sell the compounds they had developed. It was a fire sale. Brameld wondered what it would take to fish out the virology compounds he had been working on and maybe start his own company around them. He went to Miller seeking guidance.

Sitting behind his office desk, Miller shared his experiences and insights about business plans and financing considerations. By this time, Miller's own entrepreneurial curiosity had been piqued. He wasn't interested in the virology assets, but wondered if Celera had something else that could work for Pharmacyclics.

"Tell me what else Celera has sitting on the shelf," said Miller.

Brameld described a program for histone deacetylase inhibitors, known as HDACs, easily the most advanced effort at Celera, as well as the very early-stage BTK program.

The moment Brameld walked out of his office, Miller picked up the phone.

The following Monday, Miller drove up to Celera's South San Francisco offices. At the 9 a.m. meeting, Miller was direct and forceful as usual. In a conference room, a group of mid-level Celera employees went through a slide presentation for Miller about their therapeutic programs, spending most of their time on Celera's lead HDAC inhibitor compound, already being tested in patients with lymphoma in a phase 1 trial. Miller said he was not interested in hearing about Celera's virology drugs. The Celera team pivoted to discuss the BTK inhibitor program, consisting of reversible and nonreversible compounds, that targeted rheumatoid arthritis.

Miller offered up an idea: "Maybe [the BTK inhibitors] would be good to treat B cell lymphoma?"

The Celera group thought Miller's idea would never work. The meeting wrapped up after two hours.

Miller's background was in B cell lymphoma, and his wife was a lymphoma expert. The groundbreaking lymphoma drug he had helped launch, rituximab, worked by interfering with certain white blood cells (B cells) of the immune system that became malignant. Rituximab attached to these cells and removed them from circulation. Miller went home and thought about it. Maybe disrupting B cell function and signaling by blocking BTK could be another way to help blood cancer patients? There was new and related work on this idea already being done, some of it in the Stanford lab of Miller's colleague, Ron Levy, which Miller visited weekly.

After giving it some thought, Miller called Celera and said he was interested in buying the HDAC inhibitor. It easily had the most value because the drug had already advanced to a clinical trial, meaning it was being tested in patients. Miller said he also wanted a blood clotting medicine, and at the end of the call, Miller dropped another request. He wanted Celera to throw in the BTK inhibitor drugs as well. The deal came together quickly. Pharmacyclics didn't have much money, but the company's board authorized Miller to use stock to do the deal.

There was another wrinkle. Normally, pharmaceutical transactions do not involve an actual acquisition of an asset. What a company is buying is the commercial rights to a drug through a licensing agreement. The BTK inhibitor program was such a low priority at Celera that the company had not even filed patents for the compounds, including Pan's CRA-032765. It was just some white powder grunge at the bottom of a test tube. As a result, Pharmacyclics' outright purchase of CRA-032765 and Celera's other BTK inhibitor compounds was somewhat unusual. Because there was no patented intellectual property to license, the company bought the compounds and owned them wholly. The entire deal was so odd that Miller worried that someone from Celera would end up driving over to Sunnyvale and just drop a bunch of test tubes on his desk.

Instead, Celera delivered all of the program's files, including Zhengying Pan's notebook. Miller also hired some of the Celera scientists he had met during the negotiation. In April 2006, Miller negotiated to pay a rock-bottom price of $2 million in cash and another $4.5 million of stock upfront for the three programs. The total added up to $6.6 million after deal costs were factored.

In the $6.6 million transaction, the Celera team ascribed next to no value to the BTK inhibitors. Typically, the selling company retains a small percentage on future net sales of a drug. But Celera didn't even bother to secure future milestone payments from any Pharmacyclics development of the BTK inhibitor program. There was no expectation that the BTK inhibitor would go anywhere. The way members of the Celera team saw it, the company essentially included CRA-032765 in the deal for nothing.

CHAPTER 3

The Takeover

One year later, Richard Miller was frustrated and angry. He started writing down what had been bothering him. He was exasperated with the FDA and its Office of Hematology and Oncology Products. The man who led the office, Richard Pazdur, had a reputation for making it hard to get cancer drugs approved. Miller thought the FDA bureaucrats had lost track of what mattered. He was determined to do something about it.

Miller sketched out an opinion article that blasted the FDA for denying treatments to cancer patients. The gap between medicine and statistics had simply paralyzed the FDA approval process, Miller wrote. This made it too difficult to get cancer drugs approved to help dying patients. In his article, Miller specifically went through the saga of Xcytrin, his company's experimental brain cancer drug. "The FDA bases its approvals—for everything from medications for minor ailments to new cancer treatments—on the rigid application of the same outdated statistical standards," he expounded.

Miller submitted his article to the opinion pages of the *Wall Street Journal.* The newspaper published the article prominently under his name.

A few months earlier, Miller had made a long-shot bet. He directed Pharmacyclics to submit Xcytrin to the FDA for market approval by filing a New Drug Application. Miller hoped that data suggesting that Xcytrin might somewhat help patients specifically with lung cancer that had spread to the brain could sway the regulators. He knew the odds were against him, given the clinical trial failures Xcytrin had racked up. But he at least expected the FDA to give him a shot. Instead, the FDA sent him a "refuse to file" letter. The regulators were not even going to consider Xcytrin's application and denied the drug without a review. It was strike three for Xcytrin.

Miller refused to give up. In April 2007, he had Pharmacyclics file a New Drug Application for Xcytrin to the FDA over protest, an exceptionally rare way to seek drug approval in the United States. Essentially, Miller had swung and missed with Xcytrin for a third time and refused to leave the plate, contesting the strike call.

Now, Miller was escalating things further with the FDA, the government regulator that had the power to make or break his company and its experimental drugs, by taking his beef to the pages of the *Wall Street Journal*.

While Miller's argument had merit, many in the biotechnology community thought that publicly contesting the FDA's decision over Xcytrin was madness. How would Pharmacyclics be treated by FDA officials going forward? To some, Miller's quest to get Xcytrin approved seemed quixotic. They whispered about the olive-green skin discoloration the drug caused in some patients. Who would want to take a drug that literally turned you green?

But Miller was just getting started. In August 2007, he wrote a second opinion piece for the *Wall Street Journal*, arguing that "current FDA policies are discouraging the development of groundbreaking treatments for cancer and other killer diseases." Before the year was out, Miller wrote a third *Wall Street Journal* opinion piece, decrying the FDA's "cumbersome and overly restrictive policies."

//////////////

RICHARD MILLER WAS FINISHING a morning shower in a Hawaii
hotel when he got a call from Bob Duggan. Miller was not in Hawaii
on vacation. He had meetings with a biotechnology company there he
thought could do some work with Pharmacyclics.

"Richard, I own a lot of your stock now," Duggan said. "I think I
should come on our board."

"Gee," Miller responded. "Let's get together to talk about this. Let
me think about this."

Miller hung up the phone and immediately called his lawyer and
some of Pharmacyclics' board members. Duggan owned 3.9 million
shares, 15 percent of the company. The feedback Miller got was that
it made sense for Duggan to have a seat on the board. Duggan had
become Pharmacyclics' biggest shareholder and the company's stock
was not doing well. It made no sense to start a fight. Duggan hopped
onto the board in September 2007.

Three months after Duggan joined Pharmacyclics' board, Miller
received a "not approvable letter" from the FDA for the Xcytrin drug
application he had submitted over protest. For Miller, this was game
over. He had done everything he could to champion this drug and
spent nearly two decades on this journey. He had taken this as far as it
could go. As hard as it was to accept, the time had come to move on.
Even Miller could see it now.

In February 2008, Pharmacyclics announced a corporate realignment. The company was done launching new trials of Xcytrin and
would try to sell, or out-license, the drug. From now on, Miller declared
in a press release, Pharmacyclics would focus on the HDAC inhibitor
and other drug candidates it had acquired from Celera.

As Miller looked for ways to turn the page, he made a momentous decision. Its full significance was not apparent to Miller, Duggan,
or anyone else at the time. But the decision would make Pharmacyclics matter in ways that pursuing texaphyrins or a brain cancer therapy

never did. Miller decided he wanted to test out the idea that had stuck in the back of his mind since he floated it past the scientists at Celera; he wanted to test the irreversible BTK inhibitor he had purchased from Celera, CRA-032765, in human beings suffering from lymphoma, not rheumatoid arthritis.

There was a simple logic to the decision. When they are fighting off viruses or bacteria, B cells are signaled to mobilize and multiply into clones to mount an immune defense. But sometimes, these signals get hacked and improperly stimulate the activation of abnormal B cells, even though there is no threat, causing cancer in the blood like lymphoma and leukemia. Miller, of course, knew this well, and a few lines of evidence suggested that these mutated malignant B cells might rely on signaling that occurs through a pathway that runs through a protein on the surface of a B cell, known as the B cell receptor. Bruton's tyrosine kinase played a role in that very B cell receptor signaling pathway. Maybe you could stop malignant lymphoma cells from staying alive and multiplying with a drug that could safely bind to BTK and block its involvement in the pathway? It was really just a hunch, but that's what Miller wanted to explore.

Pharmacyclics had purchased two different series of BTK inhibitors: one consisted of those sticky covalent compounds that irreversibly bound to the enzyme, like the tool compound CRA-032765; the other series was made up of reversible compounds. Erik Verner, one of the chemists who had joined Pharmacyclics from Celera, worked on both compounds in the company's lab, doing investigational lab procedures known as screening assays and cellular assays and some testing in mice.

The lab work yielded little. It was a challenge to find the appropriate cell or animal models to use. But one thing that did become clear to Verner was that the irreversible sticky compounds were better at shutting down the B cell receptor signaling pathway. Verner brought the results to Miller, who agreed they should focus on developing irreversible, or sticky, inhibitors. The tool compound CRA-032765 was the most promising. The molecule was given a new code name, PCI-32765, to reflect that it was now owned by Pharmacyclics.

Verner's small study showing that some obscure compound had shut down a signaling pathway could do nothing for Pharmacyclics' stock, which had tumbled to around $2. But Miller figured it was worth $1 million or so to give PCI-32765 a go in a small clinical trial that would test the drug in lymphoma patients—the kind of cancer patients he treated weekly at Stanford, those he knew needed help.

///////////////////

DANIEL POLLYEA WAS JUST trying to catch a break at the Stanford Medical Center. With an interest in blood cancer, the thirty-year-old had shown up as a clinical research fellow after graduating from the University of Chicago's Pritzker School of Medicine. The son of a doctor in Columbus, Ohio, Pollyea was trying to navigate the rivalries and politics of the big-ego professors. He spent his fellowship working with Sandra Horning and rubbed shoulders with her husband, Richard Miller, quite a bit. In Miller, Pollyea found a supporter. He always enjoyed spending time with Miller, and the two got along well.

Wearing a tie and white coat, Pollyea was between patients one day when Miller came by and said he wanted to talk. Miller didn't have his own space at Stanford, so he took Pollyea to Horning's big office, where the two sat in the chairs in front of Horning's desk.

"I got this drug," Miller said. "It's this BTK inhibitor. My wife is conflicted, she can't run this study. She would be the logical person. I want you to run this study."

Pollyea jumped at the chance to run a real clinical trial in patients. This was exactly what he had dreamed of doing. It was a rare opportunity for a research fellow.

Pollyea opened his notebook and started writing Miller's instructions:

BTK Inhibitor
Early Step in BCR [B-cell receptor] signaling
More focused inhibition . . .
Irreversible . . . Safety problems?
Ready for man!
Work with Ranjana?

These were the first sketches of the first-in-human phase 1 trial of PCI-32765, as designed by Richard Miller, which Pollyea would run with their colleague Ranjana Advani. This first trial would not have happened without Miller. He wrote the study plan, known as a protocol, for a trial of patients with different lymphomas that were either relapsed, meaning the cancer had returned after a period of treatment and improvement, or refractory, meaning it had become resistant to treatment. Miller had written many trial protocols in the past. He wrote this one himself because there was hardly anyone else around to write it. Pharmacyclics had just cut back its headcount by 40 percent.

It was a typical dose escalation study that aimed to establish therapeutic drug levels that would be safe for patients. The plan called for patients to swallow one dose of capsules daily for four weeks and then take a recovery week off the treatment. Miller wrote the protocol while away on vacation for a few days with his wife and at times turned to Horning for advice. "What should I use as a cutoff for hemoglobin?" he would ask. "What should I use as a cutoff for platelet count?"

Among the many decisions Miller made when writing the protocol, one in particular would turn out to be critical. He decided to include in the study patients with chronic lymphocytic leukemia, the most common form of adult leukemia, often referred to as CLL.

It was a bit unusual to include CLL patients in a lymphoma protocol. But Miller had a good reason. In CLL, many of the malignant cells are in the bloodstream, whereas with most lymphomas the cancer cells are largely in the lymph nodes and other tissue. Miller wanted to be able to measure and observe how the drug bonded to cancer cells. With

CLL patients he could do this with a simple blood sample, as opposed to cumbersome biopsies, which would likely be required in lymphoma patients. Pharmacyclics went ahead and filed an Investigational New Drug Application with the FDA to test PCI-32765 in humans with different lymphomas and CLL.

///////////////////

BOB DUGGAN DID NOT like the direction Pharmacyclics had taken. For one thing, he was not ready to give up on Xcytrin, the brain cancer drug that had initially enticed him to invest in the company. And it didn't help that Duggan was losing money on his Pharmacyclics investment, at least on paper. The company's stock had now dipped below $1, and the NASDAQ stock exchange was threatening to delist it. Duggan kept pushing Miller about launching another phase 3 Xcytrin trial. Somebody had to right this ship.

Duggan had ideas about Xcytrin that came from a longtime colleague, Rainer Erdtmann, who everyone called Ramses. Tall, broad, and imposing, Erdtmann had arrived in the United States from Germany in the mid-1990s and met Duggan soon after. Erdtmann and his mother were Scientologists, and one of his mother's Scientologist friends knew Duggan's wife, Trish Duggan, and made the connection. Erdtmann had previously spent some time working as an investment banker and portfolio manager in Frankfurt.

For a while, Erdtmann worked for Duggan as a portfolio manager in Santa Barbara. They always kept in close touch, and in 2007 Duggan asked Erdtmann, now in his early forties, to do some research on Pharmacyclics. Erdtmann had little biotechnology experience, but he started digging into the Xcytrin trials. To help him on the project, he brought in a biostatistician friend who worked at a hospital. The biostatistician crunched all the data and predicted that a phase 3 trial of Xcytrin that focused on a certain subgroup of patients with metastasized lung cancer could work.

Duggan brought the statistical work to Miller, who did not buy it. Miller's experience was if you slice and dice data, you could show any result you want. When they talked, Miller found it difficult to follow Duggan's train of thought as he jumped around from idea to idea. Even though he thought Duggan was extremely smart, Miller had a hard time communicating with him. "Go try to explain Bonferroni corrections and biostatistics to Bob Duggan," Miller would say. "That's impossible." Sometimes their conversations would get a little bizarre for Miller, who claimed that Duggan once asked him if BTK was in the body. "Bob, it's in B cells," Miller responded. At bottom, Miller was simply against doing another Xcytrin trial.

To push Pharmacyclics to launch a new Xcytrin trial, Duggan launched a tender offer in May 2008 to buy up to four million shares of Pharmacyclics at $1.05 per share. The purpose of the offer, Duggan spelled out for shareholders, was to "use all available means to encourage and to urge Pharmacyclics to pursue another trial to achieve approval of the drug MGD (f/k/a Xcytrin)." Through the tender offer, Duggan ended up spending $2 million for another 1.9 million shares, increasing his holdings to 5.9 million shares.

Duggan now controlled nearly a quarter of Pharmacyclics' shares, giving him an even greater say in how the company would be run. He wanted a new trial for Xcytrin and got his way. Miller hired a doctor with clinical research experience to write the protocol and manage a new phase 3 trial for the brain cancer drug. "You never know," Miller rationalized. The business he had chosen was not black or white. "Maybe the guy is right, maybe another trial will work."

Duggan made more demands on Miller, asking him to hire Mahkam "Maky" Zanganeh to help with business development. When Miller looked at Zanganeh's résumé, he couldn't believe it. She was a dentist with no pharmaceutical or oncology experience. But Duggan had come to rely on Zanganeh, and Miller was now pressed under Duggan's thumb.

Born in Iran, Zanganeh's family had left after the Iranian Revolution, and she attended a German high school before winding up in France. Zanganeh got her dental degree at Louis Pasteur University in Strasbourg in 1997. Through a friend, Zanganeh met Duggan and started working for Computer Motion in France. While working there, Zanganeh also got her master's of business administration from Schiller International University. She spoke with a mixed Persian European accent and would focus on the smallest of details when working on a project, often leading to good results.

Zanganeh had become indispensable to Duggan. She joined Robert W. Duggan & Associates in Santa Barbara after the Computer Motion sale, and Duggan hardly made a decision without her. Knowing Duggan's feelings about his late son, it was Zanganeh who first came across Pharmacyclics and brought the company to Duggan as an investment idea. Slim and extremely fit with blond hair and brown eyes, Zanganeh, thirty-eight, would be Duggan's eyes and ears at Pharmacyclics. Miller followed Duggan's direction and hired Zanganeh as vice president of business development.

Not long after Miller hired Zanganeh, Duggan came to Sunnyvale to see Miller in his office and dumped a pile of folders on his desk. Each folder contained a résumé and background information on a new slate of people Duggan thought should be appointed to the board of directors of Pharmacyclics.

"Richard, I think we need to replace your board," Duggan said.

"What do you mean, who do you want to replace it with? It is a pretty good board," Miller said. "These guys are very good."

"Look, I got people here I want you to take a look at," Duggan responded.

Duggan thought that Pharmacyclics needed a board that would reign Miller in and make him more accountable to shareholders. Miller started to look through the folders. He didn't like Duggan's board candidates. One of them was Minesh Mehta, a radiation oncologist and one of the medical researchers who helped conduct the Xcytrin trials. Miller had never heard of the others and thought they were lightweights.

"Bob, I disagree with what you're doing. These guys are nowhere near the caliber of people I have on the board now. But I'll tell you what, I'll meet these people."

"Great idea. You need to meet these people," Duggan responded.

Over the next few weeks, Miller met with Duggan's proposed board candidates and came away thinking they would make terrible Pharmacyclics directors. They would not be able to advise him in a way that would be helpful like his current board and would just push the company in any direction Duggan wanted. When Miller reported back, Duggan said he was going to go forward with replacing the board. He would start a proxy fight and get a majority of shareholders to back him if necessary. Duggan's hard-hitting moves started to look like they were more about gaining control than anything else.

Miller called his lawyer and Pharmacyclics' other board directors. "Guys, what can we do about this?" Miller asked them. Not much. Duggan had continued to buy Pharmacyclics stock and now owned 29 percent of the shares. The company had accumulated $322 million of operating losses since inception and its stock traded for around $1. On Wall Street, Miller was seen as the culprit. The chances that Miller would win a proxy fight were slim.

Miller convened the board members at the offices of law firm Latham & Watkins in Menlo Park, about 14 miles up toward San Francisco from Pharmacyclics' headquarters. Even though he was a board member, Duggan was not invited. The directors were not enthusiastic about getting into a proxy fight with Duggan that could result in shareholder litigation and personal liability for themselves. Instead, three of Pharmacyclics' six board members chose to resign. Taking stock of the situation, Miller, who was also a director, decided he would leave Pharmacyclics with them. Angry about losing his company, Miller had no interest in talking to Duggan. One of the resigning directors, Miles

Gilburne, reported the news to Duggan, who was in Clearwater, Florida, visiting the Church of Scientology's spiritual headquarters. Duggan told Gilburne he wanted Miller to stay on—only with a board that would be less friendly to him and hold Miller's feet to the fire.

The next morning, September 10, 2008, Miller wrote a letter to Duggan, saying he was resigning the CEO position and jumping off the board immediately. The company's chief financial officer would also exit. Not long after, Miller started selling all his shares, a 6.8 percent stake in Pharmacyclics, a process that would take two to three years.

On the surface, it seemed like the founding CEO of a flailing biotech company had been pushed aside, leaving a smoldering mess for a new imperious caretaker who had little idea about what he was doing. What had Miller and Duggan been fighting about anyway? Pharmacyclics was a train wreck of a company with a failed brain cancer medicine and three cast-off drugs from Celera, one of which was a BTK inhibitor that had initially been designed as a tool compound. Nobody cared. And at this point, exhausted by the failed trials and now fighting for his own company, that included Miller. He was unsure whether his lingering curiosity—a BTK inhibitor—would have an application in lymphoma. He figured he had helped push the drug forward, just like many medicines he had been involved with before. Miller was just another founder whose company had moved on without him. The biotech world was saturated with such stories.

It didn't matter. Pharmacyclics, the company Miller cofounded seventeen years earlier, now belonged to Duggan.

CHAPTER 4

Starting Fresh

Francisco Salva arrived at Pharmacyclics' offices in Sunnyvale and was led to a cubicle, where he was handed a stack of papers. Among them was a long multiple choice test. Salva started filling out the answers. The questions probed Salva's temperament and ethics. There were no math or logic questions. The whole thing was weird. To Salva it looked like a personality test, one that happened to take three hours and resembled the kind of quizzes administered by the Church of Scientology.

Bob Duggan denied that the Pharmacyclics hiring process ever included a personality test that had been influenced by Scientology and would later say he certainly never authorized one. Either way, Salva shrugged off the experience. He had started his career as an investment banker and investor doing grunt work at Wall Street firms, focusing on biopharma. He was just an observer of the life sciences industry. For the first time, he now had a chance to get in the game and work for a biotech company. He was eager to make the transition.

Salva had already interviewed with Duggan, now the interim CEO and chairman of Pharmacyclics, who wanted Salva to join in a corporate finance role, starting as a consultant. He thought Duggan was charismatic and passionate, even though Duggan had no biopharma experience whatsoever. During the interview, Duggan told Salva he needed help raising money for a new phase 3 Xcytrin trial. Salva had been warned about this and the personality test by other Pharmacyclics employees. "Do you really want to do this?" he was asked. "Bob is going to try to get you to raise money on this dead drug."

For Salva, it was an opportunity to finally join the biotech industry. He took the job and reported to Maky Zanganeh.

When Bob Duggan ousted Pharmacyclics' board, he overplayed his hand a little. He wanted to control Pharmacyclics and make Miller more accountable, not get rid of him. But Miller had left, and Duggan was holding the bag of a cratering company running dangerously low on cash. Days after Miller's exit, Lehman Brothers, the big New York investment bank, collapsed. The financial crisis left Pharmacyclics with few options. Raising money had become impossible. Investors were running for the hills. Many small biotech companies had been forced to restructure, and some filed for bankruptcy. Pharmacyclics seemed headed in that direction as well.

Duggan decided to step up. He loaned Pharmacyclics the $5 million it needed to get through the year. He loaned Pharmacyclics another $1.4 million in March 2009. In the interim, Pharmacyclics' stock traded for as little as 57 cents. The company likely would not have survived without Duggan's loans and support of the stock.

But even with financial markets and the global economy on the precipice, Duggan found purpose in the company. He wanted to find a medicine that would change people's lives, especially those with brain cancer. "We take full responsibility for what we know and we know the work we are engaged in is work worth doing," he said at the time about his decision.

To raise cash, Ramses Erdtmann suggested to Duggan that Pharmacyclics try to sell its BTK inhibitor. Duggan didn't like the idea. "How do I know how much it's worth?" But during this period, Pharmacyclics was holding partnership discussions about potentially selling a stake in PCI-

32765 to players like Forest Laboratories. For almost no money, anybody in the biopharma industry could have bought a material ownership interest in the drug. But there was a reason the price was so low. Nobody was interested in putting a sticky BTK inhibitor in human beings.

Duggan may not have known what PCI-32765 was worth, but he knew he had to develop Pharmacyclics' only assets, its experimental drugs. The only other option was to quit. With the financial crisis raging, the company launched its phase 1 trial of PCI-32765, and Daniel Pollyea prepared to dose the first patients at Stanford Medical Center. Duggan also authorized a study of PCI-32765 in dogs with naturally occurring lymphoma.

A good number of Pharmacyclics' employees remained deeply skeptical of Duggan, who was learning a new business on the fly. Early on, he showed up to a meeting in the conference room with boxes of McDonald's chocolate chip cookies. "I am the inventor of this recipe," Duggan exclaimed as he passed them around. "I spent months perfecting it." When Duggan talked about his cookie venture, he would joke that it was his first involvement with chemistry—mixing sugar with chocolate, flour, and eggs. A few of the scientists wondered how the cookie guy would help them navigate drug discovery.

Some at the company were also uncomfortable with Duggan dropping Scientology teachings in the office and seeming to incorporate them into the company's philosophy. Duggan expounded for employees on the idea of exchange in abundance—people or businesses giving more than they received to customers or partners—and how it could lead to good things like referrals, trust, and loyalty. Duggan's habit of constantly defining words in the middle of a conversation was also seen as a teaching of L. Ron Hubbard. In a friendly manner, Francisco Salva was encouraged to attend Scientology meetings by Ramses Erdtmann, who had joined Pharmacyclics as head of finance. So Salva went to the Church of Scientology's San Francisco home, located in the historic Transamerica Building, to check out some classes. He didn't pursue it further and Erdtmann never brought it up again.

But one thing Duggan did know a lot about was patents. The successful sale of Computer Motion had largely been driven by the company's patent strategy and litigation. There would be no point in figuring out whether Pharmacyclics' drugs worked if the company didn't patent the intellectual property. Pharmacyclics' preclinical group got to work writing applications for the US Patent and Trademark Office. This included the first issued patent for PCI-32765. But it also included broader patents for BTK inhibitors written by Erik Verner that changed the molecule's core by modifying heterocycles and moving nitrogen around.

Duggan quickly got comfortable running a life sciences company and decided to become a full-fledged CEO, removing the interim designation. He liked the challenge and, more than anything, wanted the company, not just any single drug, to succeed. Why couldn't he do this? Duggan issued a mission statement for Pharmacyclics, and its first words were "to build a viable biopharmaceutical company." His plans to do so were lofty and vague—identify "promising product candidates" and develop them "to make a difference for the better."

In practice, Duggan put together an expert committee to advise him on what to do about Xcytrin. After a comprehensive review, nobody on the committee thought it made sense to start a new Xcytrin trial. The verdict was unanimous—and impossible for Duggan to ignore, especially with a plunging stock price and no money for another expensive late-stage Xcytrin trial. Duggan was single-minded in his pursuits, but he could also pivot quickly when he arrived at a decision, as he had shown in the cookie business.

"The reason that we stepped in here is no longer viable and we are going to have to carry on," Duggan would explain. In February 2009, Duggan suspended any new clinical development of the brain cancer drug. The three drugs Pharmacyclics had acquired from Celera were now the better bets by default.

To move these drugs forward, Duggan needed a chief medical officer and someone to run clinical drug development.

//////////////

AHMED HAMDY WAS WORKING at the South San Francisco offices of Elan Pharmaceuticals when he got a call from a recruiter about a job opening at Pharmacyclics. At Elan, Hamdy oversaw the clinical development of drugs targeting gastroenterological and autoimmune conditions. He was one of several mid-level therapeutic area heads at the company. Before he got the job at Elan, Hamdy had sent his résumé to Richard Miller. Now, Pharmacyclics was interested in talking to him about becoming chief medical officer, a top position. Hamdy met with Bob Duggan, who told Hamdy that he liked that this would be Hamdy's first executive role because he would be hungry.

Hamdy got the job. Sure, the company's finances were shaky. But the opportunity represented a huge promotion in title, and Hamdy figured that even if the company didn't pan out, the move could lead to other big things. The shorter commute made Pharmacyclics even more attractive. Hamdy loved living in sunny and laid-back Santa Cruz on the Pacific coast. Brutal Silicon Valley traffic meant spending hours each day driving 65 miles to Elan's offices in South San Francisco. Working at Pharmacyclics in Sunnyvale would cut that commute in half. He would even have time to hit his rowing club, located at the Lexington Reservoir, on the way.

In addition, Pharmacyclics represented a sort of lottery ticket for Hamdy. The job paid an annual salary of $315,000, with a signing bonus of $25,000, a nice wage bump from his last job. Hamdy was awarded 300,000 Pharmacyclics stock options when the stock was changing hands for a mere 73 cents a share, with assurances of more stock options to come. The low exercise price of the options meant that if the stock price climbed back to the $10 it had been worth just a few years earlier, he would be a millionaire. If the stock could return to its heights of $80 during the Miller years, Hamdy would possess some serious wealth.

With a full head of dark brown hair at age forty-five, the tall and wiry Hamdy was also a doctor, meaning he had the basic qualification for becoming a chief medical officer, or CMO, the single person who is ultimately responsible at biotech firms for making sure the interests of patients are always safeguarded. It would be Hamdy's responsibility to monitor the safety of the compounds under development and work with the investigators—the physician-scientists—who administer experimental treatments to patients. Ensuring those patients are dosed correctly would be the kind of thing that would typically be part of the job. So would staying on top of any serious safety issues. But the role also required a lot of business experience, and at a small company like Pharmacyclics, that role would be expanded. Hamdy would also be vice president of clinical development, designing trial plans, interpreting results, and writing final study reports. He would—in some way— touch nearly every aspect of the drug development process. It was a top executive-level job. For Hamdy, it was a big break. He had come a long way to earn it.

The only son of an Egyptian army general, Ahmed Hamdy grew up in Cairo, on an island in the Nile river. From his childhood apartment, he would watch rowers on the Nile float by his window. He learned the sport himself and made it as far as the Egyptian national rowing team. Slated to go to the 1980 Olympics in Russia, Hamdy's Olympic dream was dashed when Egypt decided to join the US-led boycott of those games and not send a delegation.

The Olympic disappointment was tough on Hamdy. But he had long had a passion for medicine and threw himself into it. He went to college and medical school at Cairo University, graduating in 1989 as a urologist. But the increasing role of religion in Egyptian public life became unsettling to Hamdy, as was the level of corruption he observed in Cairo's medical community. He wanted to be a man of science and felt increasingly out of place in Egypt, where personal connections seemed to matter more than merit or anything else. Hamdy wanted to go to America.

Hamdy landed a job as a visiting scientist at the Centers for Disease Control and Prevention in Atlanta (the CDC). From there, he headed to the University of Colorado for a PhD in experimental pathology, focusing on prostate cancer. Wanting to start a family and in need of money, Hamdy left Colorado before getting his PhD. He found a job in Salt Lake City with Watson Pharmaceuticals, leading clinical programs in urology.

In the years that followed, Hamdy headed farther west to California, pulled by the twin excitement of being in a place known for creating immense wealth while also working to help people in a profound way. The high-tech workers of Silicon Valley could harbor visions of great wealth while talking a good game about their revolutionary products. But really, what was the human value of another iPhone app or Facebook feature? With biotechnology, Hamdy could save people's lives. The credible mantra of biotechnology workers was always that they were in it for the patients.

In California, Hamdy first worked for PDL Biopharma before becoming a senior director at Elan Pharmaceuticals, which translated into Hamdy being a mid-level cog in Elan's drug development machine. But at Pharmacyclics, Hamdy would be the fourth-highest-ranking person at the company.

Hamdy showed up to work at Pharmacyclics in March 2009. It was a tiny outfit with forty-six employees, a minuscule drop in the Silicon Valley biotech ocean compared with the eleven thousand people working at Genentech. He quickly tried to get up to speed, working closely with Glenn Rice, who had been appointed president of Pharmacyclics. With a PhD in cellular and molecular biology, Rice had previously been CEO of various small biotech firms he had founded. What seemed to appeal most to Duggan about Rice, however, was his experience as a laboratory director at Genentech, the South San Francisco company that essentially invented the biotechnology industry. Duggan had enormous admiration for Genentech and appeared to think that anyone who succeeded there could make a meaningful impact.

Pharmacyclics had two programs in blood cancer, its HDAC and BTK inhibitor drugs, mostly in lymphoma. A urologist by training who had worked at companies focused on diverse sets of diseases and conditions, Hamdy had gotten used to learning new therapeutic areas. With his warm smile and easygoing demeanor, Hamdy operated like a smooth diplomat. He was a sweet man. People liked him. It was one of his strongest skills and an important one. To get doctors to join an early clinical trial run by a tiny company and motivate them to enroll patients, it helped to make strong connections.

Enrolling patients in a clinical trial for an unknown experimental therapy could be extremely challenging. Just the regulatory burden was enormous, involving contracts with each hospital or site, budgets, and the oversight of boards and committees. To then get doctors operating in a busy oncology practice to take a significant amount of time to talk with their patients about a clinical trial could be next to impossible. So it was absolutely crucial to make inroads with the doctors. Hamdy started sending out emails, building advisory boards, and connecting with the expert physicians in blood cancer who would need to play a role in any experimental blood cancer drug.

By this time, the first patient had been dosed with Pharmacyclics' BTK inhibitor, PCI-32765, at Stanford Medical Center. It was slow going. Weeks passed between the dosing of the first and second patient. Hamdy hoped the trial would show the drug was safe and also that it might show a sign—any sign—that it might help blood cancer patients. Hamdy really wanted to get two of the most respected chronic lympho-cytic leukemia experts to participate in the trial, John Byrd, a doctor at Ohio State University, and Susan O'Brien, a doctor at the University of Texas in Houston. Both were hungry enough for new medicines to meet with the CMO of a biotechnology outfit they had never heard of before. But Byrd and O'Brien both passed on getting involved, They explained to Hamdy that they didn't like the phase 1 trial design for PCI-32765, which seemed devised to get softball patients.

When it came to clinical trials, John Byrd had two rules: Do no harm and don't cherry-pick easy patients. He was suspicious of bio-pharma companies trying to make their drugs look good in early trials. Unless a drug is a total dud, Byrd knew, a biopharma company could manipulate patient eligibility to speed things along to phase 2. In the trial for PCI-32765, he wanted to see patients enrolled with lower platelet and hemoglobin counts, markers for poor patient outcomes. He thought the eligibility requirements for the phase 1 study were ridiculous. Doctors could allow cancer patients in the study who were not in a bad way—having received little previous treatment and with close to normal platelet counts. "You need to let real patients on study," Byrd told Hamdy in a phone call. "Call me when you are ready to get serious."

Hamdy wanted to partner with the biggest names in lymphoma and leukemia. But he also wanted to give Pharmacyclics' new trials a fighting chance, some easy wins before getting to the games that mattered. Hamdy continued through his file of leads. Two physicians high on his list were Lou Staudt and Wyndham Wilson.

////////////////////////

OVER YEARS OF WORK, Louis "Lou" Staudt had become one of the nation's most distinguished physician-scientists. In 1988, he opened his lab at the National Cancer Institute's campus in Bethesda, Maryland, part of the National Institutes of Health. There, Staudt made remarkable contributions to cancer research, particularly in the area of lymphoma. Utilizing new genomic tools, Staudt discovered molecularly distinct cancer subtypes, defining subtypes of lymphoma that, as a result, became viewed as distinctive diseases. Staudt revealed the mysteries of different types of lymphoma and, before it became known as precision medicine, pointed to different therapeutic strategies that might be appropriate for patients. Along the way, Staudt struck a career-defining collaboration with Wyndham Wilson, a brilliant lymphoma expert with an MD and PhD in neurobiology from Stanford University.

By the early 2000s, Staudt and Wilson had set out on a more therapeutic track of science, trying to figure out how to treat the new types of lymphoma they had helped identify. Around 2008, Staudt literally had an aha moment. "Maybe the lymphomas themselves depend on the B cell receptor?" he thought. Just like Miller had, Staudt also grew increasingly interested in a kinase in the B cell receptor pathway, Bruton's tyrosine kinase, the same BTK that Pharmacyclics had been focused on. Two postdoctoral researchers working in Staudt's lab found genetic evidence that B cell receptor signaling was required for the survival of lymphoma cells.

Staudt submitted these findings to the journal *Nature*. But the peer-reviewed scientific journal asked for supporting experimentation and more work prior to publication. In the meantime, Staudt had agreed to give an April 2009 talk at the annual meeting of the American Association of Cancer Research in Denver. It was unusual to present unpublished work at a medical conference, but Staudt decided to go for it. In his talk, Staudt brought to light discoveries indicating that lymphoma cells are driven by B cell receptor signaling, in which BTK played an important role. Immediately following his talk, a small group of Pharmacyclics employees in attendance bum-rushed the podium to talk to Staudt.

"Have we got a drug for you," they told him.

Staudt was one of the only people at the Denver meeting who gave Pharmacyclics' BTK inhibitor any thought. In conjunction with the conference, Pharmacyclics tried to create some buzz by formally announcing it had started treating patients in the phase 1 trial of PCI-32765. The company's preclinical team also gave a 15-minute talk at the meeting about the work they had done with their BTK inhibitor in lymphoma, including early data of the study of PCI-32765 in dogs that had naturally developed lymphoma. With the cancer of one out of four dogs partially responding to the treatment, the early data from the canine trial did not turn any heads.

Even to the people working at Pharmacyclics, it was far from clear that the drug had become a top priority. The company was certainly not a BTK inhibitor company. The drug didn't even have a formal name.

In fact, the other blood cancer drug at Pharmacyclics, the HDAC inhibitor, was getting more attention. In her role as head of business development, Maky Zanganeh had used her connections in France to negotiate a deal with Laboratoires Servier, the second-largest French pharmaceutical company. Servier bought the non-US rights to the HDAC inhibitor for $11 million up front. Servier also agreed to pay $4 million for research on the drug and agreed to another $24.5 million of milestone payments, bringing Pharmacyclics some cash.

But the company needed much more.

CHAPTER 5

Wall Street

The Trout Group had warned them, "Get ready for this one." Bob Duggan, Glenn Rice, and Francisco Salva had hired the Trout Group to advise them on potential investors, and then made a fundraising trip to New York to pitch Pharmacyclics to hedge funds and investment firms. The Trout Group told the Pharmacyclics execs that this next meeting would be different from the usual PowerPoint and Q&A. "He can be really brutal sometimes. He may accuse you of lying."

The meeting was with Wayne Rothbaum, a trader who specialized in biotechnology stocks. Another person, Thomas Turalski, would also be there. "He likes to tag team people with his friend Tommy," they were told. "Tommy works for Joe Edelman."

Amid Pharmacyclics' cash crunch and his personal loans to keep the company afloat, Duggan planned on launching a share offering in the summer of 2009 that would raise $24 million from existing Pharmacyclics shareholders. The purpose of the share sale was to fund the company's operations and help launch the drug trials the company needed to get off the ground. To entice investors, Duggan would be buying more stock alongside them by converting the $6.4 million of emergency loans he had extended to the company into Pharmacyclics shares. He would not be taking money off the table or buying shares at a cheaper price. For Duggan, this was the philosophy of exchange in abundance being put into practice.

Sitting in Wayne Rothbaum's office, Duggan knew just how to handle the situation. He had often been on Rothbaum's side of the table, a prospective investor assessing management. Even as the Great Recession hit the economy, Duggan did not believe there was ever a scarcity of money or ideas. There was only a scarcity of confidence in the ideas. The key to building confidence was to do whatever you say you are going to do and not promise to do what you can't accomplish.

Rice and Salva did most of the talking, giving a presentation on Pharmacyclics' development pipeline, including the HDAC inhibitor and blood clotting drug. Rice spent a lot of time on the BTK inhibitor, emphasizing that the drug targeted lymphoma and maybe had some applications in autoimmune disease or asthma. Chronic lymphocytic leukemia was never mentioned. "It's a more safe oral rituximab," Rice kept saying, comparing it to the famous monoclonal antibody drug used in blood cancer that had been developed by Idec, the company Richard Miller cofounded decades earlier. Rothbaum and Turalski peppered them with questions.

Rothbaum did not pay much attention to Rice, but Duggan made a strong impression on him. Duggan talked a little about his backstory, including the Ethernet company and the cookies he baked that made it to McDonald's. Otherwise, Duggan sat mostly silent. He paid close attention to what Rothbaum and Tommy Turalksi said and threw in an answer where he could.

From his vantage point, Rothbaum noted that Duggan did not pretend to know what he didn't know and listened attentively. There had been a buzz about Duggan in the New York biotech investment community—the guy whose businesses always made money. Rothbaum didn't care that Duggan had no biotech experience, and he cared even less where Duggan went to church.

Duggan came across as honest and direct. Rothbaum viewed him as a winner.

//////////////////////

IT TAKES 80 MINUTES on the Long Island Rail Road to get from Smithtown, New York, to Manhattan, but Wayne P. Rothbaum's trip to Wall Street was not as direct. He had grown up middle class in Smithtown's mash-up of Irish, Italian, and Jewish families. He played baseball and football and lived in a 1,500-square-foot home with his younger twin sisters. Rothbaum's high school football coach had a nickname for him—rabbi. It was the 1980s.

Rothbaum's father co-owned a small company that provided security services for retail stores, focusing on the product and sales while his investment backer, a jeweler, managed the finances. The jeweler ended up orchestrating transactions that diluted the elder Rothbaum's stock, and Wayne saw—and felt firsthand—that his father had been screwed. He was never going to let something like that happen to him.

Rothbaum took premed courses at the State University of New York at Binghamton, but soon gave up on the idea of medical school, graduating in 1990 with a dual major in political science and psychology. Next he headed to George Washington University to study international affairs with the hope of becoming a spy. But his dreams of international intrigue came to an end while he was taking one of the Central Intelligence Agency's entrance tests. The drab testing room suggested to Rothbaum that working for the CIA was probably not going to be a James Bond fantasy, so he didn't bother going any further with the application process.

He headed for Manhattan because he needed work. There he landed an interview with a strategic consulting firm called the Carson Group. He was shocked when he got the job.

Over the next decade, Rothbaum built the life sciences practice at the Carson Group. With an intensity that stood out even on Wall

Street, he learned the business cold and turned out to be very good at analyzing biotech assets and companies. Rothbaum even started an investment bank within the Carson Group that arranged financings for biotech companies. To help him, he hired an analyst, Tom Turalski, who had recently graduated from Columbia University, where he had studied economics and political science.

Then, in 2001, the Carson Group was sold to information and data giant Thomson Corporation. The sale represented a turning point. For years, Rothbaum had been great at advising on biotech deals. Now he wanted to become an investor in them himself. He took his profits from the Carson Group sale ($1 million after taxes) and set up his own investment firm, Quogue Capital, named after the Hamptons town on Long Island where he owned a summer home.

When it came to biotech finance, Rothbaum found a mentor in Joe Edelman. The two had first met at a Manhattan party in the 1990s and hit it off. Edelman's dry sense of humor had Rothbaum laughing all night. Thirteen years older than Rothbaum, Edelman worked as a research analyst covering biotechnology before starting a small hedge fund, Perceptive Advisors, to trade biotech stocks in 1999.

After many years on the sell side of Wall Street, where they provided services in return for fees from investors that bought and sold securities, both Edelman and Rothbaum were eager to get in the game as investors themselves. They wanted to be on the buy side. How good were they? They wanted to find out.

At one point, Edelman talked to Rothbaum about starting Perceptive together, but they decided against it. They knew enough about each other's temperaments to understand that a venture together probably would not work out. To beat the market, Edelman firmly believed that he needed a certain attitude and had to be willing to go "all-in" on his good bets. His five biggest stock positions would often make up the majority of his portfolio exposure. Rothbaum had picked up this portfolio theory from Edelman and took it a step further. He was ready to put everything on the line in one single investment. Edelman's stomach for risk, as strong as it was, did not match Rothbaum's maniacal aggressiveness.

"The only way we are going to get really wealthy is if we bet really big on our best ideas," Rothbaum would tell Edelman as they set up each of their investment operations at almost the same time. When they first got to know each other, Edelman had schooled Rothbaum about the biotech industry and investing. But soon the elder investor began learning from his protégé. Rothbaum and Edelman would talk to each other daily, swapping ideas, sharing research, and talking through different investment decisions. Every Saturday morning, they had breakfast together at a Manhattan diner. Edelman hired Tom Turalski, who had met his new boss through Rothbaum. All three men stayed in close contact. Edelman's Perceptive Life Sciences hedge fund scored a net return of 129 percent in its first year. The investment that drove the biggest chunk of this return, Enzon Pharmaceuticals, had been Wayne Rothbaum's idea.

During his years working in biotech, Rothbaum grew truly amazed with how the human body worked. He marveled at the connections and mechanisms, the chain reactions, and the interconnectedness of everything. He looked at the body as an elegant biomechanical machine made up of parts, molecular gears, cogs, and switches that could be turned on or off. This machine followed rules defined by a genetic code and electrical pathways in which kinases played an important role driving cellular activity.

When he analyzed the impact of diseases on the human machine, Rothbaum focused on the places where the machine had broken down. "Cancer is just one type of a system breaking down for various reasons," he reasoned. Rothbaum used translational science, connecting the dots from different disciplines, like biology, chemistry, and medicine, to make stock market bets based on breadcrumbs of clinical data that fed his understanding of what might make the human machine work. With a photographic memory and a job that forced him to look at the entire picture, as opposed to just a silo of medical science like lymphoma, Rothbaum believed he understood the human body as well as the doctors, scientists, and biopharma researchers themselves, if not better. He could sometimes become abrasive with those experts—like the time Rothbaum told a renowned gene therapy expert that he didn't know anything about gene therapy, horrifying Edelman, who had set up the phone call conversation between the three of them.

When Rothbaum pivoted his focus from the body to human behavior, he sometimes took a more cynical view. Rothbaum thought that people are often ruled by their insecurities, jealousies, and self-interest. Rothbaum also had a deep paranoia that led him to be extremely secretive, even by the opaque standards of the hedge fund trading world. He never gave press interviews or spoke at conferences. His philanthropic donations were anonymous. No picture of Rothbaum ever hit the Internet.

Even as he became a wildly successful trader, Rothbaum refused to have Quogue Capital raise money from investors, forgoing the big fees that made so many hedge fund managers rich. He built a trading operation with all the robustness of a hedge fund, but without the clients. He didn't want to deal with clients or answer to them.

Rothbaum would invest only his own money and not hedge against his own abilities. He owned everything. The logic of his investments. The decisions that drove them. The risk and the reward. As long as it was his money, then it was his game and he owed no one anything. The money—and the guts to lose it—bought him independence. You could say he believed in himself.

In the small Wall Street world of biotech investing, the hyperfit Rothbaum, his hair close-cropped on top and shaved to the skin on the sides, acquired a reputation for being bold in a way that matched his presence, making huge and concentrated bets on which drugs he thought were going to work. Given all the work required to properly understand and make a biotechnology investment, he just couldn't understand why any life sciences investor would take the mealymouthed approach of owning a diversified stock portfolio. In an industry where most drugs failed, portfolio theory was a sucker's game.

Rothbaum's investment operation became a blazing success in his first decade of trading. The only time his trading got him in trouble was in 2008, when federal securities regulators accused Rothbaum, then forty, of improperly shorting, or betting against, the stocks of four biotech companies by selling stock in those companies and covering the short sales with stock he bought in a share offering—a no-no. The civil action was part of a wide regulatory sweep conducted by the Securities and Exchange Commission that snagged many hedge funds, including Edelman's Perceptive Advisors. But since Rothbaum was investing only his own money, he was personally named in the sweep, whereas in every other case the SEC only cited the hedge fund firms and not the people behind them. Without admitting or denying the civil allegations, Rothbaum settled with the SEC and paid back the $782,902 he earned on trades he made in 2005 plus a penalty of $390,000. Then he got back to work.

In the summer of 2009, after listening to Bob Duggan and his team in his office, Rothbaum agreed to participate in Pharmacyclics' share offering by making a small investment. Turalski convinced Edelman to invest as well. At $1.28 a share, the stock was being sold on the cheap. Rothbaum and Edelman's Perceptive hedge fund were two of the five main investors that participated in the offering.

Duggan raised $28.8 million in the offering for Pharmacyclics, contributing more than $6 million of that amount himself by converting his corporate debt holdings. At this point, Duggan personally owned a 23.5 percent stake in Pharmacyclics, which had been slightly diluted by the new share purchases of other investors.

Over the span of five years, since his first phone call with Richard Miller, Duggan's ownership in Pharmacyclics had ultimately cost him $31.8 million to acquire, but he had saved the company and put it on reasonably firm financial footing. Now Duggan needed one of Pharmacyclics' drugs to show some promise.

//////////////////

ON THE VERY SAME day Bob Duggan publicly announced that Pharmacyclics had successfully completed its share offering—August 5, 2009—an eighty-two-year-old woman showed up at a tiny medical clinic in Springfield, Oregon.

Located in a single-floor building of a strip mall anchored by an Albertsons grocery store, the clinic was a satellite office of the Willamette Valley Cancer Institute, headquartered in nearby Eugene. The woman had been suffering from chronic lymphocytic leukemia, or CLL, which had returned after chemotherapy treatment, causing the lymph nodes in one of her armpits to inflate to the size of a golf ball.

The most common form of adult leukemia, CLL is diagnosed in 21,000 mostly older Americans annually, representing more than one-third of all new US leukemia cases each year. While defined as a relatively rare cancer, it is not rare enough. Because CLL is a slow progressing disease, about 186,000 Americans deal with it at any given time. The median age of patients is seventy-one, but it's not just an old person's disease. As many as 11 percent of CLL patients are under the age of fifty-five, so the absolute number of younger patients is still significant.

For doctors, treating CLL was both monotonous and abysmal, and to make matters worse, there had been no major medical advancements in CLL for a long while. The cancer grew slowly in most patients, who initially just kind of lived with it. Their doctors would typically see them every six months and tell them their blood tests looked good. But eventually, things would go south and one of these appointments would result in a recommendation for treatment. The tempo and conversation would then change rapidly, and there were mostly only two tools available. First off, there was the carpet bomb of chemotherapy that indiscriminately kills both good cells and bad. The second option was rituximab, the monoclonal antibody treatment developed by Richard Miller and the team at Idec. These therapies were often administered in a combination treatment program. Remissions rarely lasted for long.

For a subset of patients with a specific genetic mutation, a more brutal chemotherapy could be more effective, but even then, only the younger patients could tolerate it. Otherwise, the cancer would normally come back within two to four years. As malignant B cells collected in the lymph nodes of patients, these bean-sized glands in the armpits, neck, or stomach would swell up to the size of an orange. Patients would often lose weight and feel terrible. Some opted for bone marrow transplants to deal with associated bone marrow failure. For most patients, the disease would no longer be treatable and they would succumb to CLL or the complications from it and the chemotherapy that ravaged their immune system.

This was the situation the eighty-two-year-old woman who arrived at the Willamette clinic found herself in. Chemotherapy was no longer a viable option for her. But one of the two oncologists on-site, Jeff Sharman, suggested she participate in a new study; it was being run by a company called Pharmacyclics that had an experimental treatment, PCI-32765.

A lot of random events had come together to produce this moment. Sharman knew all about Pharmacyclics and its drug. He had known Richard Miller at Stanford, where as a thirty-one-year-old hematology-oncology fellow Sharman had first worked in Ron Levy's lab on the idea of impairing B cell receptor signaling in blood cancer. Miller frequently visited the lab, where Sharman had originally impaired B cell receptor signaling, not by blocking BTK, but by hitting a different tyrosine kinase called Syk. Some Stanford doctors thought that Sharman's work had helped inspire Miller to test a BTK inhibitor in lymphoma patients in the first place. And before he left Pharmacyclics, Miller had ended up including CLL patients in the first-in-human trial of PCI-32765 in order to more easily do assays.

Sharman had arrived in Oregon a year earlier to start a career as a practicing doctor at the Willamette Valley Cancer Institute. Meanwhile, at Pharmacyclics, the trial of PCI-32765 had been expanded under Ahmed Hamdy's direction to include a few new physician-scientists, clinical investigators who could recruit patients to the trial. Sharman had signed himself up, and he was now convincing the elderly woman suffering from CLL to be treated with Pharmacyclics' BTK inhibitor.

Sharman entered the patient into a database so she could get access to the experimental drug. He also called Hamdy. Sharman warned Hamdy that the patient's white blood cell count might increase. More white blood cells normally meant the cancer was advancing, but Sharman knew from his experience inhibiting Syk at Stanford that the white blood cell counts could eventually come down.

"Don't get alarmed," Sharman said.

The next day, the patient returned to the clinic to get her blood drawn, revealing that her white blood cell count had indeed shot up just as Sharman had anticipated. Standing in his muddy backyard that evening, Sharman called Hamdy to talk to him about it. Hamdy freaked out. Was the drug making the cancer *worse*?

"Are we causing a hyper-progression?" Hamdy barked into the phone.

But Sharman felt something else was going on, a signal beneath the noise.

"I could feel her armpit lymph nodes and they're smaller," Sharman responded.

For Sharman, swollen or firm lumps under the skin were the most surefire symptom of blood cancer, indicating that large numbers of cancerous white blood cells had gathered in the lymph nodes. The fact that the lymph nodes had shrunk meant that something good was happening. Sharman expressed confidence that the white blood cell count would begin to come down over time, just like it had with the Syk inhibitor he had worked on at Stanford, a drug called fostamatinib.

Hamdy ordered a CT scan. And indeed, the imaging showed a reduction in the patient's swollen lymph nodes of more than 25 percent.

Not long afterward, the elderly patient's lymph nodes shrunk by more than 50 percent, and she was noticeably feeling better. Her white blood cell count declined during her week off treatment. As a result, the patient was recorded to have had a partial response to the drug. Later in the fall, Sharman enrolled another relapsed CLL patient, a sixty-two-year-old who for years drove a taxi cab in Juneau, Alaska. He also experienced a partial remission while taking PCI-32765.

Back in Sunnyvale, word of the partial responses was greeted with a sense of relief. For the first few months of the trial, there had been no indication the drug was doing anything. It had not resulted in any harm, which was good, but there was no patient improvement either.

When Duggan heard at a Friday meeting about the first partial remission, he jumped up on the conference room table and danced an Irish jig. Duggan would later deny ever doing the dance. But for Glenn Rice, the moment was unforgettable.

CHAPTER 6

The Big Easy

H it by a cold spell in early December 2009, the temperatures in New Orleans dipped well into the 30s. Bob Duggan showed up in town dressed for the weather, one of twenty-one thousand attendees at the American Society of Hematology Annual Meeting, a four-day gathering known in the drug business as ASH. Duggan was not well known among the crowd and neither was his company. Pharmacyclics had only recently demonstrated an interest in hematology, the branch of medicine concerned with blood diseases.

Duggan made an indelible first impression. He stormed into the Ernest N. Morial Convention Center wearing a long, thick fur coat. Men and women dressed in standard business-casual attire marveled at him. He breezed past the hundreds of poster presentations offering new ideas and discoveries to scientists and investors. Duggan wasn't interested in them. He was a man on a mission.

Tom Turalski caught one glimpse of Duggan and felt a jolt of panic. His hedge fund had invested in a man who wore a fur coat to a medical convention. The analysts at Perceptive Advisors had been trained by their boss, Joe Edelman, to look out for even the slightest warning signs from CEOs they had bet on. Turalski and Edelman had just recently gotten spooked about an investment in a different company because the executive team behaved strangely when Turalski happened to run into them on a Manhattan sidewalk. Turalski pondered reporting this strange scene to Edelman, but decided it was not worth bothering his boss over a coat. Still, Turalski was not the only person who was having second thoughts about things.

Not long before the ASH conference, around Thanksgiving, Duggan had walked into Ahmed Hamdy's office to talk about the company's strategy for the event. Duggan had learned that medical conferences were a critical part of the biopharma industry's metabolism, where vital meetings took place and impressions were made. They needed to be taken seriously. The company had submitted a poster for the phase 1 data that had been collected for PCI-32765, the BTK inhibitor. These were early interim results of the drug's first-in-human study. Duggan was unsure whether presenting such early data would be a good idea and wondered if they should scrap the poster. Hamdy disagreed. He thought the phase 1 results would generate interest.

"You should go to ASH, you should present this data," Hamdy argued.

An excited Daniel Pollyea, the young Stanford fellow, went down to New Orleans to be the primary presenter of the poster, the first time in his career he would present data at a conference. The white and red poster detailed the experiences of sixteen patients between the ages of forty-nine and eighty-two treated with PCI-32765. Each patient had swallowed one dose of capsules for twenty-eight consecutive days, followed by one week of rest. Some of the patients had been given a higher dose of the drug than others.

The poster showed that five of the patients had experienced a partial response, meaning their enlarged lymph nodes had shrunk by at least 50 percent and several other markers had improved dramatically. Of those responding patients, two suffered from relapsed or refractory mantle cell lymphoma and one had follicular lymphoma. The other two responses were Jeff Sharman's previously treated chronic lymphocytic leukemia patients. Only three of the initial sixteen patients experienced anything close to a serious adverse event, and the other thirteen tolerated the pill just fine. Still, for the average ASH attendee, the data showed a drug in such an early stage of development that it didn't matter. On the surface, stuff like this happened often and never amounted to much.

Pollyea displayed and dutifully stood by the poster. Duggan came by. He shook hands with Pollyea and the two chatted for a while. For Pollyea, this was all thrilling. He was a mere research fellow, but he had a poster at ASH. He was hanging out with a biotech CEO.

But hardly anyone took any interest in Pollyea or his poster. Not a single doctor from the academic community ever approached him. Duggan continued standing by the poster as well, closely watching the activity around it.

At one point, Sandra Horning swung by to check on Pollyea and give her mentee some support. Duggan had of course effectively ejected Horning's husband, Richard Miller, from Pharmacyclics, the company Miller conceived of, founded, and built for seventeen years. Now they were both standing in front of a poster with the Pharmacyclics name on it. Neither Horning nor Duggan made a scene. Polished and diplomatic, Horning had just left academia and taken a high-profile job at Genentech as the global head of oncology and hematology. She had bigger fish to fry.

While the doctors and scientists mostly ignored Pollyea's poster, a Wall Street investor found his way to it, attracted almost by some invisible animal scent. Richard Klemm worked at OrbiMed Advisors, a relatively large biotech hedge fund in New York. He walked up to the poster and took a look. Reading the data presented, Klemm saw that this experimental drug owned by Pharmacyclics had generated two partial responses in chronic lymphocytic leukemia, or CLL. Partial responses in CLL, just about the most widespread blood cancer, were a rare event, and there was little to help patients when they got sick. The poster had been placed in the poster hall's lymphoma section, but here it was flashing a signal in leukemia. The early data on the poster in lymphoma did not look as interesting. Klemm called up his boss, Sven Borho, in New York. They saw that shares of Pharmacyclics had last changed hands for $2.35. OrbiMed started buying the stock the next morning. Borho bought his first Pharmacyclics share for $2.31.

Back in New York, another stock trader took note of the Pharmacyclics data in CLL. Before the stock market opened, Pharmacyclics put out a morning press release detailing the interim phase 1 results. It included some information that was not on the poster, data the company had recorded in the days after the poster had been prepared. There were another three CLL patients taking the drug who had experienced partial responses in recent days. In total, Pharmacyclics said, five out of six CLL patients on the drug had recorded partial responses.

"Holy shit," Wayne Rothbaum said to himself. "Five out of six, that's pretty amazing."

Rothbaum knew a lot about CLL and had invested in Pharamcyclics' summer share offering primarily because he thought that BTK was an interesting target. He found Pharmacyclics' results, as minuscule as they were, remarkable. This was Rothbaum's specialty, building an investment thesis out of a precious few pieces of data and being bold enough to do something about it.

While none of the medical professionals gathered in New Orleans seemed to care (they couldn't even spare a moment for the Pharmacyclics poster), Wayne Rothbaum, sitting in his office in front of his trading screen in New York, called up his broker.

"Whatever blocks you can find me, buy me up to one million shares," Rothbaum said.

While his broker tried to buy large chunks of shares from institutional market participants, Rothbaum also started buying smaller amounts of Pharmacyclics stock though his own trading platform. His broker called him back and said he had found someone willing to sell two hundred thousand shares. "Take it," Rothbaum said. "Whatever you can get, take it!"

Watching his six trading screens, Rothbaum could see the price of the stock steadily rising. Somebody else was buying the stock. The broker called Rothbaum and confirmed that another big buyer was gobbling up all available Pharmacyclics share blocks. Rothbaum told his broker to increase his bid. "I don't care what you pay, just buy it," he barked over the phone.

The other buyer was Sven Borho and OrbiMed Advisors. Rothbaum and Borho were friends. They didn't know it at the time, but the two New York investors were furiously bidding up the stock against each other.

Normally, a big volume day for Pharmacyclics' stock would mean one hundred thousand shares traded during a session. With Rothbaum and OrbiMed spurring demand, over one million shares changed hands, and the stock price rose by 17 percent in a single day. Another 741,000 shares traded the next day, and the stock closed at $2.93. Rothbaum bought one million shares. Not long afterward, Joe Edelman's Perceptive Life Sciences hedge fund would also become a big buyer of the stock.

At $37 million, Pharmacyclics' market valuation remained tiny, worth 96 percent less than it had been a decade earlier. But if you were watching closely, something about this company had suddenly interested someone—or some few—in a way worth noting.

//////////////////////

AHMED HAMDY LOOKED AT the ASH conference partly as a recruiting opportunity. He needed to build up Pharmacyclics' clinical operations. And just like that, just outside the poster hall of the ASH conference, Hamdy saw Raquel Izumi.

"That's the person I want to see," Hamdy said to himself.

Hamdy knew Izumi from their days together at PDL Biopharma. They never directly worked together—they had never even been in a single meeting with one another—but things had always been friendly between them. What they had in common at PDL was that they both reported to the same boss, and Hamdy knew that Izumi had been very well regarded.

"Raquel!" Hamdy called out.

Forty years earlier, Izumi's Colombian mother had kept her pregnancy a secret. She entered the United States with the hope that the child she was carrying would become an American citizen. Izumi was born in the United States and grew up in Northern California. When she was five, Izumi's parents divorced, and she ended up being adopted by her stepfather, a Japanese American who built a career in the US Air Force. Izumi liked to joke that from her stepfather she got a Japanese surname, a tiger dad, and military discipline. It all helped push her—a woman in an overwhelmingly male field—to a BA in biology from the University of California, Santa Barbara, and a PhD in microbiology and immunology from the University of California, Los Angeles.

Izumi had opted for the biotech industry after seeing the piddling wages in academia. She wanted to work in clinical drug development and found a path through the relatively obscure field of medical writing.

Medical doctors could get into clinical development without much trouble. But PhDs who wanted in? They generally had to become clinical research associates, a grunt job that required a lot of travel to the medical centers where patients were being dosed with experimental medicines.

With children at home, being a clinical research associate was a nonstarter for Izumi. But a mentor had sold Izumi on medical writing as a great cross-function position that involved working with everyone in the clinical development process—doctors, scientists, and regulators— and would give Izumi a bird's-eye view of how clinical development worked. The job was about generating documents, particularly for regulators and medical centers, describing research, trials, statistics, and results. And Izumi was a good writer.

Izumi worked her way up clinical development departments at biotech firms like Amgen and PDL, ultimately landing at SuperGen as a senior director of clinical operations. SuperGen had two posters at ASH, and Izumi generally liked to attend big cancer conferences. She had just taken a break after doing a lap around the poster hall when she heard a voice say her name.

Izumi recognized Hamdy and they got to talking. Izumi had no idea that Hamdy had joined Pharmacyclics, let alone that he was the CMO. Hamdy had more news for her. Quietly, like he was letting her in on a secret, Hamdy told Izumi he had been getting partial responses in blood cancer from an early trial of a BTK inhibitor drug. Izumi's eyes widened. Hamdy then gave Izumi a peek at some of Pharmacyclics' phase 1 data.

"I really want you to come and work with me," Hamdy said.

In her decade in biotech, Izumi had never been close to a cancer drug that was getting partial responses in a phase 1 trial. The chance to get in on a cancer drug on the ground floor was much more exciting than anything she had been working on. And with Hamdy as the CMO at a small company like Pharmacyclics, Izumi would have a real opportunity to contribute. She was determined to be a part of it.

Izumi marched up to her hotel room and started updating her résumé.

///////////////

DESPITE THE TEPID RESPONSE of much of the medical community, Bob Duggan left the ASH conference in New Orleans reinvigorated. Back in Sunnyvale, he prepared to interview Raquel Izumi. At a small biotech company like Pharmacyclics, it was not unusual for the CEO to interview incoming job candidates. Looking at her résumé, Izumi's 1993 degree from UCSB jumped out at him.

Duggan felt a strong affinity to the school where he had studied economics and met his wife, even though he never graduated. For years, he had been a trustee of the UCSB Foundation. Recently, he had even been invited to give the commencement speech at the UCSB graduation ceremony for the mathematical, life, and physical sciences division.

"I recently took over as CEO of a Northern California biotech company, quite frankly it was on a collision course with disaster," Duggan told the graduating class before delivering his punch line. "That's why it was available for me to take over!"

As he delivered his graduation speech, Duggan defined the word "commencement" as meaning both a day of celebration and a new beginning. He told the graduates he had recently learned from a children's book that the human body was composed of seventy-five trillion cells and that each had a job to do. Duggan had taken on-the-job learning to an entirely new level. He was literally learning about the human body from children's books.

Izumi had prepared to meet Duggan in a more conventional way. She planned to talk about her work history, PhD, and blood cancer. To her amazement, the entire interview centered around UCSB. The two talked about little else. Izumi left the interview concluding that Duggan knew little about the biotechnology industry, that he was passionate about what he was doing, and that the work meant a lot to him. She also figured that UCSB had helped get her a job as a senior director of clinical development at Pharmacyclics. She would get to help oversee the in-human trials of the BTK inhibitor and be involved in everything from study planning to timelines and execution.

After the conference in New Orleans, Duggan thought that Pharmacyclics might have hit a turning point, even if few others could detect the shift. New data of the company's HDAC inhibitor had also been presented there and garnered some attention. It was not clear which of these drugs would be the best horse to bet on, but Duggan could see that at least his options were expanding.

A few weeks later, in January 2010, the BTK inhibitor gained momentum from another push by Lou Staudt, the distinguished physician-scientist at the National Cancer Institute. Staudt's team finally published its peer-reviewed paper in *Nature*. The paper detailed the discovery that various types of lymphoma are driven by B cell receptor signaling and described this process as dependent on BTK activity. "BTK is a critical kinase for survival" of lymphoma cells, they wrote. Staudt had even conducted experiments with PCI-32765 and noted that B cell receptor signaling might respond to it.

At Pharmacyclics, Staudt's paper felt like a validation. The company featured the paper on its own website. Now, Duggan and Hamdy wanted to explore what the drug could do for CLL. Neither could possibly comprehend they were embarking on a journey that would change many lives, especially their own.

PART II

CHAPTER 7

The Next Phase

Ahmed Hamdy was walking to a gate at an airport one afternoon when his cell phone rang. On the line was Wayne Rothbaum. Hamdy had gotten used to hearing from hedge fund types. For months, he had been charged with selling Wall Street on Pharmacyclics' move into blood cancer, conducting multiple investor presentations.

Straight to the point, Rothbaum demanded to know why he should keep buying shares of Pharmacyclics when a rival firm, Calistoga Pharmaceuticals, was so far ahead.

Calistoga was a private Seattle company testing an experimental blood cancer drug, idelalisib, which targeted a different kinase, known as PI3K delta, in the B cell receptor pathway. Rothbaum was considering making a major investment in Calistoga, and his research made him wonder why he was bothering with Hamdy and Duggan.

"If I had your money, I would buy the stocks of both of them," said Hamdy.

Small biotech companies with experimental therapies essentially have two ways to try to fund their dreams. Calistoga and Pharmacyclics were prime examples. These companies can remain private and raise money from venture capitalists in successive equity financing rounds, like the kind Silicon Valley start-ups have made famous. The other option is to list on a stock exchange through an initial public offering or, in some cases, through a reverse merger into a publicly traded shell company. Public companies can issue stock to raise funds. The higher their stock prices, the more money they can raise.

At Pharmacyclics, the biggest owner of stock by far remained its CEO, Bob Duggan. But Rothbaum now owned a sizable percentage as well.

Rothbaum met with Duggan and the Pharmacyclics team in New York a few weeks after the ASH conference. He emphasized to Duggan how valuable a new treatment in CLL would be, given the relatively large number of patients. Rothbaum followed up with a letter to Duggan in February 2010 in which he laid out a regulatory path for quick FDA approval. His biggest concern was that Duggan would not emphasize the BTK inhibitor at Pharmacyclics over the HDAC inhibitor. Pharmacyclics was also working on its experimental blood clotting treatment, so its attention was spread across three different drugs. For such a small company, doing three things at once was a tall order. Rothbaum also worried that Duggan would partner with a larger pharmaceutical company to develop the BTK inhibitor, essentially selling off a piece of the drug. Rothbaum wanted Pharmacyclics to own 100 percent of such a potentially valuable product.

"I believe 32765 is a rare and unique asset. While still early, to date, the Phase 1 data is spectacular with an exceptionally clear and robust signal in CLL," Rothbaum wrote. He warned Duggan about how promising drugs often are "partnered off unnecessarily to big pharmaceuticals in the mistaken belief they needed the capital and expertise of these larger companies." Rothbaum wrote in capital letters: "DO NOT PARTNER PCI-32765."

Days later, Duggan led a conference call to update investors and stock analysts. Once the call began, Hamdy told investors that Pharmacyclics was working to start a new phase 2 trial program for PCI-32765 later in the year, but he was vague and noncommittal about exactly which conditions the company would target. Later, Duggan vaguely responded to a question from a stock analyst about potentially finding a strategic partner to help shoulder the financial burden of developing Pharmacyclics' drugs.

"When you get into business development and begin to predict the future, that road I have found in the past is paved with many land mines and a lot of dead bodies," Duggan said. "We have a policy to move all of our molecules into commercialization as fast as possible."

Then, like a slugger hitting cleanup, Rothbaum jumped on the line. He focused on the BTK inhibitor. Rothbaum said Duggan had three choices: going it alone, finding a partner, or selling the company. Rothbaum observed that going it alone would result in the biggest possible reward, but based on the way Duggan had answered the earlier investor question, it seemed like Duggan was intent on finding a partner. Rothbaum used Celgene as an example of a biotech company that did not partner on its key products or sell itself early on, and it became one of the biggest biotech companies in the game.

Duggan pushed back on Rothbaum's idea. He noted that Celgene issued stock along the way to fund its drug development programs, which also diluted the rewards of early shareholders. "If you look at Celgene, I think over the last ten years, they've gone from 45 million shares to about 450 million. There's dilution one way or another. You can provide someone with territorial rights. You can provide shareholders with equity."

"And you'll probably have a $28 billion market cap," Rothbaum replied snidely. Celgene's path had resulted in a massive valuation in the stock market that had benefited shareholders.

"Exactly right," Duggan snapped back.

Duggan sensed that Rothbaum didn't fully appreciate his ability to execute and make things happen. And for all he had poured into this company—his excruciatingly personal mission—Rothbaum's dismissiveness didn't sit well.

"Wayne, I'm here and others are here on the same terms you are," said Duggan. "We want to make this company viable—and this is the management team in place."

Duggan was just getting started.

"A year ago or six months ago, we had a negative net worth. Today, we have over $30 million in the bank . . . Our shares traded a few thousand shares a day. Today, they trade a few hundred thousand shares . . . But most importantly, our drugs in the clinic are driving the results . . . most importantly, the patients are pleased. These are three-time losers, typically. You get told you have cancer. You go home in tears, you come back hoping a drug will solve it, you find out, no, that didn't work. You try a second one, sorry, didn't really work. You try a third one, oh, it worked, now you've relapsed. How about a fourth one. Only 3 percent of Americans that have cancer are willing to subject themselves to what we do. But in our last cohort, in our BTK, it was standing room only where they enrolled in one day."

Rothbaum remained unmoved by Duggan's speech.

He inferred that Duggan would be inclined to partner on the development of the BTK inhibitor by selling the rights to a portion of the drug's future profits and he didn't like it. In biotech, Rothbaum believed, asset dilution could be far more costly than equity dilution. In other words, he thought that selling off a piece of a drug in return for required funding would leave you worse off than if you sold shares of the company that owned the drug to obtain financing. Rothbaum had his own ideas about how to conduct drug development and run a biotech company—and he was as strong-willed as Duggan.

But Duggan never did anything he didn't want to do. Rothbaum was just a trader, and all he could accomplish at this point was to squeeze out more practical information on which he could base his investment decisions.

So Rothbaum started to drill down on the crucial next phase of the BTK inhibitor's development. If handled correctly, Rothbaum thought it could change the fate of the company and hundreds of thousands of cancer patients. But if mismanaged, the drug would probably be abandoned for good, just another promising medicine that hit a dead end. Even if the BTK inhibitor was a lifesaving cancer drug, no one would ever know it if Pharmacyclics didn't make the right decisions to get through this next stage. All the promise could be undermined by a poorly designed study.

Rothbaum asked about the phase 2 trial Hamdy had mentioned earlier in the call. He demanded to know what condition exactly it would target. But Hamdy remained evasive. "There isn't yet a specific design that I can share with you to describe our phase 2," Hamdy said.

///////////////////

AHMED HAMDY STOOD IN front of the group of doctors he had invited to the Garden Court Hotel in Palo Alto, California. Some of the foremost experts in chronic lymphocytic leukemia had made the trip. Hamdy wanted them to be clinical investigators, doctors under whose immediate direction PCI-32765 would be administered to patients in a trial. Armed with the interim results of the phase 1 study, Hamdy had been able to generate strong interest in this advisory board meeting.

To kick off the meeting, Bob Duggan had first addressed the group, introducing them to Pharmacyclics, the company he now rightfully called his own. He spoke about the death of his son and how that tragedy had led him to Pharmacyclics. There was no mention of Richard Miller in the short corporate history. Duggan had turned the meeting over to Hamdy and sat at the back of the room. Hamdy introduced himself as well as Raquel Izumi and started to present the phase 1 data. He also had Jeff Sharman, who had flown down from Oregon, walk everyone through the experiences of his CLL patients on the drug. Hamdy then made some recommendations about clinical trial design.

Some of the doctors now in the room, like John Byrd at Ohio State University and Susan O'Brien at the University of Texas, had only a few months earlier rebuffed Hamdy because the phase I trial seemed to cherry-pick patients. But Hamdy had assured both of them that Pharmacyclics was now ready to meet their high standards.

The relationship between a biotech company and physician-scientists is a delicate dance requiring mutual trust: the companies need to trust that the doctors are truly interested in the experimental therapy and committed to their study, while the doctors need to trust that the science is sound. None of the doctors in the room really liked Hamdy's trial ideas, which they found overly complicated. But Byrd and O'Brien did home in on an interesting sawtooth pattern in the data.

In the phase I trial, the patients took the capsules daily for four weeks, followed by a week of rest when they did not take the drug. For the four weeks on the drug, the data showed the patients' enlarged lymph nodes shrinking and their white blood cell, or lymphocyte, count shooting up. This elevated white blood cell count, called lymphocytosis, is typically viewed as a bad sign that the cancer is advancing and getting worse. On the week off the drug, the patients' white blood cell count came down. Then the patients would take the drug again and the white blood cell count dramatically went up again. This created the up-and-down sawtooth pattern that Byrd and O'Brien found significant. Even though the elevated white blood cell counts would scare most doctors, Byrd wondered if this sawtooth pattern might be a good sign. He noted that with each new cycle on the drug, patient white blood cell counts never reached their previous peak.

Byrd and O'Brien were aware of work that had been done by Jan Burger, a physician-scientist colleague of O'Brien's at the University of Texas. Burger had analyzed blood samples of patients taking fostamatinib, the same Syk inhibitor drug that Jeff Sharman had tinkered with while he was a fellow at Stanford. Importantly, Burger had shown how B cell receptor signaling enhances crucial survival signals coming from outside the CLL cells, the *external* tissue zone around them, such as the lymphatic tissue and bone marrow. Byrd had experience working with another B cell receptor signaling inhibitor being tried in blood cancer, Calistoga's idelalisib. While Calistoga and Pharmacyclics were competing with each other, Byrd had an impartial role. He didn't care which company brought a drug that could help his patients, and he could use knowledge he attained working on one company's drug to inform him when he worked on another. For Byrd, it was all part of a larger scientific pursuit. Byrd recalled that Calistoga's drug also initially drove up the lymphocyte count in patients.

Byrd wondered if Pharmacyclics' drug was mobilizing the B cells in the bone marrow and lymph nodes to move into the bloodstream. Forced out of their protective and stimulative niches, the B cells would be more vulnerable in the blood. It would be easier for PCI-32765 to find and confront malignant B cells if they were exposed in the bloodstream rather than buried inside bones and lymph nodes. Byrd thought the sawtooth pattern could, over time, result in an overall downward trend and diminished amount of disease. Another reason Byrd was encouraged was that the patients in the phase 1 trial experienced very few adverse events and none were severe.

Intrigued by the data, Byrd and O'Brien recommended a new and very simple phase 1B/phase 2 trial of CLL patients who had been failed by previous treatment and elderly CLL patients who were just initially starting treatment. Standing silently for a moment, Hamdy listened very carefully to what they were saying and paused before speaking. He then played down his initial clinical trial ideas, shrugging them off as just a straw-man proposal. He quickly threw his support behind the suggestions being advanced by Byrd and O'Brien. The rest of the meeting was spent designing a relatively large trial that would simply try to determine if the drug worked in CLL.

Byrd was impressed with how things came together. Pharmaceutical and biotech companies would sometimes thank doctors like him for their input and continue down whatever path they had chosen. Hamdy was listening to the expert doctors in the room. He was very good at listening. Byrd left Palo Alto motivated to enroll as many CLL patients in the trial as possible.

///////////////

JOHN C. BYRD GREW up in a small town, Augusta, Arkansas, located in one of the poorest corners of America. The son of a glazier who ran a small glass company, Byrd's family managed to stay above the poverty line—but not by much. Neither of Byrd's parents went to college. Recognizing that their son was bright and not being challenged in the town's public school, Byrd's parents sent him to Catholic boarding school in Arkansas starting at age fourteen. For some years, he needed a scholarship to attend. He found that living away from home could be difficult. Byrd also struggled with a stutter that seemed to get worse as he got older. Sometimes, when he had a hard time finding words, the wrong ones would pop out.

Byrd studied chemistry at tiny Hendrix College in Conway, Arkansas. To pay for medical school at the University of Arkansas, he joined the army, which brought him to Washington DC's Walter Reed Army Medical Center in 1991. He loved his years in the army, where he could mix clinical research with caring for patients and shooting an M-16 assault rifle at a shooting range. Sometimes, he would grab food from the cafeteria named after Ogden Bruton, the former chief of pediatrics at Walter Reed in the 1950s. There, Bruton treated a boy who could not fight off common childhood diseases. The doctor discovered that the boy had a disorder that kept his body from producing mature B cells, impeding his immune system. Decades later, the enzyme responsible for the disease would be discovered and named after him, Bruton's tyrosine kinase, or BTK.

At Walter Reed, Byrd became an oncologist specializing in leukemia. It angered him that CLL patients had so few treatment options. "We've got to do better," he would say. In the army, Byrd developed a keen hatred of chemotherapy. He witnessed the pain and anguish it put patients through, the damage it would do to both the body and the mind. His antipathy only grew more intense during his mother's chemo, which had been prescribed to fight a cancer that ultimately took her life.

Chemotherapy was the enemy. It had to be replaced by treatments that were more humane. Because it hitches a ride in the bloodstream, chemotherapy circulates throughout the body and kills splitting cells no matter where they are found. Cancer cells divide more often than healthy ones, so it is more probable that chemotherapy will find and destroy them. But, inevitably, chemotherapy attacks healthy cells as well. This whole medical approach could literally be traced back to the devastation of World War II, when research on mustard gas led to medical science that advanced chemotherapy as a way to kill cancer cells. The method was far from exact and created a lot of collateral damage. While he was in the army, Byrd became determined to help patients go beyond this form of treatment. He was amazed how many doctors and scientists were also motivated by this goal. Finding new therapies that target only cancer cells and did not kill healthy cells had become the holy grail of cancer drug development.

After a decade, Byrd retired from the army with a rank of major. He moved to Columbus to join the faculty at Ohio State's College of Medicine in 2001, and by the time he started working on the Pharmacyclics clinical trial, he had become director of the hematology division, directing over fifty faculty members, and leader of the leukemia research program.

Over the years, Byrd's Catholic faith grew stronger. He would come to believe that God wanted PCI-32765 to get developed in order to help patients. At Ohio State, he had a huge machine to make that happen: the Arthur G. James Cancer Hospital, usually known just as The James, one of the nation's largest cancer hospitals. This was no single-floor clinic next to the Albertsons. Byrd had a large staff of doctors, nurses, and administrators and was prepared to throw this institutional weight behind the Pharmacyclics trial.

For her part, Susan O'Brien, who worked at the nation's biggest cancer center, the MD Anderson Cancer Center in Houston, also tapped into the enormous resources at her disposal to support the Pharmacyclics study.

Hamdy and Izumi got working on the new phase 1B/phase 2 trial that had been fleshed out by the advisory board in Palo Alto. Hamdy and Izumi wrote the trial plan, designed to dose 130 CLL patients to gauge the effectiveness and safety of the drug. The trial was not randomized, meaning there was no control group of patients getting a different drug or placebo. There were only two dosing levels.

At a small upstart organization like Pharmacyclics, Izumi proved to be invaluable. At every biotech company she had worked at after Amgen, regardless of her formal role, Izumi found herself writing up documents for the regulators and medical researchers, distinguishing herself by her ability to write thoroughly, compellingly, and quickly. Energetic with flowing brown hair and green eyes, Izumi's no-nonsense approach combined dedication and toughness. Because she was a scientist with clinical operations experience, Izumi could take all the data and seamlessly write protocols, filling out all the science boxes but also writing out a plan that could be implemented at a medical center or hospital. Izumi got things done—and, vitally, she made it easy for others to get things done, unlocking and cracking open every door for the various medical counterparts to walk right through.

Hamdy and Izumi wanted to enroll as many patients as possible as quickly as they could in their trial. With her background in medical writing, Izumi supercharged this effort by generating documents. She churned out documents for the FDA, she churned out documents for the ten medical centers participating in the trial, and she churned out documents for state governing bodies. These documents presented scientific information to physicians and regulators, ranging from doctor brochures to study plans, trial contracts, safety reports, patient information leaflets, and answered questions posed by regulatory staff. The engine of drug development requires a well-defined road map, and Izumi was communicating the rules of the road to the patients, researchers, doctors, health professionals, and regulators. In this maze of locked doors, she had all the keys.

The pattern repeated itself at Pharmacyclics, where Izumi—and the astonishing bandwidth of information she held in her head—got PCI-32765 flowing to 130 desperate patients. Hamdy and Izumi complemented each other well. Hamdy had a firm grasp of the big picture, maintaining his relationships with the key doctors and as an MD handling the medical responsibility of the trial. Izumi's incredible work ethic and detail-oriented approach accelerated the effort. Hamdy and Izumi liked working with each other and found moments to laugh together to break the stress. It took them fifty-seven days to get the trial up and running in April 2010, much faster than the average clinical trial start-up period of five to six months. Soon it was enrolling patients at breakneck speed.

At Ohio State, John Byrd had an elegant way of explaining to patients how the drug might work for them. As they sat in an examination room, he would walk over to the light switch and turn it off. His finger, he said, was like a tyrosine kinase inhibitor drug. When the light was on, the cancer was spreading. When he turned the light off, the cancer halted. Then Byrd would tape the light switch off. The tape was like an irreversible inhibitor, he said; that's how this experimental new drug worked. Then Byrd told patients that chemotherapy could also turn off the light, but instead of a finger or tape, it was like using a sledgehammer. Many of these patients had experienced the sledgehammer. They were happy to try the tape.

Hamdy kept an air horn in his office. Each time a new patient enrolled in the trial, Hamdy would emerge from his office and set it off, giving the office in Sunnyvale a loud jolt.

Duggan constantly demanded updates. He walked around the office, sometimes clutching a dictionary. With the mentality of an investor, Duggan hired consultants to double-check and, sometimes, question what Hamdy and his staff were doing. In preparation for meetings with Duggan, Hamdy memorized the latest developments in the database for each patient on trial, ready to answer any questions Duggan or the consultants threw his way.

It was a high-pressure environment. From time to time, Duggan would walk into Izumi's office and ask to see the latest patient information, glancing at her computer screen over her shoulder. Izumi did not mind. She was impressed by how hard Duggan worked to understand what was going on. But every now and then, Duggan's more eccentric nature would pop up. One time he tried to talk to her about how cells move at the speed of light. Izumi brushed it off. The trial had started and she had work to do.

///////////////////

WAYNE ROTHBAUM REMAINED ENTHUSIASTIC about Pharmacyclics' BTK inhibitor. Others on Wall Street were starting to sniff out the opportunity, too. Pharmacyclics' stock kept rising. In June 2010, the company issued shares to investors for $6.51 apiece, raising $50.8 million for operating expenses. Rothbaum was a buyer and by the end of August 2010, he held a 5 percent stake, becoming the second-biggest shareholder of Pharmacyclics after Duggan. Joe Edelman also bought more stock, and his Perceptive Advisors hedge fund held a stake that was just about as large as Rothbaum's. The difference was that Edelman was buying many of those shares with other people's money, and Rothbaum was only using his own. Rothbaum was convinced of the connection between kinase inhibition in the B cell receptor pathway and the treatment of CLL. He also invested in Calistoga and its idelalisib drug in a big way, leading a $40 million financing round announced in June 2010 that gave him about 10 percent of the private company.

Around the same time, Pharmacyclics presented updated data from the initial phase 1 trial of PCI-32765 in Chicago at the American Society of Clinical Oncology's annual meeting. It now showed that eight out of the first thirteen CLL patients in the study experienced partial remissions. After the data had been presented, Pharmacyclics held a dinner reception for doctors and investors. John Byrd made sure to show up and met Rothbaum there for the first time.

As people sat down at round tables to eat dinner, Ahmed Hamdy began giving a presentation about the clinical program for PCI-32765. As he did, some investors pressed Hamdy about why Pharmacyclics had not increased the daily dose being tested in patients until it hit a maximum tolerated dose—the highest dose of a drug that does not cause bad side effects. They wondered why Pharmacyclics was not trying to find the perfect therapeutic window that would confer the most effectiveness with the least possible amount of toxicity. Maybe Pharmacyclics was leaving some of the drug's effectiveness on the table? The drug might be even better if more of it was given. Hamdy argued it was not necessary because the lower doses had achieved 90 percent target inhibition of the BTK signal and there was no need to push the safety envelope with patients. Rothbaum listened intently. Privately, he had made the same point to Duggan earlier. Rothbaum entered the fray and argued that it made scientific sense for the company to find the maximum tolerated dose.

The dinner had grown tense. Duggan stood and calmly walked over to Rothbaum's table. He grabbed Rothbaum by the arm, squeezing his bicep and twisting it firmly. Duggan then leaned in close. "We are considering it," Duggan whispered in Rothbaum's ear. "Now, just shut the fuck up already."

CHAPTER 8

Fired

In October 2010, a desperate and hurting Robert Azopardi made the short trip from Long Island to Manhattan's Upper East Side. At age sixty, Azopardi had an appointment with Richard Furman, an oncologist who ran the chronic lymphocytic leukemia research center at Weill Cornell Medicine. The appointment was Azopardi's last hope. After several rounds of chemotherapy, his doctor had run out of ways to keep his CLL at bay. Azopardi had been told he had three months to live and advised to prepare for hospice care. As a last-ditch effort, he had been directed to Furman.

Azopardi's wife brought him in a wheelchair to one of Furman's examining rooms. The enlarged lymph nodes in Azopardi's back pressed on his sciatic nerve, causing him to bend over from the excruciating pain. He had not walked in months. The lymph nodes on both sides of his neck and under his arms had also swollen up. At the appointment, Furman told Azopardi he was a candidate for a clinical trial of PCI-32765. "I don't know if it's going to help you," Furman said. "But it's worth a try."

About four weeks into treatment, Azopardi woke up in the morning and did not feel the familiar pain running down his leg. For a moment, he wondered if he had died.

After a month of taking the drug, Azopardi returned to Manhattan and sat waiting in Furman's examining room. When Furman walked into the room, Azopardi got up and stood straight. "Hey doc," he said. "Look at me."

Azopardi's improvement had been so dramatic that Furman called Ahmed Hamdy personally to tell him about it. Clinical information about trial patients, who are assigned a number to protect their privacy, is fed into an electronic database, but discussions are always being conducted between sponsoring companies and physician-scientists.

Furman was not alone. Hamdy had been hearing these kinds of stories anecdotally from the MDs scattered across the country. He kept getting verbal reports of shrinking lymph nodes. Raquel Izumi heard about one patient who had started receiving hospice care prior to taking the drug. He felt so good he went out and bought himself a Harley-Davidson motorcycle.

At Ohio State, where John Byrd had been furiously enrolling patients on the phase 2 study, many patients taking Pharmacyclics' BTK inhibitor were seeing their enlarged lymph nodes disappear. Word of the drug had been circulating at the participating medical centers, and new CLL patients were rushing to get into the trial. At Pharmacyclics' Sunnyvale offices, origami was hung at the entrance for each patient who responded to the drug.

When Byrd and his team started to enroll patients at The James in Columbus, Ohio, they started seeing a distinct pattern. As patients started swallowing the pill daily, their white blood cell counts would shoot up and their lymph nodes shrink. Other physician-scientists, like Susan O'Brien in Houston, Richard Furman in New York, and Jeff Sharman in Oregon, were all experiencing the same thing.

In the initial small phase 1 trial, patients had stopped swallowing the drug after four weeks of treatment and took a week off. During the week-long break, their white blood cell count would drop. Then the patients would start a new four-week cycle on the drug, followed by another week off. Patient white blood cell counts rose and fell, accordingly. With the phase 2 trial design, however, the CLL patients were no longer taking a weeklong break. But without the time off, the white blood cell count of most of the patients rose and remained elevated. At Pharmacyclics, Hamdy and Izumi continued to worry that this was a bad sign. If nothing else, this lymphocytosis meant disease progression by the traditional criteria for CLL.

Byrd, O'Brien, Furman, and Sharman knew what they were doing. They took the lymphocytosis seriously, but did not want to ignore other positive signs. The lymph nodes of many of the CLL patients on the drug were indisputably getting smaller. Other important markers, like their platelet, neutrophil, and hemoglobin counts, were often rebounding from dangerously low levels. In a world dominated by data and statistical analysis, the experience of seeing and feeling the dramatic reduction of the lymph nodes in patients counted for something. The patients, who ultimately made the decision, wanted to stay on the drug, even after being told about the higher lymphocyte count. For them, it was simple. They felt so much better.

In her Sunnyvale office, Raquel Izumi also kept trying to figure out what was going on. One key marker, the white blood cell count, went in one direction, while just about every other key marker went in another. She shared the same fear that Hamdy had expressed to Sharman at the very start. Could the drug be making the disease worse? According to the traditional "response criteria," patients were only considered to be improving if their lymph nodes shrank and their lymphocyte count was reduced by 50 percent. The doctors on the front lines started to wonder if maybe they needed new criteria. Maybe seeing smaller lymph nodes was enough?

In December 2010, the Pharmacyclics team headed to Orlando, where the annual ASH conference was being held. A year earlier in New Orleans, the company had one simple poster for PCI-32765. This time around the drug had a much higher profile at the conference with three abstracts for oral presentation and a poster. The blood cancer community had taken notice of Pharmacyclics, and the data being released on

PCI-32765 in Orlando, while still small, intrigued them even further. The company pooled information on forty-five CLL patients treated with the BTK inhibitor from the initial phase 1 trial and the phase 1B/2 trial. The analysis showed that 80 percent of the evaluable patients saw their lymph nodes shrink dramatically. From that standpoint, the treatment looked incredibly promising.

There was one catch. Pharmacyclics explained that by traditional metrics, the response rate was much lower, under 50 percent—mostly because of those pesky white blood counts. Pharmacyclics claimed that data from the phase 1 trial suggested that the white blood counts decreased over time as patients continued to take the drug and that by taking the drug longer, patients could potentially achieve partial remission.

The data released in Orlando and the way it had been described by Pharmacyclics was controversial. Some people thought that Pharmacyclics and a group of doctors had conjured up a new response criteria to fit the data that had been generated. But the data piqued the interest of yet more investors on Wall Street, especially Felix Baker and his brother, Julian Baker, who together ran a New York hedge fund that specialized in biotech stocks. With his PhD in immunology from Stanford University, where he also completed two years of medical school, Felix Baker had his Baker Brothers Advisors start buying up Pharmacyclics' stock, which finished the year hovering around $6.

On the flip side, Wayne Rothbaum didn't like what he was seeing. He got spooked by the information Pharmacyclics released. Like doctors John Byrd and Jeff Sharman, Rothbaum also had experience with idelalisib, the drug that targeted a different kinase in the B cell receptor pathway and that had gotten much further ahead in the drug development process. Rothbaum's position as a 10 percent owner of Calistoga, the company behind idelalisib, entitled him to be a board observer, and he feared he had a view into the future of PCI-32765.

Calistoga's drug was not working as well as he had hoped. From the start, idelalisib also caused the white blood cell counts to shoot up. For the most part, patients taking idelalisib over a long period of time would eventually see their white blood counts come down to the pre-drug baseline, but they did not go much lower. The drug never really cleared the cancer cells out of the blood.

Rothbaum worried that the elevated white blood counts in patients in the second trial of PCI-32765 were a bad sign. He thought it could be an early indication that the ultimate safety and effectiveness of Pharmacyclics' drug wouldn't be good and that there was not all that much difference between Pharmacyclics' drug and Calistoga's drug. It could also mean that disrupting B cell receptor signaling might be a dead end.

Rothbaum had trained himself to never remain anchored to any investment thesis and to always take into account new information that challenged it. Now he was starting to lose his conviction in Pharmacyclics.

Rothbaum and his hedge fund buddy Joe Edelman sold most of their Pharmacyclics shares and made a tidy profit. It was a decision that would redefine Rothbaum's life.

//////////////////////

AHMED HAMDY HAD AN idea that he just could not let go of. The initial phase I trial had included nine patients who suffered from mantle cell lymphoma, a nasty blood cancer that is both rarer and faster growing than CLL. Seven of those nine patients responded to the drug—at least partially. Now Hamdy wanted to launch a phase 2 trial of PCI-32765 in patients suffering from mantle cell lymphoma.

Getting Duggan on board for an expensive phase 2 trial took some convincing. Duggan had hired Gwen Fyfe as a consultant and gotten her a seat on Pharmacyclics' board of directors. Fyfe had just left Genentech, where she had spent more than a decade playing a role in the company's most prominent cancer drugs, rising to be vice president of oncology development. One of the drugs Fyfe had worked closely on was rituximab, which Genentech had developed with Idec. Hamdy's idea was falling flat with Fyfe as well as the other Genentech veterans Duggan had hired.

In general, the Genentech gang lacked confidence in Hamdy because he was a urologist, while Fyfe and the others were oncologists with special training in blood cancer. Mantle cell lymphoma is an exceptionally difficult and rare disease. Fewer than three thousand Americans are diagnosed with this cancer annually, making it one of the smallest patient populations in lymphoma. Financially speaking, it is a tiny market. Pharmacyclics would be taking a huge risk for a potentially small-dollar reward that would help relatively few people. Considering Pharmacyclics' limited resources, the Genentech gang preferred the company to keep laser focus on CLL, the most common form of adult leukemia. The CLL patients who needed help numbered in the hundreds of thousands. The company could turn to mantle cell lymphoma later.

Of course, Hamdy wanted the company to use its resources wisely and make sound financial decisions. But the way Hamdy saw it, patients diagnosed with mantle cell lymphoma were at the time essentially defenseless. By the time they were diagnosed, the cancer had often already found its way to the lymph nodes and bone marrow. Hamdy felt they had an obligation to help these patients as well, even though there were relatively few of them. He also thought it made sense from a strategic perspective.

Normally, the FDA requires new drugs to undergo lengthy and costly head-to-head trials against existing disease therapies to gain market approval. In the case of mantle cell lymphoma, where few treatments existed, Hamdy felt the FDA would likely grant accelerated approval, meaning Pharmacyclics would not need to put its drug in a large and expensive head-to-head trial. It would only need to show that PCI-32765 was effective and safe.

Having an effective drug approved by the FDA, even in a small market, would have immense value. It could make it easier to get the drug approved for other conditions. Hamdy argued that they should prove that the drug worked, that it safely and effectively blocked BTK in mantle cell lymphoma, and rush it to market. Once they did, then regulatory approval could be secured for other indications, like CLL.

Hamdy pushed his strategy through, and together with Izumi, he designed and launched a phase 2 trial of the drug in mantle cell lymphoma patients.

Unfortunately for Hamdy, however, his next decision took him down the wrong path. Against the advice of the Genentech veterans, Hamdy amended a trial protocol to boost the dosing amount of PCI-32765 in some patients to see if they were getting the most out of the drug's effectiveness, the move Wayne Rothbaum had suggested. The drug ended up not showing more effectiveness in patients who received the higher dose, but it did cause an increase in white blood cell counts, which some worried would be seen as another negative for the drug.

The rift between Hamdy and the former Genentech executives was growing wider. To them, the urologist didn't know what he was doing. And the stakes—life, death, and money—were getting appreciably higher.

////////////////////

PETER LEBOWITZ HAD BEEN at his new East Coast job for three weeks before being tasked to fly out to Northern California to visit a small company based in Sunnyvale. The new head of blood cancer at Johnson & Johnson's Janssen pharmaceutical unit, Lebowitz had been hired from another giant company, GlaxoSmithKline, to beef up Janssen's oncology drug pipeline. The idea was to find early-stage drugs being developed by smaller biotech companies and strike partnership deals with them. Paul Stoffels, J&J's pharmaceutical research and development chief, had come up with a plan to scout new drugs. He called it Project Playbook. It organized each disease in a Bullseye chart, shaped like a shooting target. The Bullseye chart for blood cancer consisted of twenty-five experimental drugs, and PCI-32765 was at the outer ring, meaning it was early on in its development.

But even though Pharmacyclics was on the outer ring, Peter Lebowitz was intrigued and called Bob Duggan, curious if the small start-up might be holding a winning lottery ticket. Meanwhile, Duggan needed money, at least a billion dollars to cover lab costs, clinical procedures, on-site monitoring, staff and administration, patient recruitment, statistical analysis, and regulatory compliance. So he gladly took the call from Lebowitz and other representatives from big pharmaceutical companies that wanted to partner with Pharmacyclics on its BTK inhibitor.

Duggan had Hamdy work with Ramses Erdtmann on a presentation for the big companies. They prepared to present to Celgene, Novartis, and J&J's Janssen unit. Hamdy also set up a secure data room equipped with a computer where executives of these big companies could camp out and review the data for themselves.

After hearing a presentation given by Hamdy and others, Lebowitz spent three days in the data room. During his part of the presentation, Hamdy had emphasized the trial he had just started involving mantle cell lymphoma patients, hoping to create traction for his approach in the minds of potential partners.

"Mantle cell could be our first indication approved," Hamdy said. "We should be focusing our resources on getting the mantle cell approval while we're still running the CLL trial." Gwen Fyfe, who also attended the presentation, interjected and stopped Hamdy in his tracks.

"I disagree with that," said Fyfe, adding that the company should put most of its energy behind the CLL trial.

During a meeting break, Lebowitz approached Hamdy to tell him that the mantle cell idea had merit. For some, the display of internal strife would have roused suspicion, but it didn't dissuade Lebowitz. He left Sunnyvale for the flight back to the East Coast, certain that his giant company should do everything it could to beat out its rivals for the drug. "We have to get this one," Lebowitz wrote in an email to his boss.

Duggan seemed pleased. The negotiations with the big pharmaceutical companies had gone well. His CMO had kept in close contact with Lou Staudt and Wyndham Wilson at the National Cancer Institute, and Hamdy was on the cusp of getting the NCI to sponsor two trials of PCI-32765 in patients with non-Hodgkin's lymphoma and multiple myeloma, giving added credibility to the drug.

Together with John Byrd's team and Pharmacyclics' preclinical group, Hamdy was also finishing up some important scientific work that would soon be published in *Blood*, the peer-reviewed medical journal published by the American Society of Hematology. The article described how PCI-32765 inhibited a key signaling pathway within CLL cells. But the article also showed that in addition to targeting the CLL cells themselves, the drug prevented CLL cells from responding to survival signals coming from the zone outside the cells. There were at least two mechanisms enabling the drug to combat CLL.

In a meeting to discuss the data of the higher-dosed CLL patients, Duggan put his hand on Hamdy's shoulder and told him things would work out fine when the data came out at an upcoming conference. "You're a good guy," Duggan said.

In April 2011, Duggan called Raquel Izumi into his office. Izumi had been working tirelessly to enroll patients in the trials of PCI-32765. Duggan knew how hard she had been working because he was also constantly in the office, pushing his employees to move with entrepreneurial speed and zeal. He told Izumi she would be getting a pay raise of nearly 30 percent, the biggest in Izumi's career. "Raquel," Duggan said, "you are a linchpin for this organization."

At the same time, Duggan couldn't resolve in his head the rising tension between Hamdy and Fyfe. It was a distraction. They openly disagreed with one another on things and just didn't seem to work well together. Pharmacyclics had one shot to bring its emerging BTK inhibitor drug to market, and Duggan wanted to collapse timelines and swiftly move Pharmacyclics from being an early-stage development company to a late-stage development company. That was the next big step, and Duggan was eager to take it. In his mind, partnering with a big pharmaceutical player would accelerate things further. It would also be necessary to change the composition of his staff. Pharmacyclics president Glenn Rice, who was experienced with early-stage drugs, was on his way out. Francisco Salva had already been pushed aside.

Duggan prided himself on being the kind of business executive who could make tough and unemotional decisions. He was always prepared to abruptly change his mind when he thought he could head off a problem that could threaten his success. Nothing and nobody was sacrosanct. He rarely suffered regrets. He was the CEO of Pharmacyclics and the chairman of its board. He owned more than a fifth of the company's shares. He had absolute power over Pharmacyclics. All of Pharmacyclics' employees were working for Duggan, and they all knew they were there at Duggan's whim.

On a Thursday in May 2011, Duggan decided to have a talk with Hamdy.

Duggan said he considered Hamdy to be an early-stage guy and that he was thinking about hiring someone above him on the development side with more late-stage experience. Duggan explained the simple facts to Hamdy as Duggan saw them. Hamdy was not a hematologist, Pharmacyclics was now a blood cancer company. It needed experts in this area. A misstep now could sink the entire effort.

Hamdy knew that Duggan disliked the disagreements with the Genentech gang, like the quarrel over targeting mantle cell lymphoma. Part of the problem was that Hamdy took a small-company approach to things, trying to do several things in tandem at all times, sometimes without much consultation. The fast pace was efficient but could also get messy. Fyfe and the former Genentech drug developers had cut their teeth at a big corporation. They often did things sequentially and in a regimented fashion.

Hamdy went home for the weekend thinking they would figure things out.

//////////////

SITTING IN HIS OFFICE the following Monday morning, Ahmed Hamdy tried to focus on the work that needed to get done. Before he managed to get going, Maky Zanganeh walked in with a message. "Bob wants to talk to you," she said.

Hamdy got up and walked to Bob Duggan's office, just two doors down from his. He didn't notice that Pharmacyclics' head of human resources was also in the room. The moment Hamdy sat down, Duggan got to the point.

"We're going to have to let you go," Duggan said.

Bewildered and shocked, Hamdy managed to ask why he had just been fired. Duggan didn't really answer. But privately, he had seen the rift growing between Hamdy and the Genentech veterans and it simply had to stop. He had arrived at the conclusion that despite previous sentiments and conversations, this was the only way.

The entire conversation lasted less than 30 seconds.

Hamdy got up to leave. That's when he noticed the human resources person walking beside him. She escorted Hamdy out of Pharmacyclics' offices to his car. Hamdy drove next door to the parking lot of the Fry's Electronics store. He sat there in his car for hours trying to figure out what to tell his family.

Despite some of the office disagreements and rivalries, Hamdy did not see this coming. Now without a salary, he started thinking about his finances and his Pharmacyclics stock.

The letter of employment Hamdy had received when he started working at Pharmacyclics in 2009 was five pages long and he remembered it. The letter granted Hamdy stock options to buy 300,000 shares at a strike price of just 73 cents per share. It stipulated that 75,000 of the options would become exercisable after Hamdy finished his first year at Pharmacyclics; the remaining 225,000 options would become exercisable and vest thereafter in thirty-six equal and successive monthly installments, meaning Hamdy would have to work at the company for four years before he got them all.

The letter added one more detail about the options: "All vesting under your option will cease upon your termination of employment." Lastly, the letter made clear that Hamdy's employment was "at will" and that the company could terminate his employment "at any time for any reason, with or without cause." It was a standard Silicon Valley contract. Hamdy hadn't hired a lawyer, and he signed it when he got it.

Hamdy wondered if Duggan might have been thinking about recapturing all of Hamdy's super cheap unvested options when Duggan had decided to remove him. The firing would cause Hamdy to lose 137,000 of those options that had not yet vested. Hamdy planned to sell the stock options that had vested to finance his family's life until he figured out what would happen next. He would just have to forgo any further upside in Pharmacyclics' stock.

That same day, Izumi was summoned to see Duggan.

Izumi did notice the human resources chief in the room before Duggan started speaking. She sensed what he would say before he said it. But she still had trouble believing he would actually speak the words. Then Duggan told Izumi she wasn't needed anymore either.

One month earlier, Duggan had given her the biggest salary bump of her career. Now she was being fired. Izumi ducked into a bathroom stall as she was being escorted out of the building to text her husband about what had just happened. "Babe, you are not going to believe this . . ." When she emerged, her eyes still wide with disbelief, Izumi was told she would never be allowed to enter the office again.

CHAPTER 9

Partners

R aquel Izumi opened her eyes in a Chicago hotel room she couldn't afford. It was being paid for by a friend of hers, or rather the company that employed her friend. Izumi had spent days lying listless on her couch after being fired. She felt like she had just done the best work of her career—maybe the best work she would ever do. And this was the result. She knew that she had likely been fired as part of the Hamdy purge, but that didn't dull the sting of being escorted to her car like some kind of criminal. Finally, her husband told her to get up. It was time to move on.

Izumi traveled to Chicago to attend the American Society of Clinical Oncology's annual meeting. John Byrd would be presenting the PCI-32765 data for chronic lymphocytic leukemia in a big oral presentation, and Izumi wanted to be there. The problem was Izumi had to pay her own way and money had become tight. She had gotten herself to Chicago and found the hotel room to stay in. One of her friend's colleagues had decided to skip the conference's Monday morning events, and Izumi borrowed his identification. Wearing a conference badge bearing a male Indian name, Izumi snuck into the massive McCormick Place Convention Center. She headed straight to the Arie Crown Theater and sat in one of the five thousand seats just before Byrd started giving his talk at 9:30 a.m.

To Izumi, the data looked incredibly encouraging. The interim results of the phase 1B/2 study consisting of eighty-three CLL patients showed that after six or seven months of treatment, the elevated white blood cell counts started to fall and the disease began to clear out of the blood. Two-thirds of elderly patients whose CLL was being treated for the first time partially responded to the drug. Many of the other previously untreated patients had seen their lymph nodes shrink substantially. A less impressive amount—just under half—of the CLL patients on the trial who had been failed by other treatments experienced a partial response to PCI-32765.

Only three patients on the study had to stop taking the drug due to modest diarrhea, nausea, and vomiting, and a mere three patients had their cancer progress. By any criteria, these were small numbers.

For Izumi, the moment was profoundly bittersweet. Izumi had played a pivotal role in a drug that she believed would help cancer patients. Her name was on the abstract of the research published in the *Journal of Clinical Oncology*, which accompanied the presentation. She was so proud, and so sad, robbed of the opportunity to keep working with this incredible medication. The drug would be moving on without her. As Byrd went on with his presentation, Izumi sat in her seat at the Arie Crown Theater and cried.

Shortly after Byrd's presentation, Wayne Rothbaum went to his scheduled private meeting at the conference with Bob Duggan, Maky Zanganeh, and Gwen Fyfe to talk about the new data that had just been presented. It was a beautiful sunny day in Chicago and the meeting took place outside. Rothbaum had sold more than half of his Pharmacyclics shares months earlier, but he remained a shareholder and very much engaged. As was often the case, Tom Turalski was at Rothbaum's side. Rothbaum sat down and turned to Duggan.

"I just have one question, and, obviously, it's not my business and I understand if you can't answer it," Rothbaum said. "What happened to Ahmed? I thought he was really good."

Duggan looked up and stared at Rothbaum before speaking. "Wayne, all I'm going to say is, when you're rowing a boat, everybody needs to row in the same direction."

The data presented at the meeting really made it look like the drug was making a clinical difference for CLL patients and that the lympho-cytosis issue—the troubling elevated white blood cell count—that had spooked Rothbaum had become less of a threat. There may have been a sneaking suspicion on his part that he'd sold a large part of his position too soon, but Rothbaum could not bring himself to go back into the stock and buy back the shares he had sold now at a higher valuation. Neither could Turalski's hedge fund boss, Joe Edelman.

Rothbaum tried to rationalize his way out of the situation. In his mind, he tried to poke holes in the strength of the data. The drug had still been tested in a relatively small community of patients. Its long-term safety and durability remained unclear. Most of the CLL patients in the second Pharmacyclics trial had only taken the drug for six or seven months. The interim data could be the result of cherry-picked patients.

But something else was going on. When Rothbaum first started buying Pharmacyclics stock, it traded between $1 and $2. Now, it changed hands for $8. He had sold a big chunk of his Pharmacyclics stock for around $6, booking an investment gain of roughly 300 per-cent. Even if it was the logical choice—and Rothbaum prided him-self on being logical—psychologically, buying the stock back now at a higher price was incredibly difficult.

But a few big pharmaceutical companies assessing the potential of PCI-32765 with fresh eyes were coming to a different conclusion. They were hungry to buy and control as much of the drug as they could.

/////////////////

BOB DUGGAN SAT IN the Pharmacyclics conference room and started reading the definition of a word from the dictionary aloud. Sitting with him, the heads of the company's different functional groups listened attentively. They were getting used to this routine. The weekly executive session at Pharmacyclics always started out this way. Duggan would define a word and philosophize for a short while about how the definition could be relevant to what they were trying to accomplish. Sometimes, he would espouse his business tenets. Duggan would emphasize three key criteria with which to approach any business decision: quality, time, and cost. Quality was the most important thing, Duggan preached. A high-quality experiment created value. Hiring quality people created value. A company that produced awful computers generated awful profit margins. It was the same in biotech. Duggan implored his executives to figure out how they were going to produce the highest-quality output and understand how it would impact time and cost. Could they collapse time or cost? High costs or extended time would be worthwhile if they produced a lot of quality and return on investment.

Then Duggan would turn the meeting over to Maky Zanganeh. Like a prize fighter bursting into the ring, Zanganeh would start firing off questions and directives, quizzing each executive and demanding updates—boom, boom, boom. Has the letter been sent to the FDA? How many patients have been enrolled in that clinical trial? Did the employee candidate accept the offer? Do you have an update on the project? Not everyone could survive this room, and those who could not handle it would often quit or be fired.

Duggan would soon promote Zanganeh to the position of chief operating officer. But even before he did, it was clear that Zanganeh had become the second-most powerful person at Pharmacyclics—the person Duggan valued above all others. Exceptionally smart and a shrewd negotiator, Zanganeh had Duggan's complete trust. Together, they challenged long-held industry assumptions and made sure to keep in close contact with the investment community—people like the Baker brothers, Felix and Julian, whose hedge fund had become Pharmacyclics' second-biggest shareholder. Both Duggan and Zanganeh worked extremely hard—they lived and breathed Pharmacyclics.

A big chunk of the organization reported directly to Zanganeh. When the company leased a nearby two-story building to accommodate its growing number of employees, Duggan made sure to put Zanganeh's office next to his. He extensively renovated their two offices with polished blond wood floors and glass walls. A private glass door was installed between their offices so they would not have to go out to the hallway to visit one another. Zanganeh's office chair had been placed so she had a view into Duggan's office, where she could see him sitting at the long wooden table he had installed. It was an incredibly close relationship. Their bond was hard to ignore, and over time, Duggan started to publicly refer to Zanganeh's child as his own son.

A young and recently hired project management director, Maria Fardis, quickly figured out that trying to differentiate between Duggan and Zanganeh was a grave mistake. If you were dealing with one of them, you were dealing with the other. They were one. Duggan could be charming and liked to keep things light, while Zanganeh hammered away on tiny details. Together, they ran the company to their personal strengths. Fardis could not comprehend how some people at Pharmacyclics did not grasp this.

With a PhD in organic chemistry from the University of California, Berkeley, as well as an MBA from Golden Gate University, Fardis had joined Pharmacyclics from Gilead Sciences, the big biotechnology company. Born in Iran, Fardis found the opportunities open to her in America exhilarating. She was determined to make the most of them. Ambitious and capable, Fardis assimilated well into Western culture and was determined to be a star in her field, though the lilting Persian accent that shadowed her words was a constant reminder of her past.

Duggan always tried to hire people like Fardis. "Never hire a person who depresses you," Duggan would tell people who brought him MIT-trained scientists or Harvard doctors, no matter how brilliant. "I couldn't wait for that guy to leave." The way Duggan saw it, scientists also had to be salespeople, who could sell a study and convince doctors to put their patients on it or sway other people in the development process, like regulators, to do what was required. He wanted extroverts like Fardis. Fardis also bonded over her shared heritage with Zanganeh, and the two spoke Farsi in the office, sometimes even in meetings.

It was not unusual for Zanganeh to have open conversations in languages others could not understand. Sometimes in meetings, she would turn to Ramses Erdtmann, the other prominent Duggan loyalist on staff, and make comments in German. Duggan, Zanganeh, and Erdtmann relished bringing an outside perspective to biotechnology. Nobody could argue that Duggan didn't know business. But operating in such a highly regulated industry made pushing boundaries complicated at times. When scrutinizing expenses, Erdtmann would ask in his German accent, "Are we buying the Volkswagen or the Mercedes?" The analogy, which might be mundane in the context of real estate or autos, was not always appropriate for biotech. During one meeting discussing efforts to increase patient trial recruitment, Zanganeh floated the idea of giving the doctors who recruited the most patients some sort of reward, something like a car. At a different point, Duggan wondered why Pharmacyclics could not put together an advertising campaign to promote its experimental drug to potential trial patients. Duggan questioned things. Why couldn't they get a discount on the CT scans they were ordering for patient trials? The life sciences veterans had to carefully explain that these tactics were industry no-nos, as there could not be bias in the decision of whether to enroll a patient in a clinical trial. Duggan and Zanganeh mostly accepted the pushback, but kept prodding people to be innovative.

///////////////////

DESPITE THE MOMENTUM, THE realities of the business dictated that Pharmacyclics needed yet more money and yet more expertise to develop PCI-32765, and Bob Duggan was certain a partnership with a big pharmaceutical company would be the best way to attain both. It would be expensive to get financing from the stock market, where

Pharmacyclics shares were still quite modest at $11 in the fall of 2011, valuing the entire company at less than $800 million. It wasn't just guys like Wayne Rothbaum and Joe Edelman who had grown cold on the Pharmacyclics story. Pharmacyclics' BTK inhibitor still did not generate much excitement on Wall Street.

The lymphocytosis issue continued to muddy the prospects of the drug for many hard-core biotechnology investors. OrbiMed Advisors, which had initially bid up the stock when Rothbaum was trying to buy it, would soon also sell its position. Duggan had gone to New York in the summer to drum up more investor interest, but many investors saw Duggan and Pharmacyclics as an oddity. The abrupt firing of Ahmed Hamdy, who had played a prominent role talking to Wall Street types, had made some investors further skittish. And Duggan continued to be outlandish. At a clambake beach party that the Trout Group hosted on a cold August evening in the Hamptons, Duggan took off his shirt, donned swimming trunks, and dove into the Atlantic Ocean. The other attendees stayed on the shore of Flying Point Beach clean, dressed, and pressed while Duggan splashed around alone in the waves.

On the other hand, Duggan had created interest among some big pharmaceutical companies. This interest was far from overwhelming. Not every pharmaceutical company wanted to negotiate with Duggan. AstraZeneca, the big British-Swedish pharmaceutical conglomerate, took one look under the hood at Pharmacyclics and swiftly backed away. But Celgene, Novartis, and Johnson & Johnson's Janssen unit persisted. Discussions went on for months.

There were some core things beyond money that Duggan wanted out of any partnership he struck with a big pharmaceutical company over PCI-32765. He was insistent that Pharmacyclics keep control of the drug's commercial operations in the United States. Duggan wanted Pharmacyclics to build its own US sales force and generate revenues in the world's biggest market, where he could slap the Pharmacyclics name on the pill bottle. Keeping regulatory responsibility for the drug in the United States also mattered to him. Duggan planned on always having Pharmacyclics' staff in the room with the FDA. If the drug was to get approved, it would be Pharmacyclics' regulatory strategy that would get the job done.

For Duggan, the idea was to build a viable company. He had made this the first goal of Pharmacyclics' mission statement. Duggan also wanted Wall Street to see the BTK inhibitor as Pharmacyclics' drug. Whether or not it ever came time to sell Pharmacyclics, the company needed to look like a robust operation and not just a royalty stream flowing off the back of a biotech whale.

As hard as Duggan bargained on these points, not everyone was willing to concede them. The price Duggan was demanding to partner on PCI-32765 was not cheap, exceeding the entire market valuation of Pharmacyclics itself. Some of the corporate executives involved in the negotiations from Novartis and Celgene simply were not going to spend big dollars and let these characters with no life sciences experience— Duggan and Maky Zanganeh—run the show.

It was with J&J that Duggan found the most willingness to conduct a partnership on his terms. The words of Peter Lebowitz, the blood cancer head of J&J's Janssen Pharmaceuticals—that the company must do everything possible to get this drug—had been heeded at the highest levels of the organization. Paul Stoffels, J&J's global head of pharmaceutical research, started flying out to Sunnyvale from the East Coast to negotiate directly with Duggan.

The power dynamic in biopharma was shifting, and Stoffels was early to sense it. This was why he had hired Lebowitz. The big pharmaceutical companies were becoming more dependent on medicines developed by smaller and narrowly focused biotechnology companies. Fewer of J&J's drugs were being created in-house, and its development pipeline would soon become dominated by drugs first pushed forward at other companies. This was a seismic change that had just started sweeping the industry.

A large bespectacled man whose dark eyebrows increasingly did not match his graying hair, Stoffels quickly bonded with Duggan, and the two drove a deal forward. J&J's lawyers and business development staff argued on contractual points. Then there was a final negotiation in the offices of the Palo Alto law firm Wilson Sonsini. When they were done, Duggan and Stoffels simultaneously stood and grasped each other's hand as their lieutenants clapped.

The deal Duggan struck with Stoffels made the two men partners and provided Pharmacyclics with more than $1 billion.

The two companies agreed to collaborate to develop PCI-32765. J&J bought half the future worldwide profits of the drug for $975 million in upfront and milestone payments, including $150 million paid right away. J&J's Janssen also agreed to cover 60 percent of all development costs. Essentially, J&J would be paying for the development of the drug.

Duggan succeeded in having Pharmacyclics retain control of American commercial and regulatory operations. The drug's US revenues would be booked by Pharmacyclics and shown on its financial statements; J&J would mostly handle commercialization and regulatory activities outside the United States. Pharmacyclics even retained a role in the drug's manufacturing. There were a few technical points Duggan did not win. He failed to keep sole control of certain functions like safety reporting of the drug and medical affairs, but these were small potatoes. The way Duggan saw it, the J&J deal would finance Pharmacyclics' participation in the development of PCI-32765, give the company an international footprint to sell the drug that Pharmacyclics could never build by itself, and give the drug the credibility that could only come from a prominent pharmaceutical company like J&J.

Duggan put Fardis in charge of the relationship with J&J. For both Duggan and Fardis, the partnership symbolized an important step in what they were trying to achieve. Fardis's rapid ascent at Pharmacyclics made her one of the most important people at the company.

Pharmacyclics had preserved the ability to give PCI-32765 a formal generic name, and Duggan had a vision for it. Duggan found that generic drug names, which adhered to a recognized nomenclature, lacked flare. He understood that after a drug got approved, the marketing department would help give a new medicine a catchy brand name, with a capital letter in front and a memorable cadence. But there were rules. The generic name for Pharmacyclics' drug would need to include the label "tinib" to designate it as a tyrosine kinase inhibitor and "bru" to identify the kinase it blocked, Bruton's tyrosine kinase. How could he make a mouthful like "brutinib" attractive?

Duggan wanted the drug to be seen as a groundbreaking product. Like many CEOs, Duggan admired Steve Jobs and the way he made his technology gadgets ubiquitous, like the iPhone and iPad. Duggan plucked the lowercase "i" from Apple's products and put it in front of his cancer medicine's required components: ibrutinib.

CHAPTER 10

Going Dutch

I n the days after Ahmed Hamdy was escorted out of Pharmacyclics, he started commiserating with Francisco Salva, who had also been cast aside by Bob Duggan. In his darkest moments, Hamdy would feel like he had been targeted and scammed. But at this precise moment, Salva was having lunch with Hamdy and doing his best to turn things around, for the both of them.

"Forget about Pharmacyclics," Salva told him. "What do you really want to do for the next five years?"

Hamdy thought about Salva's question. "I really want to develop good drugs," he replied.

"So let's just do that," Salva blurted out.

Hamdy looked at Salva in disbelief. "Are you out of your mind? How are we going to find the drug or fund it?" Salva thought for a moment. "You've done it at Pharmacyclics. Why can't you do it again?"

Salva knew, as surely as Hamdy did, that this was mostly happy talk. The odds of achieving anything like they had at Pharmacyclics were near zero.

That same evening, Hamdy received a call from Raquel Izumi. After the highs and lows of Pharmacyclics, Izumi couldn't imagine life with a boring corporate job. Izumi was under personal financial pressure, but she needed the rush of being part of the biotechnology vanguard. She had read a paper by someone she knew who was at the Huntsman Cancer Institute in Salt Lake City. "He has a BTK inhibitor. Do you want to go get it for autoimmune indications or multiple myeloma?" Izumi asked.

"Hold on," said Hamdy, taken quite aback. "What are you saying?" Izumi repeated herself.

She wanted to license the drug at the Huntsman Cancer Institute and start trials in patients with rheumatoid arthritis. This was the very same condition ibrutinib had originally been designed to target by the chemists at Celera Genomics. Based on what she learned from ibrutinib, Izumi thought this BTK inhibitor could also work for multiple myeloma, a kind of blood cancer.

Hamdy thought he was being punked. "Did you talk to Francisco today?"

Izumi had not.

"I just spoke to Francisco. And he wants to find a compound and start a company," said Hamdy.

Hamdy marveled at their hubris. But Izumi and Salva's determination overwhelmed him. Many biotechnologists go their entire careers without developing a single successful drug. What were the chances lightning could strike twice?

The next day, Hamdy, Izumi, and Salva met in San Carlos, California, at Le Boulanger Bakery & Café, a sandwich shop on Laurel Street, the town's main drag. As the trio discussed their new pipe dream, Hamdy got a call.

It was Wayne Rothbaum.

Hamdy put his phone on speaker. Rothbaum was direct as ever.

"Ahmed, what are you doing next?"

Salva had sparked the dream. Izumi identified the drug. Rothbaum had the money. It had all come together—almost completely by chance—in less than forty-eight hours.

The Pharmacyclics refugees formed a new company, Aspire Therapeutics. They met regularly at the bar of the Rosewood Sand Hill hotel
in Menlo Park, which in addition to being a hot Silicon Valley meeting
place also offered free Wi-Fi. The practicalities of their start-up situation were not lost on the intrepid trio. They needed to start from the
beginning, they needed to build a broad base of investors to support
their new initiative, and they needed to reintroduce themselves to the
market. There was only one place to do that—the J.P. Morgan Healthcare Conference.

In most of America, JPMorgan Chase & Co. is known as the
nation's biggest bank. But in the biopharma industry, J.P. Morgan
stands for one thing: the most important conference and networking
event of the year—the industry's Super Bowl. In January 2012, Hamdy,
Izumi, and Salva joined the pilgrimage north to San Francisco for the
conference.

There were 395 drug companies officially presenting to investors at
J.P. Morgan in 2012. Aspire Therapeutics was not one of them. Instead,
Aspire had been relegated to Biotech Showcase, a less prestigious side
conference. While the J.P. Morgan conference took place at the luxuri-
ous Westin St. Francis Hotel on San Francisco's Union Square, Biotech
Showcase took place at the Parc 55 Wyndham, four blocks away. Still,
Salva had rented a suite and set up some meetings to talk about the
inhibitor out of the Huntsman Cancer Institute.

One of the people who walked into the suite was Edward van Wezel.
"Are you the guys from Pharmacyclics?" he asked in a Dutch accent.
Hamdy, Izumi, and Salva nodded.
"I am really not interested in your drug."
Van Wezel was the managing partner of a Dutch venture capital
firm called BioGeneration Ventures, specializing in funding European
biotech start-ups. Van Wezel dismissed the group's pitch on the com-
pound from Huntsman. He was interested in something else.
"I've run into these scientists," van Wezel said. "It would be inter-
esting to have you guys come take a look."

////////////////////

ON THE SURFACE, THE sleepy town of Oss seems like something of a backwater, surrounded by cow and pig farms. About an hour's drive southeast from Amsterdam, the town has 92,000 people, a few windmills, and Catholic churches, in contrast to the Protestantism that dominates the rest of the country. Once each year, Oss' Carnaval celebration lights up the town. Otherwise, it's mostly overlooked. But wedged between Oss' modest houses, made of red brick and terra-cotta roof tiles, lies Pivot Park, a cradle of modern cancer science that has impacted the world in a way few people realize.

Pivot Park is the biopharma campus where a local slaughterhouse owner had founded a company called Organon in 1923. Their first product was insulin extracted from the pancreas of pigs. Both the slaughterhouse and Organon became part of Akzo Nobel, the massive Dutch chemicals conglomerate. Like most huge multinationals, Akzo Nobel would regularly acquire and divest various units. In 2007, it was Organon's turn to be flipped. Akzo Nobel sold the company, now a broad human and animal health business, to New Jersey–based Schering-Plough for $14.4 billion.

Around the same time, a talented Organon chemist working in Oss, Tjeerd Barf, had been focusing his attention on BTK inhibitors, much like the scientists at Celera Genomics had done. Barf's major supporter was a man named Allard Kaptein. With graying hair and glasses, the tall and thin Kaptein was a popular biologist at Organon's Oss complex. The kind of group leader a chemist like Barf always preferred to work with, Kaptein had a sharp sense of humor and knew how to bridge chemistry with biology in a way that spurred early drug development. As Barf and his team advanced work on the BTK inhibitor, Kaptein eventually headed a second team of about a dozen additional scientists. This was a gifted group, each of whom was juggling multiple projects. Some of them were also excited about a different cancer therapy that blocked a protein called programmed cell death receptor 1, or PD-1.

Both the BTK and the PD-1 projects were being run out of the same Oss building. Kaptein's group focused on making a particularly selective molecule, meaning it would block BTK and little else. It was not clear that such an approach made sense. But the chemists hoped a cleaner, or more selective, compound would limit toxicity while treating rheumatoid arthritis. They came up with a thing of beauty: a warhead that irreversibly bound to BTK while hitting only four other kinases, five fewer than ibrutinib. They tested it in a mouse with rheumatoid arthritis and the mouse's condition improved. The drug was given a code name, SCH 2046835.

As the scientists in Oss went about their work, they were oblivious to the corporate negotiations underway across the Atlantic Ocean. In 2009, only two years after they became part of Schering-Plough, the entire Schering enterprise was gobbled up by Merck & Co., an even bigger New Jersey pharma giant, for $41 billion. Merck did the deal for many reasons, but mostly so it could get its hands on Schering's allergy spray, Nasonex. In the process, Merck also acquired Organon's complex in Oss, including Kaptein, Barf, their BTK inhibitor, and the PD-1 project. Merck had little interest in what had been going on at its new and remote Dutch outpost. The Oss complex was just another asset to be bought and sold.

On top of being irrelevant to Merck's mission, Kaptein's BTK project struck a bad chord within Merck. As a policy, Merck didn't like covalent compounds that irreversibly stuck to their targets. And unfortunately for the Oss team, this was exactly what it had designed with its BTK inhibitor. Senior management in New Jersey thought that drugs like this could staple onto off-target proteins and become dangerous to patients. They were concerned about irreversible drugs leading to hapten formation, an immune response that could create serious side effects, such as anaphylactic shock. Merck especially did not like the idea of these drugs in patients with a nonlethal disease like arthritis. The risk was simply not worth it for Merck.

Within a few months, the BTK program in Oss ground to a halt.

Merck started looking to shut down its newly acquired complex in Oss. Kaptein, Barf, and their team members would soon be laid off. But Kaptein and Barf believed that they were onto something special. They decided to create a company called Covalution BioSciences— and its first matter of business was to extract their BTK inhibitor from Merck.

///////////////

LIKE MANY DUTCH FATHERS, Allard Kaptein had a son who played soccer. They lived in Zaltbommel, about a 30-minute drive from Oss on the A2 motorway leading to Amsterdam. Kaptein's twelve-year-old boy played for the local soccer club, Nivo Sparta. After one of his son's games, Kaptein huddled in a canteen area to stay dry during a rainstorm. As his son showered and changed, Kaptein started making small talk with one of the other Nivo Sparta dads, Hans van den Bighelaar. The fathers had driven their boys to the game together and just watched them run up and down a soggy field. They talked about the layoffs at Oss and Kaptein's dream of grabbing his BTK inhibitor on his way out the door. But he needed money and was not shy about admitting it. Van den Bighelaar said he knew someone from his long-distance running club who might be helpful: a biotech venture capitalist named Edward van Wezel.

Kaptein set up a meeting with van Wezel and sent him Covalution's business plan for the BTK inhibitor. By that time, Kaptein knew about Pharmacyclics' and ibrutinib's success in chronic lymphocytic leukemia, so he included blood cancers along with rheumatoid arthritis as potential conditions to target. Kaptein and Barf drove up the A2 motorway to Naarden, just outside Amsterdam, to meet van Wezel in his office. Van Wezel was impressed with their ideas and presented them to his investment partners. He was greeted with skepticism. Bio-Generation Ventures was a small fund and developing a cancer drug was an expensive business. Ibrutinib was already far ahead in its treatment of blood cancer, and they would be starting from zero by licensing this drug from Merck. Van Wezel would not give up so easily.

Van Wezel headed to Leiden University, the oldest university in the Netherlands, popularly associated with the Dutch Golden Age of the seventeenth century. He had made an appointment to see Stan van Boeckel, a part-time chemistry professor who had just been laid off as Organon's medicinal chemistry chief. Van Wezel headed to the Academy Building, a former neo-Gothic church on the banks of the Rapenburg canal. The building's "sweat room" is where generations of students waited for their test results and, upon receiving diplomas, made their mark by signing their names on the wall. In this ancient building, with its cherry-colored bricks, leaded-glass windows, and clock tower, van Boeckel greeted van Wezel. Then he shared his thoughts. The compound, van Boeckel said, was one of the best he had come across in his career.

Preparing for his annual trip to San Francisco for the J.P. Morgan summit, van Wezel spotted the name Ahmed Hamdy. Partnering with the former chief medical officer of Pharmacyclics might be extremely helpful, van Wezel thought. A few weeks later, van Wezel was inviting Hamdy, Izumi, and Salva to meet Kaptein and Barf.

///////////////

AHMED HAMDY, RAQUEL IZUMI, and Francisco Salva showed up in New York without a clear idea of what they were doing. Their big meeting was on Fifty-Seventh Street in Midtown Manhattan, just two blocks south of Central Park. The thing with the Dutch was in the background, and this meeting in New York was far more pressing.

They took an elevator to the fifteenth floor of the prewar office building, the home of Quogue Capital. Wayne Rothbaum greeted them but had little patience for niceties. Hamdy had sent Rothbaum the data on the BTK inhibitor at the Huntsman Cancer Institute that Izumi had found.

Rothbaum had reviewed it and had a strong opinion. "It's garbage."

He nearly threw them out of the office. Shocked, the three tumbled out of Rothbaum's office and down to the street. The Hunstman Institute compound seemed dead.

Not long after, the trio returned to New York. The thing with the Dutch was now in the foreground. With few cards left to play and little else to do, they were here to meet Edward van Wezel and the two Dutch scientists, Allard Kaptein and Tjeerd Barf. This meeting took place in a nondescript conference room at a Midtown Manhattan law firm. They were an unlikely and motley crew. Van Wezel was the only person in the room who had a full-time job. Kaptein and Barf had paid their own way to New York, making sure to take the cheapest flight available, a connector through Iceland. The two Dutch scientists even shared a hotel room. Meanwhile, Izumi's husband had seen his job at a biotechnology company go sideways, and he was also now out of work. For a period of time, Izumi and her husband tried to make ends meet by going on unemployment insurance, but with two kids and a Silicon Valley mortgage, their financial situation had become precarious.

Despite these kinds of pressures, the group hit it off from the start and the atmosphere relaxed. Kaptein and Barf presented a short slide deck that proposed licensing not only their BTK inhibitor, but also two other molecules created by the group at Organon and ignored by Merck. Most of the discussion centered around the BTK inhibitor. The preclinical data dazzled Hamdy. He turned to Izumi and they gave each other a look.

Van Wezel noticed their excitement. Hamdy and Izumi said that the Dutch compound looked like it was much more selective than ibrutinib, a drug they knew very well, to say the least.

They took the Dutch through a potential development program. Van Wezel was an experienced team builder, and he had an early feeling that this would be a good one. The two sides had different expertise—the Dutch were preclinical scientists and the Americans were clinical practitioners—so nobody felt threatened. Van Wezel suggested an even partnership, split 50-50.

The group, a mix from California and the Netherlands, dined together happily that night at the Mediterranean restaurant Fig & Olive. With the prospects of very limited side effects because of its selectivity, Hamdy believed they could take the Dutch BTK inhibitor and revolutionize the treatment of autoimmune conditions. The market for rheumatoid arthritis was huge, much bigger than the market for blood cancer. Hamdy understood the excitement of his new team to tackle a treatment for blood cancer, but he preferred to stay away from directly competing with Pharmacyclics. He was wounded; and he never wanted to hear Bob Duggan's name again.

Before leaving New York, Hamdy wanted to check one last thing. Just in case. He worked up the nerve to call Rothbaum again and described the compound in the Netherlands.

Rothbaum was intrigued.

The investor immediately picked up on the potential of the selective nature of the molecule. Two weeks before, he had been all but thrown out of they guy's office. Now, Hamdy had Rothbaum's full attention.

Hamdy told van Wezel about Rothbaum. Eventually, the two would speak by phone. Each time they did, Tom Turalski also seemed to be on the line. "Tommy's here, too," Rothbaum would bellow. Van Wezel liked that Rothbaum had extensive experience with the B cell receptor signaling pathway, but he had no idea about Rothbaum's potential financial firepower. There was virtually no publicly available information about Rothbaum, even on the Internet. He was like a ghost.

Everyone on the team saw salvation in the Dutch molecule. Kaptein and Barf wanted vindication for their work, something they would never receive from Merck. Hamdy and Izumi saw a drug that might be better than ibrutinib. Van Wezel would take pride in putting together another superb team. And Rothbaum—well, Rothbaum had something to prove. Mostly to himself. He knew he had been right about BTK inhibitors, but he had given up on ibrutinib too soon. This was his way back in.

But a large problem remained. The Dutch still hadn't secured the rights to the drug they wanted to develop. It belonged to Merck & Co.

CHAPTER 11

/

Genius

B ob Duggan stood in front of a large projector screen wearing a blue button-down shirt and holding a wireless presentation remote control. He faced a group of Pharmacyclics employees sitting in rows of chairs that had been laid out perfectly in a large room at corporate headquarters. Duggan started talking about the word "genius."

"I was stuck in the dictionary definition of the word genius," Duggan said, adding that the textbook definition of the word described a genius as someone extraordinary. "When I got into the etymology of the word and I looked at it, it was a totally different picture. In fact, it was the polar opposite—it says innate, inborn, inherent characteristic— that's not extraordinary, that's ordinary, that's inclusive."

Duggan had organized an entire employee program at Pharmacyclics around the twenty-four genius qualities outlined by Alfred Barrios that had been made required reading by L. Ron Hubbard, the founder of the Church of Scientology. For Duggan, Barrios's genius principles provided an incredibly valuable approach to business and life and could be a competitive advantage to those who embraced them. Duggan had licensed the Genius materials from Barrios before the author died, and this corporate class was an important part of the Pharmacyclics program he had launched. "We are all geniuses when you really get into the word," Duggan said. "That's the revelation that I want to bring out here at Pharmacyclics."

As Duggan spoke, slides flashed on the projector screen behind him. "AN IDEA TO LIVE BY: Turn on your Genius Characteristics," one of the slides said. Duggan told the employees of his biotechnology company that the genius principles had been taken from an article that had first been published in the *National Enquirer*. The slide presentation then went through each one of the twenty-four genius characteristics. The slide for optimism, for example, said: "Geniuses never doubt they will succeed. Deliberately <u>focus</u> your mind on something good coming up."

Duggan prepared decks of Genius flashcards with the different characteristics on them that he distributed to Pharmacyclics employees. He wanted them to know these qualities. In addition to the flash-card training, he also sent out Genius exercises and topics that could be discussed at Genius workshops. In annual performance reviews, Duggan would talk about genius characteristics and ask people which ones they had met and which were their favorites. Was it enthusiasm or persuasion? Or maybe they had practiced individualism?

Some Pharmacyclics employees recognized the Scientology overtones in the Genius program. For his part, Jesse McGreivy had gotten used to his monthly Genius meetings. He tried to get as much out of the meetings as he could. A doctor trained as a hematologist-oncologist, McGreivy had worked as a clinical researcher at a major biotech company, Amgen, before being hired to run clinical work for Pharmacyclics' critical BTK inhibitor program. Attending these monthly meetings had become part of McGreivy's job. He had been assigned a Genius partner, Paula Boultbee, recently hired to run sales and marketing. Less open-minded about the Genius meetings she attended with McGreivy, Boultbee went along with it and tried to go through the training professionally.

During his one-on-one Genius meetings with Boultbee, McGreivy would fill out forms and answer questions tied to the Genius principles. The way McGreivy and Boultbee both saw it, Duggan was trying to instill a corporate culture of positive thinking, no different from the life coaches or other corporate culture initiatives they had encountered over their careers. McGreivy recognized the self-help roots of Scientology and took to heart Duggan's message that people had an inner potential that could be unleashed to make them more than they thought they could be. This was not just talk. Duggan had become hugely successful and had overcome the devastating death of his son to build something positive and potentially life changing. He had the will to lead a company developing an oncology drug even though he had no previous experience in the life sciences. Duggan had been doing exactly what he was preaching.

But not everyone at Pharmacyclics felt this way. For some Pharmacyclics employees, the Genius training seemed tangential to the main focus of getting ibrutinib to patients. At a minimum, some employees thought the Genius training ate up their valuable time. Others also became intimidated by what they considered to be the creep of Scientology into the company. The Church of Scientology had come a long way from its counterculture roots in Southern California, where in the 1970s it was sometimes seen as something people graduated to after experimenting with recreational drugs. It had become a controversial religion in America, surrounded by heaps of news coverage detailing allegations that the Church mistreated its members and acted belligerently against its critics. One might argue that the track record of other religions hadn't been so great. But some Pharmacyclics employees strongly believed there was no place for any religion in the workplace, especially a workplace dedicated to science. Alice Wei, a high-level regulatory consultant Duggan hired, thought a corporate line of separation had been crossed. In a private conversation with Duggan, she spoke up about her feelings. Duggan was respectful about Wei's concerns, but it did not deter him from pushing the Genius program forward.

////////////////

BOB DUGGAN DID NOT fill the office with Scientologists. That was not his style. In fact, Duggan claimed he never brought any aspect of Scientology to the Pharmacyclics workplace. He was adamant that the Genius program had nothing to do with Scientology. After all, the man who came up with the Genius principles, Alfred Barrios, was a clinical psychologist. Duggan thought that Genius principles like "be curious" or "improve your perception" could be found in Judeo-Christian tradition. "Do you know what the definition of religion is?" Duggan asked. "The word is 'religio,' it means consciousness, the condition of being conscious. That's a good thing."

Still, Duggan was proud of his Scientology beliefs and open about his connections to the Church. For a while, he kept a photo of John Travolta, one of the Church's most famous members, on a table in his office. He would sometimes drop the name of another prominent Church member, Tom Cruise, into conversation. After he saw Cruise charging through a Dubai hotel wearing a flashy blue suit in the movie *Mission Impossible: Ghost Protocol*, Duggan had to have it. "I am going to get that suit!" he told colleagues. Duggan later showed up to a Pharmacyclics party dressed in the lustrous blue outfit.

For some at Pharmacyclics, Duggan brought a fresh way of conducting the drug development business, sparking energy and purpose that resembled a Silicon Valley technology start-up. He didn't take a salary or award himself any options, ensuring that his fortune would rise or fall based on the stock he had purchased himself. Most drug developers eschewed this mentality. Duggan quickly picked up the esoteric jargon of the biotech industry and rapidly learned the various aspects of his new business. McGreivy would give Duggan highly technical presentations and was amazed at how Duggan sensed the one or two most important aspects. Through hiring and rapid promotions, Duggan liked to give people new opportunities, but also made it clear that he was not afraid of change or turnover in the employee base.

There was no such thing as tenure at Pharmacyclics. "I helped in hiring and also helped in relieving people of their jobs," Duggan would say. "If it is contentious in the company, somebody has to be able to do that."

No matter how people felt about the level of influence of religion in the workplace, it was hard for some to ignore the parallels between the culture at Pharmacyclics and a cult. Pharmacyclics had a brash and charismatic leader, and the employees were possessed with a deep belief in ibrutinib, the drug they were working on, and a strong sense of purpose. The long office hours and Duggan's Genius program added to the sense of fervor. It was also a volatile environment. Duggan quickly anointed people as his favorites and fired people or pushed them aside just as fast if he felt it was needed. Ahmed Hamdy and Raquel Izumi were just the beginning.

When Hamdy and Izumi were fired, people at Pharmacyclics were shocked. But after a while, they got the message: no one was safe. Some, like Erik Verner, quit because they thought the office had become toxic. Even people who seemed powerful, like the consultant and board member Gwen Fyfe, quickly disappeared from Pharmacyclics after losing favor with Duggan. Others, like Brett Villagrand, at one point the commercial lead for ibrutinib, were outright fired after clashing with Duggan or Maky Zanganeh. Other executives, like Joshua Brumm, vice president of finance, were fired for less obvious reasons. Cindy Anderson had been hired to run clinical operations, a pivotal role at the time, but barely lasted a year. Rebecca D'Acquisto got hired at Pharmacyclics as a lowly corporate recruiter and within four months was running human resources. A few months later, D'Acquisto was gone. Corina Hughes worked at Pharmacyclics as head of contract administration and procurement. As exciting as it had been for her to see CT scans of shrinking lymph nodes, she became disenchanted with the unstable workplace and left.

Lori Kunkel, the chief medical officer who replaced Ahmed Hamdy, played a crucial role by smartly and creatively driving the ibrutinib clinical trial program forward and dealing with safety issues that arose with the drug. A respected hematologist-oncologist with CMO and Genentech experience, Kunkel had worked on rituximab and thought ibrutinib could duplicate its success. The drug had a way of attracting talent, and Duggan called Kunkel a "genius." But Kunkel had to constantly report to Maky Zanganeh about everything she was doing. Zanganeh demanded relentless updates on the clinical development process, and Kunkel found herself summoned on a nearly daily basis to Zanganeh's office. This irritated Kunkel. She didn't like being micromanaged and started to resist informing Zanganeh about each new development. Kunkel pointed out that her contract said she reported to Duggan. She started dreading coming to work in the morning. A year and a half after starting as CMO, Kunkel quit.

//////////////////////

JESSE MCGREIVY WAS SITTING in a conference room when he was interrupted by Bob Duggan, who ran in wearing glasses and holding a piece of paper. President Barack Obama had just signed a law creating a new experimental drug designation for the FDA called "breakthrough therapy." Pharmacyclics needed to conduct clinical trials that would clearly demonstrate the effectiveness and safety of its drug to regulators who had the power to approve it for the US market. Duggan thought the new designation could help Pharmacyclics by giving the company additional opportunities to communicate with FDA regulators during the approval process. He was always looking for ways to collapse timelines and thought breakthrough status could create shortcuts through the regulatory process. Congress created the designation in response to the kind of criticisms made by Richard Miller and others that the FDA had not been expediting the development of drugs that indicated substantial improvement over existing therapies. It was not like McGreivy and the rest of the clinical development team were unaware of the new regulatory tool, but Duggan immediately pushed them to pursue it in a way their big development partner, J&J, never did.

Breakthrough designation was not in itself a goal, but it could help Pharmacyclics reach its goal of obtaining market approval for its drug quicker and easier. Pharmacyclics applied for breakthrough designation for ibrutinib in mantle cell lymphoma, even though the drug did not seem to produce as lasting a remission for those patients as it did for chronic lymphocytic leukemia patients. The company also sought breakthrough therapy designation for CLL patients who had 17p deletion, a chromosomal abnormality associated with resistance to chemotherapy, and Waldenstrom macroglobulinemia, a rare lymphoma. Pharmacyclics became the first company to obtain three breakthrough therapy designations for the same drug.

Finding a shorter regulatory path was a nice first step, but Pharmacyclics now needed to successfully race through it. The company had to launch a battery of large trials involving hundreds of patients to generate the kind of data that could lead to FDA approval in three different blood cancers. This push would raise the clinical budget for ibrutinib to nearly $1 billion.

For a company like Pharmacyclics, several kinds of clinical trials had to be conducted to secure different regulatory market approvals, each of which played an important role. The regulatory strategies of biotechnology companies were truly elaborate games of chess, weighing the needs of regulators and countering the moves of rivals. To obtain full FDA approval for ibrutinib in certain blood cancers, these trials included phase 3 registration studies that pit ibrutinib against other drugs. Full regulatory approval was not the same as accelerated approval.

Accelerated approval greenlighted medicines for the treatment of diseases fast, based on the results of smaller groups of patients that could reasonably predict clinical benefit. In serious diseases, the FDA could even issue accelerated approval based on single-arm studies—trials made up entirely of patients who received the drug, without a control group receiving a comparative therapy or placebo. But in such cases, the expectation among regulators was that further comprehensive testing in a large and randomized study with a control group would confirm things and lead to full approval. This is what the FDA wanted to see.

As a result, the clinical development team designed RESONATE, a phase 3 randomized controlled trial of 350 patients with relapsed or refractory CLL. It put the drug against ofatumumab, a monoclonal antibody already approved to treat CLL. At Pharmacyclics, the feeling was that ibrutinib would beat the pants off ofatumumab. To get access to ofatumumab for the trial, Pharmacyclics struck a supply agreement with GlaxoSmithKline, the pharmaceutical company that sold it. Another phase 2 trial tested the drug only in CLL patients with 17p deletion, the chromosomal abnormality associated with resistance to chemotherapy. Duggan skillfully raised $200 million by selling Pharmacyclics' rising stock, which together with the cash coming in from J&J was enough to cover the company's portion of the tab while also building out a new commercial sales force.

Some at Pharmacyclics butted heads a bit with their counterparts at J&J, who were launching trials of ibrutinib in combination with other drugs that had already been FDA approved. Driven by many important successes, combining drugs was a very popular strategy in the life sciences. J&J's approach could be less risky because the trial would not sink or swim on ibrutinib alone. Nevertheless, people at Pharmacyclics could not comprehend why anyone would want to combine ibrutinib and its dazzling data with another drug in cancers like CLL. If anything, they thought the combinations would likely dilute ibrutinib's effectiveness rather than enhance it. Duggan and Zanganeh agreed that ibrutinib would be more likely to work best by itself as a single-agent therapy.

Among CLL patients, the word was out: Ibrutinib could save your life. Brian Koffman, himself a doctor, helped spread the message through the popular online blog he maintained about his life with CLL. He moved for three months from Southern California to Columbus,

Ohio, so he could get into an ibrutinib trial as one of John Byrd's CLL patients. On his third day on ibrutinib, Koffman was taking a shower when he touched the disfiguring lymph nodes under the beard he had grown to conceal them. They felt smaller and softer. Byrd eventually sent Koffman home for three months at a time with a supply of ibrutinib. It was Koffman's most precious possession. He would fly home to California with the battleship gray capsules in his pocket, just in case an emergency might force him to exit the plane quickly without his overhead bag and belongings.

Patients on online message boards and support groups started talking up the drug. Those who were on the therapy told about their health improvements. They would exchange information about doctors who were participating in ibrutinib trials. With the Internet revolutionizing cancer treatment, empowered patients were often bringing ibrutinib to the attention of their doctors.

The stories eventually reached Rothbaum, who also kept a close eye on Pharmacyclics' rising stock price. Hearing about ibrutinib's promise and watching Pharmacyclics' stock fly put Rothbaum in a deep funk. The tendency for people to prematurely sell assets that have increased in value is known in behavioral finance as "the disposition effect." For Rothbaum, this pill had become almost too bitter to swallow. He took his medicine chronically, whenever he checked the computer screen that displayed the stocks he tracked. The symptom it caused was regret. Rothbaum became withdrawn and stopped socializing with friends. His mood became dark. People who knew Rothbaum began to wonder what was wrong with him. His wife grew concerned, and for a time, Rothbaum even stopped trading stocks.

It wasn't just the money. How could it have been? He was already obscenely rich by most people's standards. No, Rothbaum had lost an intellectual test. He had picked up on ibrutinib and the BTK inhibitor story very early, almost before anyone else. He knew the science inside and out. It drove him nuts that he had seen it and not had the courage of his convictions. Rothbaum kept replaying the decision to sell, reverse engineering his mistake. He had betrayed his entire investment philosophy of making big bets that could really count. At bottom, he had panicked and been wrong.

"We all make mistakes," Rothbaum tried to tell himself.

But this wasn't just a mistake. It was the worst trading error of his career. The question was, what would he do about it?

CHAPTER 12

Truffle Pig

Wayne Rothbaum could not understand what he had been hearing. Sitting on an ottoman in a lounge area of Chicago's giant McCormick Place Convention Center, Ahmed Hamdy had just said he no longer wanted to license the Dutch BTK inhibitor owned by Merck. Rothbaum had huddled for a moment with Hamdy, Raquel Izumi, and Francisco Salva at the bustling annual American Society of Clinical Oncology conference. Tom Turalski was there, too.

"We are thinking about changing to something else. It's a ROR1," Hamdy said, pronouncing the drug's name like the cry of a lion, "roar one." He was referring to a tyrosine-protein kinase transmembrane receptor that had emerged as another potential blood cancer target.

Rothbaum and Hamdy were just getting to know each other as close colleagues. Previously, their relationship had been defined by their roles in the biotech industry. Rothbaum had been a stock investor who owned shares in a company where Hamdy was an executive. Their relationship was cordial and arms-length, even defined by specific stock trading rules. The two had come to respect and like one another as practitioners. But now they were trying to work together and the stakes were high. It was a much more intimate and revealing experience.

How did we go from starting a BTK company with a promising molecule to a RORı, Rothbaum asked himself. Several months had passed since Rothbaum had met this group in New York, and this was not the update he had expected. Rothbaum and Turalski looked at each other as Hamdy kept talking.

"There is this molecule from the Karolinska Institute in Sweden. It's considered one of the most exciting targets. We were talking to them about licensing."

"And you are going to put this into the BTK company?" Rothbaum asked.

Hamdy responded that he wanted to start a company only around this Swedish compound. Rothbaum started asking more questions.

"Where did you find this molecule?"

Hamdy pulled out a poster that contained some data. "We just saw it at the poster session," Hamdy said. "We were talking to the person."

Rothbaum felt like he was in some bad movie. "Wait, what are you talking about? We spent months on this one molecule and you just met somebody at a poster session from an academic research facility in Sweden . . . and you are going to drop the BTK. What am I missing here?"

Rothbaum looked at the poster. "This is horrible," he said. "What's going on?"

Hamdy took a deep breath. He said he had spoken to Allard Kaptein and Tjeerd Barf. Merck had decided they were not going to give them the autoimmune arthritis rights of the BTK inhibitor. The pharmaceutical company would only license the cancer rights. "I can't do this without the autoimmune rights," Hamdy said. "I have decided to pass on it."

Rothbaum felt his hair turning white. He took the Swedish poster and threw it on the ground. "Ahmed, what is wrong with you?" Rothbaum asked. "I don't give a shit about autoimmune rights now. Let's focus on cancer. Cancer is where we need to focus. This is crazy."

Hamdy's cold feet had nothing to do with the prospects of the drug in cancer. He was terrified of Bob Duggan. As long as they were developing a BTK inhibitor for rheumatoid arthritis, they would not be going up against Pharmacyclics and Duggan. An obvious blood cancer play would put Hamdy on a collision course with his former boss. The idea scared him.

Rothbaum did not understand this dynamic. But he did understand what he had to do. "I don't know what the fuck this is, you just met these people," Rothbaum said, adding that he would find a way to get the autoimmune rights from Merck one day. "I'm going to take this molecule and work with [the Dutch.] You have a choice. Either you call them right now, or I am going to call them and do it without you."

Hamdy thought about it. He knew the best play here was for the Dutch BTK inhibitor to be a fast follower to ibrutinib in blood cancer, a second class of treatment that built on ibrutinib's proof of concept by having improved properties. It could capitalize on the pioneering work done developing ibrutinib, but also be structurally unique in a way that could make a material difference to patients. Lipitor had famously been the fifth cholesterol-fighting statin drug introduced to the market, but it still became the top-selling pharmaceutical product of its generation. For the approach to work, the Dutch drug would have to work better, safer, or both. The logic behind what Rothbaum wanted to do was inescapably sound. On the other hand, the fear of Duggan was somewhat irrational. The thought of missing out, again, dawned on Hamdy and he decided to get back on board. "Okay, I will call them," he said.

After their huddle, Rothbaum continued to do the rounds at the five-day conference in Chicago. His itinerary included a meeting with Duggan and others at Pharmacyclics. By this point, Rothbaum knew that Duggan had become a potential rival, but Duggan didn't have a clue. At the meeting, Rothbaum asked about another company, Avila, that had been trying to develop a BTK inhibitor. Its early first-in-human trial in blood cancer patients was not panning out. The Pharmacyclics team, which had no idea about what had been going on in the Netherlands, laughed. They said the problem with the Avila drug was that it was too selective. It was not hitting some of the kinases that bolstered the blocking of BTK, helping to drive ibrutinib's good results. They called it ibrutinib's "secret sauce."

Leaving the meeting, Rothbaum started to panic and question the idea of selectivity. Maybe BTK was not the key target at all? This was all still new science. Maybe blocking BTK was not the only thing powering the effectiveness of ibrutinib? Maybe it was better to be promiscuous rather than selective? In the middle of the day, Rothbaum rushed up to his hotel room to research the kinome map. Ibrutinib hit tyrosine kinases like EGFR and ITK that the Dutch drug did not. The Dutch drug hit the BMX tyrosine kinase, but less than ibrutinib. Maybe some of these targets were important?

Rothbaum was getting spooked about a BTK inhibitor drug—again. He called up Hamdy and started grilling him. But Hamdy remained adamant that BTK was the target that made ibrutinib work, and not any of the other kinases it hit. Something must be chemically off with the Avila drug. "It's BTK, it's BTK," Hamdy kept saying. Slowly, he talked Rothbaum off the ledge.

Earlier that week, it had been Rothbaum who kept Hamdy from redirecting the entire project. Now it was Hamdy's turn to keep Rothbaum on track.

Back in the Netherlands, van Wezel had been working for months to secure the rights to the BTK inhibitor. It's not easy to convince a huge pharmaceutical conglomerate to sell, or out-license, you a compound, even one it doesn't want. But the team had two things going for it. For starters, Kaptein and Barf had influence with senior leadership at Organon, who pushed Merck to sell the drug. Then there was politics. People had taken to the streets to protest Merck's decision to close research and development at Oss, eliminating two thousand Dutch jobs. The protesters carried signs that read "profits grown, jobs cut." Preferring to avoid conflict with a major European government, the American pharmaceutical giant began discussions with the Dutch government about divesting its unwanted Dutch assets and leaving them in Pivot Park.

One of the assets that Merck started negotiating to sell was the PD-1 inhibitor that some members of Barf's team had worked on. Somehow, PD-1 landed on a list of drugs Merck was looking to out-license. It even made its way onto a term sheet that valued it at an extremely low number. But late in the negotiations, Merck abruptly stopped the sale of the drug. That PD-1 inhibitor went on to become Keytruda, an immunotherapy that would be used to treat at least sixteen different cancers, most prominently lung cancer. Former president Jimmy Carter was one of the one million grateful patients. It became Merck's top-selling product, generating $14.4 billion in sales in 2019, nearly one-third of Merck's revenue and growing. For all intents and purposes, Merck *was* Keytruda. That Merck ever acquired and retained the drug came down to dumb luck.

For his part, van Wezel had been put in touch with a Merck director of corporate licensing in Whitehouse Station, New Jersey. Licensing out the BTK inhibitor was far from the director's top priority. Nobody at Merck thought much about the molecule. Van Wezel had sent the licensing director a term sheet. As a placeholder, he wrote in a nominal sum for the up-front payment: $1,000. From time to time, emails would go back and forth. At one point, Merck indicated it would only license the drug for cancer, ensuring it would not compete with any of Merck's existing drugs in other therapeutic areas, like rheumatoid arthritis.

If it had not been for Kaptein and Barf's allies at Organon, and a healthy dose of Dutch government pressure, the whole thing would have collapsed. But van Wezel finally closed the deal in 2012, promising Merck approximately 5 percent of any net revenues the drug generated. Nobody at Merck changed the initial cash payment on the term sheet.

The drug was purchased for an up-front payment of $1,000.

///////////////

BEGINNING WITH HEWLETT-PACKARD, THE myth of the Silicon Valley company starting up in a garage has been popularized in technology culture. Apple, Google, and many others followed. But the evolution of a biotechnology company, even one from Silicon Valley, typically does not take this path. There's sensitive equipment, regulations, and big costs involved. Nevertheless, the two-car garage of Raquel Izumi's 2,600-square-foot house in San Carlos, California, had been converted into a chemistry lab. Izumi's husband, Todd Covey, and their two young children painted the garage interior white and cleaned it thoroughly. It was the cleanest area of the house. Covey ordered lab equipment, like a cell culture hood, and parts from Home Depot to build a biological safety cabinet. For $50, he snagged an incubator and bought carbon dioxide (CO_2) from a beer company. At one point, Izumi used her credit card to buy human stem cells online that were delivered to the house. Covey stored them in liquid nitrogen, with the gas sometimes emitting through the sides of the garage door. With the final season of *Breaking Bad*, the nation's hottest television show at the time, Izumi told her kids to keep the garage doors closed, just in case the neighbors got suspicious. The man who lived next door was, in fact, an FBI agent.

In addition to being Izumi's husband, Covey was an excellent biologist. He also needed a job. Wayne Rothbaum and Ahmed Hamdy enthusiastically welcomed him to the team. The launch of the new company, which would merge Aspire Therapeutics with Covalution BioSciences, had been delayed for several months. Van Wezel was sorting out funding issues in Holland. Rothbaum couldn't launch an equity funding round until van Wezel was ready.

Meanwhile, Hamdy, Izumi, Salva, and the Dutch scientists had put their lives on hold to work on spec in places like Izumi's garage. Their savings were dwindling. Without funding, they could accomplish little. They all needed Rothbaum's help to keep their dream alive.

Rothbaum floated a $1.6 million loan to the team, since the cash flow situation of the founding employees had become so tight. He said he would later roll the loan into the first equity round of funding. The money enabled Hamdy to start work on the chemistry and manufacturing of the drug and to begin mapping out some preclinical testing.

Hamdy and Izumi decided to test the drug against ibrutinib in healthy mice. A scientist Izumi knew at Stanford said he had a few extra mice and could sneak her into the animal medical testing facility at the university. To test the two drugs, Izumi would need to perform oral gavage, using a needle to deposit the experimental medicines through the throats of the mice into their bellies.

Lab mice are surprisingly difficult to obtain. Izumi had not done work like this in years, and she was nervous about making a mistake and killing the precious mice her scientist friend had given her. She decided to get a mouse from a nearby pet store and practice in her home's garage lab. At the store, she picked up a cage and a mouse. When she got to the checkout, Izumi was handed a form to fill out. The store did not sell feeder mice. She had to attest that she was buying the mouse as a pet and not as food for a snake or any other purpose. Standing at the register, Izumi did not know what to do. She signed the form, bought the mouse, and gave it to her kids as a pet. They named her Shaniqua.

Izumi soon found herself in a run-down part of town, in a dingy store with dim lighting that sold feeder mice. Izumi purchased five mice, but she took a liking to one of them and adopted the mouse, named Lucky. That left four mice for her practice and a growing set of mice as housemates.

As for the four remaining feeder mice, Izumi soon learned that she had not lost her touch. She was ready for her stealth mission at the animal testing facility at Stanford. Izumi's contact ushered her and Hamdy through the security doors. They put on white coats and entered a lab. Being careful not to arouse suspicion, Izumi went to work and treated her mice. The next day, they snuck in again and were able to see the results. The experiment showed that the Dutch BTK was not only effective, but even more potent than ibrutinib, tamping down B cell activation at a lower dose. After the days in her garage and the nights worrying about paying bills, Izumi now saw a viable path forward.

Van Wezel finally figured out a solution to his funding issues, so there was money on the way—though only a modest amount. The pressing question became, what would they call themselves? The biotechnologists agreed to simply call the company Acerta Pharma. Acerta was an acronym that stood for the first initials of the California and Dutch founders—Ahmed, Cisco, Edward, Raquel, Tjeerd, and Allard. Everyone but Rothbaum. It never even crossed their minds to include Rothbaum. In fact, that's what annoyed him the most. If the California and Dutch founders of Acerta thought that Rothbaum was going to play the role of passive, dumb money, they were dead wrong.

The founders of Acerta looked to push the company hard straight out of the gate. Rothbaum became chairman of Acerta and immediately led the initial equity funding of $6 million in early 2013. It had been structured as the first phase of a multipart Series A financing round. The other investors were van Wezel's BioGeneration Ventures, Joe Edelman's Perceptive Advisors hedge fund, the provincial Dutch development authority, and a California-based investment fund.

Rothbaum and Edelman had been stock traders. Now the two New Yorker investors were morphing into venture capitalists, putting money in a private start-up company at the founding stage. Traditionally, hedge funds did not operate this way. But guys like Rothbaum and Edelman had noticed that the most promising new companies were not seeking early financing from the stock market. If those companies became successful, investing at the beginning would be the best entry point and provide for the largest financial return. A very small number of hedge funds specializing in technology trading had already made the transition, starting with Chase Coleman, whose New York hedge fund operation, Tiger Global Management, had invested in Facebook when the social media giant had still been a private company.

Now, Rothbaum and Edelman were bringing this same mindset to biotechnology, helping to open a new spigot of money that would soon flood the industry. Rothbaum had already invested in Calistoga in its late stages of financing as a private company. With Acerta, Rothbaum and Edelman invested at the very beginning. Tom Turalski, the analyst at Edelman's hedge fund who had started his career working for

Rothbaum, joined Acerta's board as Edelman's representative. Within a few years, hedge fund investors across Wall Street would make bets and inject capital into private biotechnology start-ups.

Hamdy became Acerta's CEO and chief medical officer, and Izumi its clinical development head. Francisco Salva started out as the finance head, while the two Dutch scientists, Allard Kaptein and Tjeerd Barf, ran preclinical development and drug manufacturing. Acerta was founded as a Netherlands-based company under Dutch law because van Wezel's fund had raised some Dutch government money for the deal and needed to invest in a Dutch company. They called their BTK inhibitor drug ACP-196—standing for Aspire Covalution Pharma-196.

After Acerta's formation, Kaptein and Barf issued a press release announcing their new company. They had been fired from big pharma and endured many months of uncertainty. Now they had successfully extracted ACP-196 from Merck, secured financing, and were eager to move their drug candidate forward.

Rothbaum went ballistic over the press release. He wanted to operate in complete secrecy. Rothbaum was an Internet ghost—virtually unidentifiable. He expected Acerta to be run the same way. Acerta didn't have a website, and future press releases were prohibited. New hires were not allowed to name their new employer on their LinkedIn profile. "Only the paranoid survive," Rothbaum explained to Izumi. Rothbaum had very specific ideas about how to make a company like this succeed. It was up to Hamdy to implement them. Keeping everyone in line would be one of his most challenging tasks as CEO of Acerta.

///////////////

WAYNE ROTHBAUM'S GRANDFATHER RAN a wholesale locksmith business and traveled across the United States selling his wares. On each business trip, he would bring bagels or some other New York food delicacy as a warm personal touch to his customers. Rothbaum picked up on this tradition and emulated it, bringing whatever hot food fad had hit New York City. In 2013, it was Baked By Melissa cup-cakes. He showed up in Thousand Oaks, California, with white boxes of them, handing them around in a conference room at the headquarters of Amgen, one of the nation's biggest biotechnology companies.

Christian Rommel, Amgen's vice president of oncology research, stood and introduced Rothbaum to his troops. "I've known Wayne for a while," Rommel said in his thick German accent. "He's a truffle pig. If anyone is a truffle pig, it's Wayne Rothbaum." The room of about twenty people went silent. Taken aback, Rothbaum grew visibly upset and turned to Tom Turalski, who had made the trip to Thousand Oaks with him.

"Tommy, did he just call me a pig? Did he just insult me?" a startled Rothbaum asked. Turalski recognized that Rommel had been referring to the European tradition of using a hog to sniff out valuable fungi. "Don't worry. It's a compliment," Turalski said.

The Acerta team, funded by Rothbaum, had decided to take on Pharmacyclics and its amazing-looking drug—a daunting task. To defray the risk, Rothbaum had been trying to sniff out ways to beat ibrutinib in blood cancer. While he was in Thousand Oaks to meet the larger Acerta team, Rothbaum was also negotiating with Amgen to license a PI3K delta inhibitor drug that was undergoing a first-in-human clinical trial. The drug blocked the same kinase in the B cell receptor pathway as Calistoga's idelalisib drug. Rothbaum thought combining Acerta's more selective BTK inhibitor with Amgen's PI3K delta inhibitor might produce stronger responses in patients. The Amgen drug could also hedge Acerta's bets just in case the BTK inhibitor blew up.

After the meeting in Thousand Oaks, Acerta licensed Amgen's PI3K delta inhibitor to be used in combination with the BTK inhibitor. Acerta paid $5 million up front and royalties of between 6 and 8 percent of any future net sales. But there was a catch: Amgen insisted on the right to buy back the two-drug combination if the proposed medicine actually worked. In such a situation, Acerta would still get a decent return and Rothbaum needed the hedge.

The other transaction that happened early on at Acerta involved intellectual property. On the surface, it may not have seemed as important, but it would turn out to be crucial. ACP-196 had been patented at Merck. But when lawyers working for Rothbaum searched the patent literature to determine whether Acerta had freedom to operate, they stumbled on an existing patent oriented toward a different family of proteins. This patent seemed to cover Acerta's drug—but also ibrutinib. The patent had come out a few years earlier from OSI Pharmaceuticals, a company on New York's Long Island that had been purchased by a Japanese pharmaceutical firm. Acerta worked with a third-party firm that surreptitiously approached OSI on Acerta's behalf to see if the patent could be obtained, and Acerta ultimately purchased it for $225,000.

In California, Hamdy and Izumi moved their lab equipment from Izumi's garage into office space in San Carlos. They converted part of the office space into a laboratory and later expanded into an adjacent warehouse. Then they started their work from square one. Though Acerta had been able to acquire the rights to the BTK inhibitor, Merck had not transferred much of the data related to the drug. As a result, all the initial preclinical work had to be repeated.

At the same time, Hamdy had connected with some of the same doctors who had been key investigators on the ibrutinib trials, like John Byrd, Susan O'Brien, and Richard Furman. Hamdy knew the move would inevitably alert Bob Duggan about Acerta's plans in blood cancer; but without these doctors, getting any traction would be difficult. Their support would be critical.

The doctors were happy to hear about this project from Hamdy, whom they deeply trusted. Just as they were convinced ibrutinib would usher in a new era for CLL treatment, these expert CLL doctors knew there was room for improvement. The side effects of Pharmacyclics' drug were hard to tolerate for some patients, who were often elderly and more sensitive to issues that younger patients might be better able to bear.

Other drug developers had started efforts to develop a safer and more effective BTK inhibitor and were already reaching out to this group of doctors to sign up. But Hamdy shared his data and convinced them that his selective BTK inhibitor would be the most likely to help patients in a significant way. Byrd and the other doctors thought the drug appeared to truly be different from ibrutinib and potentially better—and Hamdy and Izumi's involvement gave them even more confidence. With the ibrutinib breakthrough, Pharmacyclics had proven that BTK inhibition was a blood cancer game changer. But the drug had initially been designed as a tool compound, not a medicine that would be used to treat humans. It made sense to Byrd that the concept could be taken to the next level.

With Byrd's help, Hamdy and Izumi initiated a study of Acerta's BTK inhibitor in a small number of dogs that had naturally developed lymphoma. They needed blood samples from a healthy dog to prepare for the study, so Izumi had blood drawn from her pet collie, named Ally. The study's resulting 25 percent response rate matched ibrutinib's early preclinical canine tests. Despite the early concerns that a promiscuous drug that hit a few kinases was some sort of "special sauce," it seemed that being clean and more selective could hold the key to success for the Acerta team.

Working furiously, Hamdy and Izumi prepared to file an Investigational New Drug Application with the FDA by the end of 2013. It had only been ten months since Acerta secured its initial equity funding—lightning fast for a skeleton-staffed start-up. Once the application was filed, Acerta was ready to go into the clinic.

CHAPTER 13

Master Switch

The frustration ate away at Terry Evans. He felt helpless. This was his last hope to stay alive and nobody seemed to care. The sixty-five-year-old retired IT manager for the City of Long Beach, California, had agreed to participate in Pharmacyclics' RESONATE trial hoping to get access to ibrutinib. But when Evans showed up for his appointment at the University of California, San Diego, a computer algorithm randomly assigned him to the control group receiving ofatumumab. The patients in the control group knew they were getting the antibody treatment because it is administered intravenously.

Evans had schooled himself on chronic lymphocytic leukemia. He had earned an honorary PhD in cancer. Like most CLL patients who had desperately researched every possible treatment, Evans understood that ofatumumab would not help him. Had his doctor's appointment been scheduled on a different day or time, the computer might have assigned him to the ibrutinib arm of the trial. This was his life hanging in the balance. Sure enough, seven months after he started taking ofatumumab, Evans's lymph nodes inflated and other markers went in the wrong direction. Evans prepared for the worst.

The RESONATE trial had been designed to include some 175 patients in a control arm because it had become clear at Pharmacyclics that the FDA would not unleash a new class of drug on the entire large CLL population without data showing overwhelming safety and efficacy. John Byrd, the Ohio State physician-scientist and principal investigator for the trial, agreed with this overarching decision. But he agonized over another design element of the study. The trial did not allow for patients assigned to the ofatumumab arm to cross over to the ibrutinib arm of the trial if the antibody treatment failed them.

When it came to new cancer drugs, the FDA regulators usually spoke to drug developers in black-and-white terms. They would make clear to the biopharma companies what they expected to see. This time in meetings with the FDA, surprisingly, the Pharmacyclics team found the regulators had been notably gray on the crossover issue. The RESONATE trial's primary measure, or end point, was the progression-free survival of patients—the drugs' ability to stop the cancer's advance. This was the primary scientific question the study had been set up to answer, and the trial would continue for months and even years until the data arrived at an answer. But the trial had been designed with a secondary end point—overall survival—and if patients could switch back and forth between the two drugs, the survival outcomes could be skewed. The regulatory discussions left the Pharmacyclics team little choice. There could be no crossover. Once the drug got regulatory approval, any patient who wanted the drug could get it, as long as they were still alive.

At Ohio State, there had been a debate about what to do about the RESONATE trial. Byrd knew he was rationalizing things, but thought the trial would hopefully give half the patients he enrolled access to ibrutinib when he had no other worthwhile treatment options to offer them. For Byrd, it was excruciating to see "control patients" die. As the trial went on, he pushed back on the crossover issue with Pharmacyclics and the FDA and promised himself he would never again be put in such a terrible situation. At MD Anderson in Houston, Susan O'Brien pushed even harder. O'Brien published a piece in the American Society of Clinical Oncology's *ASCO Post*, saying it was wrong for the FDA to prohibit crossover after the disease of patients taking ofatumumab had progressed.

"Here's the harsh reality: There are people on the control arm of RESONATE who will probably have disease progression and die," O'Brien wrote. "Presumably, that is what the FDA believes is necessary to document survival . . . I think it's unfortunate."

Richard Pazdur, the FDA's oncology chief, issued a response in the *ASCO Post* in which he clarified that the FDA had not opposed crossover and encouraged companies to provide patients access to promising therapies. With the FDA on board, Pharmacyclics amended its trial plan and allowed patients like Terry Evans to cross over and get ibrutinib capsules. They worked. Evans would continue taking them for many years.

Pharmacyclics also wanted to work toward getting ibrutinib approved as a first-line treatment, rescuing patients from the horrors of chemotherapy. To seek this approval, Pharmacyclics launched a second big RESONATE trial in 2013 that tested the drug against chemotherapy in previously untreated elderly patients. By this point, some physician-scientists became deeply uncomfortable about putting their patients on any therapy other than ibrutinib. Richard Furman, the influential CLL doctor at Weill Cornell Medicine in New York, refused to participate in the RESONATE-2 trial. He had become confident that ibrutinib was a phenomenal drug and thought it would be unethical for any of his patients to be randomly chosen for chemotherapy.

Furman held the FDA accountable for the lives put at risk by forcing Pharmacyclics to conduct another expensive study to gain approval for first-line treatment in CLL. The trial did allow for patient crossover, but Furman was concerned there would be an increased chance of death for patients initially treated with chemotherapy.

With more and more patients now on ibrutinib, some side effects emerged. Reports trickled in of patients suffering adverse events, mostly mild ones like diarrhea, joint pain, and bruising, although these could be difficult for older patients to tolerate.

There were also more serious side effects. In some patients, the drug seemed to induce irregular heartbeats, known as atrial fibrillation, as well as subdural hematoma, the gathering of blood between tissue layers wrapping the brain. Both conditions can be life-threatening. Pharmacyclics developed a medical management plan to deal with these issues and kept patients out of the trials if they had preexisting atrial fibrillation or were taking blood thinners. The irregular and rapid heartbeat occurs when the heart's two upper chambers chaotically beat out of coordination with the two lower chambers, putting patients at risk for heart failure or stroke. Doctors were warned about these heart and bleeding events so that they would monitor their patients carefully.

///////////////

IN JUNE 2013, THE *New England Journal of Medicine* published the results of the phase 1B/2 trial of ibrutinib for eighty-five relapsed and refractory CLL patients, the study that Ahmed Hamdy had first spoken to the expert doctors about in a Palo Alto hotel three years earlier. The data were sensational, and the physician-scientists now had a much better idea about what was going on. The paper described BTK as being like a master switch. Switching off BTK beat the cancer cells back. Some of the patients in the trial had now been taking ibrutinib for nearly two years. Seventy-one percent of the patients in the study had seen their lymph nodes shrink and their white blood cell count decrease. This was considered an "overall response"—almost the best result Pharmacyclics could hope for. Another fifteen patients had seen their lymph nodes shrink, but their white blood cell count remained high. Even patients with the troublesome 17p deletion abnormality responded well to the drug. The side effects were shown to be modest, with very few people having serious adverse reactions. "Ibrutinib was associated with a high frequency of durable remissions in patients with relapsed or refractory CLL," the paper concluded.

On Wall Street, the *NEJM* paper generated a lot of excitement. Ibrutinib seemed to be very good at tamping down CLL in a reasonably safe way. Here was a cancer medicine that really made a difference, extending life in CLL patients in a way no other available medicine could. For financial investors, the beauty of the drug from an economic perspective was that even though the drug worked, it didn't work too well. Ibrutinib was not a magic bullet cure. The cancer was never fully cleared from the blood and rarely went away completely. There were few complete remissions. It was, in crass terms, a subscription model. Patients would need to take a pill once a day, every day, for a long time—years.

As analysts at banks and hedge funds plugged the numbers into their spreadsheets, the financial projections for ibrutinib kept rising. The analysts took the relatively large number of CLL patients and multiplied it by the sky-high price that similar cancer drugs commanded in the market. Then they tried to estimate how long those patients would continue taking the drug. The analysts figured the drug could generate billions of dollars. By the end of the summer of 2013, Pharmacyclics' stock soared to $123, and its market valuation touched $9 billion.

The savviest biotech investors clamored to get a piece of the action. Pablo Legorreta, a former investment banker who had set up a New York firm to buy pharmaceutical royalty streams, made a creative kind of bet. Celera Genomics, the company that had given away ibrutinib years earlier, still retained a small piece of future sales of the drug, as had been outlined in the deal struck by Pharmacyclics founder Richard Miller. Quest Diagnostics, the big medical lab operator, had purchased Celera for $650 million in 2011, and this future royalty stream had come along in the deal. Right after the *NEJM* paper came out, Legorreta's firm, Royalty Pharma, swooped in and bought Quest's rights to a slice of ibrutinib's revenues for $485 million.

Still, not everyone involved in the Pharmacyclics story was thrilled. The *NEJM* paper listed John Byrd as its first author, followed by Susan O'Brien, Richard Furman, and Jeff Sharman, among other doctors and Pharmacyclics employees. It did not list Ahmed Hamdy or Raquel Izumi as authors. Hamdy and Izumi were only mentioned in the acknowledgments, even though they designed and initially implemented the trial itself. For Izumi, being published in the *New England Journal of Medicine* was a career and life goal, and she felt that meaningful recognition had been unjustly stolen from her.

It is a general operating procedure in medical research to give credit to doctors and scientists involved in a peer-reviewed medical paper. Even if they die prior to publication, researchers are generally listed as authors if they were involved in the effort. At Pharmacyclics, it had become something of a trend for people to be left out. Richard Miller, the founder of Pharmacyclics, who had written the protocol for the initial phase 1 trial of ibrutinib, and Daniel Pollyea, the Stanford fellow who had run that trial early on, also had their names left off the final paper of the study when it was published in the *Journal of Clinical Oncology*. They remained angry about it, too. Miller felt like he was being purposefully written out of the ibrutinib story. In fact, Bob Duggan always maintained that Miller had nothing to do with the development of the drug. A month after the CLL study results were published, *NEJM* published the promising results of the phase 2 trial of ibrutinib in relapsed mantle cell lymphoma patients. It neglected to list Hamdy and Izumi as authors once again.

For Hamdy, there was also the matter of money. With his personal finances overleveraged, Hamdy had exercised his vested Pharmacyclics options when he was fired and sold them for $1.1 million. It was a huge mistake.

Had he held onto just those shares, they would have been worth $20 million in the summer of 2013.

The absolute amount of money Wayne Rothbaum had left on the table was on a whole other level. Rothbaum had made serious money on Pharmacyclics. But the cost of his decision to sell early now approached $300 million.

There was only one way for Rothbaum to make up for it.

PART III

CHAPTER 14

Approved

Ahmed Hamdy was trying to put his son to sleep when he got an incomprensible audio message on his cell phone from Bob Duggan, who seemed to want to check in on him.

It was not clear to Hamdy what Duggan wanted or why he called. The message was ambiguous. Hamdy had not heard from Duggan since being fired from Pharmacyclics, and to Hamdy the whole thing was creepy and even threatening.

On a morning soon after, Hamdy saw a suspicious-looking white van parked outside the gated community where he lived. He called up Wayne Rothbaum in a panic to tell him about the van and play him the audio message.

Hamdy was scared of Duggan. He knew that stepping back into Duggan's world would leave him open to attack—but Hamdy always assumed it would be a corporate or legal attack. Now he wondered if he could also face an actual intrusion into his personal life. Hamdy thought again about trying to steer his new venture away from cancer treatment but knew his new team would never agree. He was trapped in a self-inflicted spiral of nerves.

Hamdy confided in the Acerta team and explained what had happened. Most of the others were not as shaken. Some listened to the audio message and thought it may have been an accidental pocket dial. Over time, Duggan became something of a boogeyman at Acerta. Staff would joke that team members should watch out for lurking white vans. Duggan's close ties to the Church of Scientology and the aggressive way it was known to go after its adversaries fed the uneasiness. Anxiety only increased when an Acerta laptop mysteriously vanished from the trunk of a car in the Netherlands. The thief had left other more valuable items behind.

There was no evidence that Duggan or Pharmacyclics had been involved with any of this. Duggan always said he didn't care about what Acerta was doing and that he wished his former colleagues well. He claimed to have never left an audio message for Hamdy. Some people at Acerta thought Hamdy had an overactive imagination.

In one sense, Pharmacyclics and Acerta were in a race. Each had a BTK inhibitor that seemed to stop CLL, and both were ultimately seeking FDA approval. But Duggan and Pharmacyclics had a massive head start. Whether or not Duggan knew or cared about the work being done at Acerta had no impact on Pharmacyclics' forward momentum. In the summer of 2013, Duggan's clinical and regulatory team at Pharmacyclics mapped out a bold strategy to seek accelerated approval from the FDA for two conditions, mantle cell lymphoma and chronic lymphocytic leukemia, where patients had received at least one previous treatment. Even though Pharmacyclics had still accumulated only a small amount of data involving relatively few patients, the company thought that the quality of the results could lead to two simultaneous accelerated approvals.

Urte Gayko, Pharmacyclics' head of regulatory affairs, had planned out critical parts of the strategy while on a plane returning to California from a meeting with FDA regulators. Pharmacyclics took ibrutinib clinical trial data involving both mantle cell lymphoma and CLL patients and put them together in a single New Drug Application package. All the data came from the two phase 2 trials originally designed by

Ahmed Hamdy and Raquel Izumi. The new Pharmacyclics team was able to leverage the results from these two small trials for the accelerated approval program of the FDA.

In the case of the CLL regulatory submission, the clinicians took the data of forty-eight patients from the phase 1B/2 trial who had taken ibrutinib at what seemed like the optimal dose and submitted it to the FDA. This New Drug Application for CLL was dicey. It was one thing to seek accelerated approval for mantle cell lymphoma patients. There were not too many of them and they had few options. But CLL was one of the biggest indications in blood cancer. At any given time, there were about 186,000 Americans diagnosed with CLL. There were a lot of people at risk. Asking the FDA to approve a drug for so many people based on the data of forty-eight patients in a single-arm trial was asking a lot.

In October 2013, Duggan flew with Maria Fardis, Jesse McGreivy, Urte Gayko, and the rest of his clinical development and regulatory executives to White Oak, Maryland, for a crucial meeting at FDA headquarters with senior regulators. They were joined by senior J&J executives like Peter Lebowitz. Having the J&J people present at the FDA meeting conferred immediate legitimacy and political force on anything the Pharmacyclics staff put forward. This had been one of the reasons Duggan had wanted to partner with an established pharmaceutical company in the first place. Some at Pharmacyclics sensed the power of J&J when, at the tail end of an earlier meeting, an FDA official had casually asked a J&J person if the company could lobby Congress to increase the FDA's staffing levels. Interactions like this made the Pharmacyclics team feel like insiders.

Richard Pazdur, chief of oncology and hematology at the FDA, presided over a discussion involving fifteen FDA regulators. It was the first time Pazdur had personally attended a Pharmacyclics meeting. Pazdur's reputation had changed dramatically since Pharmacyclics' founder, Richard Miller, wrote those opinion pieces in the *Wall Street Journal*, blasting the methods of Pazdur's office for blocking promising cancer treatments. Congress's breakthrough designation program had helped Pazdur's team work more closely with the biopharma industry. In addition, Pazdur's wife, Mary Pazdur, an oncology nurse practitioner, had been diagnosed with ovarian cancer. Her personal experience with cancer, which ultimately claimed her life, changed Pazdur and helped set him off on what he described as "a jihad to streamline the review process and get things out the door faster."

The pharmaceutical industry was ready to join Pazdur's crusade. With new cancer drugs costing, on average, more than $100,000 annually per patient in the United States, biopharma companies would soon spend as much as $31 billion in a given year to research and develop them, more than three times the amount directed to any other therapeutic area. To a large degree, the industry focused on developing targeted small-molecule therapies, like ibrutinib, that infiltrate cancer cells and interfere with their genes and proteins.

Though nominally on opposite sides of the table, Duggan and Pazdur found themselves as allies. Cancer had profoundly affected their lives on a personal level. The disease had changed them both. In fact, the reason Duggan and Pazdur were in a room together talking about ibrutinib was that Pazdur's office had repeatedly rejected the brain cancer drug Richard Miller had championed, leading to Duggan's takeover of Pharmacyclics. But even though Pazdur had declared a "jihad" on the red tape that held up drug approvals, he remained an indefatigable regulator, focused on the smallest details and concerned for public safety. The split was evident during his meeting with Pharmacyclics.

During the meeting, the regulators expressed concern about the small number of patients, just forty-eight, who had been tested at the proposed dose in a common leukemia. Even to the Pharmacyclics team, much of the submission seemed like a hodgepodge of phase 2 data. The FDA officials asked if the underlying study had initially even been intended to gain regulatory approval. The Pharmacyclics team admitted that it had not. The regulators made it clear that the phase 1B/2 trial didn't have the breadth of information and checks that were expected, like an independent verification of radiological assessments. The application in CLL, they said, was flawed.

"Dr. McGreivy," Richard Pazdur said, his voice rising as he spoke to Pharmacyclics' chief medical officer. "Let me tell you about bias."

For a hardcore regulator like Pazdur, bias is what you get when you submit a single-arm dataset, one in which all the patients received the same treatment and the results are not compared with patients who received an alternative treatment or no treatment. The regulators always preferred a large randomized trial with a control arm that could fully demonstrate the effectiveness of a drug. There was enough evidence indicating that ibrutinib had the potential to save lives. But not enough work had been done to fully show its efficacy and safety compared with other treatments or placebos. Pazdur was the gatekeeper protecting American lives from drugs that could be harmful and opening the gates to let pass those that could be game changers for patients.

"In the end, the FDA is in an impossible situation, and I have been in that impossible situation. You are either approving drugs too fast, you are approving drugs too slow," is how Pazdur would explain it. "But what we try to do is establish a balance of safety and efficacy."

As Duggan listened on at the meeting, the regulators altered the bold plan Pharmacyclics had put forward. Pazdur's team said they would split Pharmacyclics' new drug application to allow for different timelines for the CLL and mantle cell lymphoma approvals. The accelerated mantle cell lymphoma approval would be completed earlier, they said. When it came to CLL, which Pharmacyclics knew was the big financial prize, the regulators suggested that the company submit interim data from the ongoing RESONATE trial that had been testing ibrutinib in patients in a randomized trial against another drug, ofatumumab. The regulators had dealt Duggan and Pharmacyclics a big setback.

Patient enrollment in the RESONATE trial had initially been slow until Maky Zanganeh shifted all of clinical operations over to Fardis, who seemed to magically fix the problem. Fardis drove the process and, in this instance, pushed to open more clinical sites more quickly. She had a way of cutting through the red tape that surrounded her. The speeding up of the RESONATE trial now proved crucial. Pharmacyclics would absolutely need the results of that trial as quickly as possible.

/////////////////

BOB DUGGAN LEFT WHITE Oak, Maryland, intent on making the most out of an accelerated approval in mantle cell lymphoma. The FDA officials had indicated that an approval for ibrutinib in CLL may not come soon.

Duggan knew about the importance of being quick to market. At the Sunnyvale offices, Paula Boultbee had been gearing up for the commercial launch of ibrutinib. Duggan had hired her for this exact purpose. Working for Novartis in 2001, Boultbee had helped lead the successful product launch of Gleevec, the groundbreaking drug used to treat chronic myelogenous leukemia. It was the first kinase inhibitor approved by the FDA.

Excited to repeat the Gleevec success with ibrutinib, Boultbee relocated her family from Southern California to Silicon Valley. Before the FDA meeting, she had been preparing a go-to-market plan for both CLL and mantle cell lymphoma. Now she had to quickly adjust and refocus everything from promotional materials to websites solely on mantle cell lymphoma.

Under Boultbee's direction, ibrutinib would be reborn and launched to the market with a brand name: Imbruvica.

Boultbee had also been entrusted with the crucial work being done around the pricing of Imbruvica. A pricing study had been conducted, benchmarking Imbruvica against other drugs in the market, particularly medicines for rare cancers, including bortezomib and lenalidomide, two other oral drugs that had been approved for mantle cell lymphoma. To get more guidance, Pharmacyclics held talks with prominent health insurance companies. Boultbee helped come up with a price range and, together with Duggan and Zanganeh, conducted discussions with J&J over this vital issue. They had arrived at a price of about $91 per capsule and expected patients to take a single dose of four capsules once each day, adding up to $10,900 per month.

Two years earlier, Ahmed Hamdy had predicted that ibrutinib might gain regulatory approval by focusing on mantle cell lymphoma. He and Raquel Izumi had designed the phase 2 study showing its effectiveness, and he had been fired, in part, for pushing this line of thinking too far. In November 2013, Pharmacyclics received a letter via email from the FDA. The fourteen-page document, carrying the blue letterhead of the Department of Health and Human Services and the digital signature of Richard Pazdur, granted Imbruvica accelerated approval for mantle cell lymphoma patients who had received one prior therapy. This was the news Duggan had been waiting for.

The approval generated newspaper headlines, with media organizations emphasizing Imbruvica's $131,000 annual price tag per patient, making it one of the most expensive cancer medicines in the United States. These kinds of price tags were sparking a popular backlash against biopharma. Soon, Americans would have the same low opinion of pharmaceutical companies as they did of tobacco companies. In an interview with the *New York Times*, Duggan pointed out that mantle cell lymphoma is a disease that afflicts only eleven thousand Americans at any given time. He argued that Pharmacyclics and J&J would not have spent nearly $1 billion developing Imbruvica if they could not price the medicine at such a level.

Back in Sunnyvale, the FDA approval ruined Thanksgiving and Christmas. Leadership was thrilled, of course, but employees had to put holiday plans on hold as the company revved up its commercialization engine. Duggan wanted to capitalize on the moment and the spotlight. Yes, the drug was expensive, there were not enough mantle cell patients to make it a blockbuster, and encouraging doctors to prescribe the drug would take time and work. On Wall Street, some investors were disappointed that a big CLL approval appeared to be delayed.

Duggan sent out a directive to his sales force: He expected $42 million in revenue from the drug in the final weeks of the year. His sales team had seven weeks to make it happen.

Michael Crum, vice president of sales at Pharmacyclics, was dumbfounded. Since being hired eleven months earlier, he had assembled a high-quality sales team, including a young, ambitious sales director, Yasser Ali. But Duggan's revenue projection was crazy, Crum thought. What's more, Duggan had tied the sales incentive compensation for Crum and his team to the $42 million figure. By contrast, J&J, which owned nearly half of Imbruvica's net revenues, had forecast $14 million for the same period.

Ali ran an analysis and determined there would be absolutely no way to meet the revenue forecast. The drug had been approved only for American mantle cell lymphoma patients who previously received another treatment. And there weren't enough of them. Crum, Ali's boss, argued that the only way to meet the sales goals was to actively market the drug off-label to desperate patients suffering from CLL. Such off-label marketing could get sales reps in trouble with regulators, maybe even law enforcement. It seemed to them like Duggan had set the sales targets as if he were still running one of his other companies, like his bakery operation. But Pharmacyclics wasn't selling cookies.

According to a lawsuit he would later file against Pharmacyclics, Crum got a voicemail from Duggan saying the sales forecasts were not negotiable and reminding Crum that his performance-based stock options were linked to hitting the $42 million sales goals. The voicemail was left on a Thursday in November, and Crum found it threatening, his legal complaint said. In case he didn't get the message, Crum got an email the same day from his manager, Paula Boultbee, reiterating Duggan's position. Over the weekend, both Crum and Ali reported the situation to Pharmacyclics' compliance department, an act they expected would remain confidential.

On Monday morning, Crum was on his way to a meeting when he ran into Duggan, who pulled Crum into his office. For more than two hours, Duggan tried to set Crum straight on the sales forecast. The way Crum told it in his legal complaint, Duggan badgered and swore at him. Crum claimed he feared not only for his job, but for his safety. Crum was so shaken that he hid at home, "sick" for the next two days. He was hoping Duggan's temper would subside. Ali kept going into the office and wound up in a meeting that included Duggan and Zanganeh. At the meeting, Duggan brought up the sales forecast and Crum's inability to stretch himself to meet the challenge.

According to a lawsuit Ali later filed against Pharmacyclics, he pushed back at the meeting, arguing that it would be wrong to tie compensation of the sales force to a revenue forecast that would push sales reps to target off-label patients. Duggan pointedly turned to Ali and asked him if he had brought up the issue with the compliance team. Ali admitted that he had done so. "Traitor," Duggan responded, scolding Ali for not coming to him first.

While he was at home, Crum got word that Duggan wanted to get together with him outside of the office. Crum decided it would be better, safer, to meet Duggan back in the office. When he got there after the Thanksgiving weekend, Crum was fired. Ali was fired, too. The wrongful termination lawsuits Crum and Ali filed in California state court against Pharmacyclics were settled without any admission of liability.

///////////////

BOB DUGGAN'S AMBITIOUS SALES projections for Imbruvica were never met. J&J's estimates turned out to be dead-on. In the last three months of 2013, Pharmacyclics generated $13.6 million of net revenue from Imbruvica. But as Duggan rang in a new year, everything else started breaking his way.

Early on in 2014, the independent data monitoring committee of

the big phase 3 RESONATE trial stopped the study early. The committee members had seen enough. Imbruvica had beaten the pants off
ofatumumab. Patients taking Imbruvica saw their CLL stop progressing, and they lived longer. Pharmacyclics immediately submitted this
incredible interim data from the RESONATE trial to the FDA, hoping
it would tip the scale.

A month later, in February 2014, Urte Gayko, Pharmacyclics' regulatory chief, was sitting in her office when she got an email from the
FDA. It included a letter informing Pharmacyclics that the FDA had
issued an accelerated approval of Imbruvica. Gayko got up from her
desk and walked over to a large blue metal bell she had bought for $100
and mounted on the wall outside her office just for this moment. As
she rang the bell, people started cheering and gathering in the hallway.
Duggan and Maky Zanganeh joined them in celebrating the key market approval for Imbruvica. Duggan marveled that the CLL approval
had come almost five years to the day after Pharmacyclics had dosed the
first patients with Imbruvica.

This was gigantic news for Pharmacyclics, for Duggan's revenue
prospects, and for people suffering from CLL. The FDA had only issued
a limited, "accelerated" approval for patients who had previously been
treated with a different therapy. But the FDA's phrasing was important.
Often, an accelerated approval required cancer patients to "fail" a prior
therapy, meaning they had to endure a round of chemo and then get
even sicker when their cancer progressed. But under this accelerated
approval, patients could game the system, receiving a so-called "first-
line" therapy like chemo for a few days and then immediately start taking Imbruvica. And what patient wouldn't? Imbruvica worked.

Ohio State's John Byrd, the principal investigator of the RESO-
NATE trial, said, "Rarely does a drug come along with so much potential to help CLL patients." The FDA's Richard Pazdur took a victory lap,
proclaiming that the FDA was using tools like the accelerated approval
program and "rapidly making this new therapy available to those who
need it most."

Bob Duggan, a man who had never worked in drug development before, had taken a targeted small-molecule cancer medicine from a first-in-human clinical trial, through the financial crisis, to attain two transformative regulatory approvals in five years. He had coalesced Pharmacyclics' focus solely on a BTK inhibitor that had become Imbruvica, overseen the launch of more than forty clinical trials, collapsed conventional industry timelines, and managed an aggressive regulatory strategy. People were cast aside in the process, dreams broken, strategies co-opted, and companies overtaken. But it was undeniable that Duggan had done the unimaginable and produced something that was saving lives.

In biotech circles, a parlor game emerged. Had Bob Duggan simply gotten lucky or was he good? What would have happened had Duggan not thrown a financial lifeline to Pharmacyclics in 2008 and pushed on with the first clinical trial of Imbruvica? When a *Forbes* article weighed in with a headline describing how "a lucky drug" had made Duggan a billionaire, Duggan became frustrated. His business track record could not be brushed off so easily.

Around the time the accelerated CLL approval arrived, Duggan was approached for the first time by the CEO of a biotechnology company about a corporate merger. Duggan conducted preliminary talks with the company and then abruptly called them off.

Nevertheless, the overture started to shift Duggan's strategic outlook. He began to think seriously about cashing out. This shift was nurtured by Wall Street investment bankers, who whispered in Duggan's ear that a single-product biotech like Pharmacyclics would eventually be pushed by its shareholders to sell itself before the patent clock on Imbruvica really started to tick and the company lost market exclusivity for its drug. Such demands would be hard to resist. Nor did he have many other options. If he bought a new drug to develop, stockholders would respond with fury and trade down the stock price. And Pharmacyclics did not have the capabilities to start a new drug program from scratch. Duggan could either control the inevitable sales process or be overwhelmed by it.

Duggan's decisions would eventually be driven by finding the right time to exit. Pharmacyclics would be able to command the highest price only after it had demonstrated the ability to generate some $1 billion in revenue. If Duggan sold the company at any point before this milestone, his would-be-buyers, the big pharmaceutical companies, would not pay top dollar. He needed to whet their appetite for massive revenue growth at just the right time. Whether it was chocolate chip cookies, Ponderosa steaks, or lifesaving cancer drugs, Duggan knew this game well. And he knew it wasn't yet time to make a deal.

//////////////////

THE SNOWFALL WOULD NOT have registered as an extraordinary weather event in Boston or New York, but this was Houston, where people were not accustomed to the cold and sleet. From sunny California, Raquel Izumi had been working—once again—with Susan O'Brien, the expert chronic lymphocytic leukemia doctor at Houston's MD Anderson Cancer Center, to recruit trial patients to go on Acerta's BTK inhibitor drug. But Izumi was still one bureaucratic signature away from enrolling the first patient.

The winter of 2014 had been challenging for the gang at Acerta. The twin approvals of Imbruvica demonstrated how far ahead Pharmacyclics had advanced. What's more, Ono, a large Japanese pharmaceutical company, had released data on a rival BTK inhibitor it had been working on that looked good. At the same time, Acerta had been working for weeks to launch the first-in-human trial of its BTK inhibitor. Progress had been slow.

Even though Ahmed Hamdy had forged strong relationships with leading CLL doctors, like O'Brien and John Byrd, who had signed on as clinical trial investigators, the company had not yet enrolled a single patient. Hamdy had become particularly nervous about Byrd, who had been singing the praises of Imbruvica but had not seemed overly engaged in finding suitable patients for Acerta. After Byrd agreed to participate in Pharmacyclics' trial, he had enrolled patients hand over fist. Hamdy worried that Byrd would be less enthusiastic this time around, especially as the Imbruvica approval meant that the drug could be prescribed for any relapsed CLL patient, not just the ones enrolled in a Pharmacyclics trial.

Wayne Rothbaum had led the start of a $37 million Series A equity financing at the end of 2013 as the clinical program kicked off, and with the money came more pressure. As always, Izumi had been feverishly writing up documents for regulators and medical centers to get the Acerta trial going. Without the documents, nothing would happen. Finally, O'Brien had identified a patient candidate, a sixty-two-year-old woman in Houston suffering from CLL.

This was no cherry-picked softball patient. In truth, at the start of a first-in-human trial, she was the kind of patient biopharma companies tried to avoid. Hamdy took one look at her condition and sighed. "That's a train wreck," he thought. The patient had failed several previous treatments, including a bone marrow transplant. Her bone marrow was 100 percent CLL cells. Inflated lymph nodes disfigured the right side of her neck. She had pancytopenia, meaning her counts for all three types of blood cells—red blood cells, white blood cells, and platelets—were dangerously low. (For some CLL patients, especially those who had endured a lot of chemo, white blood counts could get low instead of high.) She had been getting infusions of red blood cells and platelets on a regular basis. The woman's suffering was acute. She was barely clinging to life.

All that stood between her and the experimental Acerta drug was one administrative signature. Izumi and the staffer in the MD Anderson contract office had been trying for days to get a hospital official to sign the patient enrollment contract. Meanwhile, the patient was dying. Frustrated, the staffer grabbed the contract and walked out into the sleet to find the administrator and get the signature.

But as soon as the first patient was enrolled, she suffered what is known as a serious adverse event. This can range from a hospitalization, to a life-threatening experience, to death. O'Brien had no choice and hospitalized the patient, who was extremely sick and now suffering from inflamed and bleeding gums. This turn of events had Hamdy on the phone with O'Brien right away. They carefully went through the patient's vitals and symptoms. After much analysis, Hamdy and O'Brien both agreed to keep the patient on the drug. The bleeding gums seemed linked to the patient's overall deteriorating condition rather than the new medicine.

Hamdy and O'Brien watched this woman carefully for two weeks. During this time, she was released from the hospital. And then, over the ensuing days and weeks, she was spending a lot less time at the hospital in general.

After another fourteen days, Izumi received pictures showing that the inflated lymph nodes deforming the patient's neck had shrunk to the point where she looked completely normal. The patient had become transfusion independent, meaning no more needles or tubes to boost her red blood cells and platelets.

It was a dramatic response. As the weather warmed up in Houston, the patient felt so good she even started gardening again.

"It is really something," Izumi said to herself. Because of her experience with ibrutinib, Izumi knew this outcome had been no fluke. The drug had produced this amazing response even though it was a more selective BTK inhibitor than the Pharmacyclics drug. A feeling of excitement and relief rushed over her.

As usual, Hamdy called up Rothbaum to report. "It's working," Rothbaum said. "It's real." For Rothbaum, this one patient outcome was proof that promiscuity was not the key. Pharmacyclics' nonselective approach was not required for BTK inhibitors to work.

Rothbaum sat in his Manhattan apartment and thought about what to do next. It was clear that Imbruvica had no secret sauce. BTK was the thing, and his drug stopped BTK more efficiently than anything else in the world. He didn't need to wait like a scientist to see more empirical evidence. This one patient was enough.

Rothbaum called up Hamdy and told him they needed to go big. He wanted to launch a broad clinical program, including trials of the drug in a wide array of B cell malignancies. As many blood cancers as they could find. Even though Acerta did not have the commercial rights, he wanted a rheumatoid arthritis program, too. He wanted a trial combining the BTK inhibitor with the drug he had acquired from Amgen. Rothbaum wanted Hamdy to hire as many people as possible. He wanted the world.

"Don't worry about money—you're in a unique situation because you will always have access to funds," Rothbaum said. "We need to catch up to Pharmacyclics."

CHAPTER 15

Demoted

Wayne Rothbaum's voice began to rise. Ahmed Hamdy and Francisco Salva looked at each other. It had been a long day, and as night descended on Acerta's office in San Carlos, California, Hamdy and Salva both knew they would not be leaving soon. Conversations with Rothbaum were seldom short, especially when he was upset and yelling. They were trying to work out financial models for a patient trial. Even though Rothbaum was more than 2,000 miles away in New York, his presence was overwhelming. Rothbaum accused Hamdy and Salva of making mistakes and covering for each other, his indictments emanating from a speaker phone.

Everyone at Acerta had come to learn they would be subject to Rothbaum's fury if his questions and expectations were not fully met. His controlling nature could not bear the thought that there were facts, events, moments he did not know or could not govern. Both Hamdy and Salva had become used to working for demanding financiers. They had gone from Bob Duggan to Rothbaum, but Rothbaum was a different Wall Street animal because he knew more about the science and the business of biotech.

Salva endured the outbursts stoically. Rothbaum had a tremendous amount of his own money on the line—more money invested than Salva could ever imagine earning in a lifetime. But Hamdy resented these episodes. They made him uncomfortable. As Rothbaum continued screaming, Salva turned down the speaker volume.

Rothbaum had begun to exert more and more control over Acerta. Hamdy knew to reach out to Rothbaum at every milestone, to report every breakthrough and ray of light. But now, with this fledgling success, Rothbaum's control became that much more present. The geographical distance between the Dutch and California teams was irrelevant. Acerta's scientists were separated by half the world but their head of operations resided in New York.

In fact, Rothbaum would call Hamdy from the East Coast at just about any time, seven days a week. The only hours Hamdy could count on his phone not vibrating were between 1 a.m. and 3 a.m. in California. These conversations were stressful. "Have you heard from John?" "Did the patient come in for a CT scan today?" "Do you have the new data results?" "Did you do that budget?"

Izumi felt pressure as well. Rothbaum had figured out that Izumi possessed a unique skill set that could propel Acerta's efforts. As the company prepared to launch new clinical trials, Rothbaum insisted that only Izumi write the study protocol plans for them and be the person who amended those plans when needed. At Pharmacyclics, Izumi had driven Imbruvica's early clinical development forward and the same thing was happening at Acerta.

Rothbaum could not believe how fast Izumi could write these protocols. They married the clinical aspects of drug development with regulatory requirements perfectly. Rothbaum also found her work incredibly compelling. Izumi's protocols were beautifully written scientific stories. But this extra appreciation of her work also brought extra scrutiny. Rothbaum would give Izumi a hard time about issues as small as where she inserted a comma in a document. Such was the extent of his attention that staff frequently found it difficult to end conversations with Rothbaum. He managed to keep them on the phone until he was satisfied, and there was always something else to discuss. On one late-night call with Rothbaum, at around 11 p.m. in California, Rothbaum went silent on Izumi. She found it unusual until she realized he had fallen asleep.

Izumi was no stranger to pressure. She felt like patients might live or die as a result of what she was trying to accomplish; she could remember once sitting at an airport bar during a layover talking to the woman sitting next to her, who worked in clothing design. "When things get really stressed at work, we always say, 'calm down, it's not like we're curing cancer,'" the woman had said. "But you, you're the one. You *are* curing cancer!" This urgency was at the heart of Izumi's every success and every failure.

At Acerta, however, the pressure rose to another level entirely. Rothbaum's hard-driving style and the intensity of the work began to negatively impact some of the Acerta team. Hamdy sometimes felt despondent, and Izumi's husband began to worry about her health.

Despite the pressure, the team was making progress. Soon after Susan O'Brien had signed up the first patient in Houston during a snowstorm, John Byrd in Ohio came through with the second. Rothbaum had been worried that doctors would not want to participate in another BTK inhibitor trial after Imbruvica was approved. But Byrd assuaged Rothbaum's concern and began enrolling a steady stream. Richard Furman in New York was also active in Acerta's clinical program. It didn't take much salesmanship from the doctors to get patients to participate in the Acerta trial. The out-of-pocket costs of ibrutinib, even for patients on Medicare, were incredibly steep. Patients on Acerta's study received its BTK inhibitor for free. More importantly, perhaps, Byrd and the other doctors saw dramatic patient responses in the initial six patients who took the drug. Acerta's drug seemed to work. It would save their patients' lives.

Rothbaum had Acerta set up weekly patient trackers for him so he could follow the data as it flowed through the electronic databases. He knew each patient not by their name, but by their assigned number in the clinical trial database. It made little difference that Rothbaum was no scientist and held no medical degree. He followed each lymph node and blood count. But the patient trackers made Hamdy exceedingly uncomfortable. From Hamdy's perspective, such data should only be circulated after it had matured and been properly vetted. In Hamdy's mind, there should have also been a line between the scientists and clinicians in the field and the financial backers who supported them.

But Acerta was a private company, mostly owned by Rothaum and his hedge fund friends. Like Duggan before him, Rothbaum felt that this biopharma company was his and saw no reason why he couldn't keep track of every crumb of data from the academic medical centers. He needed the information to make sound business decisions for Acerta.

Rothbaum's entire identity had become wrapped up in Acerta. He took a step back from trading stocks and mostly focused on the company. For years, he had been an interested spectator of biotechnology companies. For the first time, Rothbaum was now deeply involved. To speed things up, he wanted to make sure Acerta did things in parallel and not sequentially. From the preclinical work in the laboratory to tax strategies, Rothbaum had a hand in almost everything. Sometimes his obsessiveness yielded important results. For example, Rothbaum knew that Amgen had the right to buy back the combination of the Dutch drug and its PI3K delta inhibitor. But with the early strong result of the BTK inhibitor as a single therapy, Rothbaum wanted to tie up loose ends. He negotiated with Amgen to own the combination outright. It cost Acerta $30 million, but Rothbaum felt owning the upside was worth the cost.

Rothbaum made another big catch when he learned that Acerta, as a Netherlands-domiciled company, qualified for a Dutch innovation box, a status that could reduce the corporate tax rate to 5 percent. This consideration had been overlooked at Acerta, which had planned to move its official domicile to California. At the time, US pharmaceutical companies were rushing to merge with European companies to obtain such tax advantages. Rothbaum's persistence helped save Acerta from losing it.

But Acerta had some problems that Rothbaum could not resolve, and it drove him crazy. The company's drug manufacturing efforts, which relied on a contractor, hit multiple snags, leading to clashes between Rothbaum and Tjeerd Barf in the Netherlands. Barf was an incredibly talented chemist, but he was not a process chemist. Barf did not have extensive experience with the chemistry, manufacturing, and control methods needed to produce large quantities of drug to feed Acerta's ambitious clinical program. In these trials, the BTK inhibitor would be chronically administered, day after day. They needed a lot of it.

The reality of opening a slew of clinical trials coupled with the fact the the the capsules would be swallowed by patients daily for months, maybe years, created a unique supply challenge. Deeply cost-conscious, Barf had been reluctant to pre-order bulk quantities of certain difficult-to-produce starting materials required to manufacture the drug. This caution delayed mass production by months, and production issues at the contract manufacturer exacerbated the situation. If Acerta couldn't supply the patients enrolled in the trials, the patients would be forced to discontinue treatment. Such an outcome could kill Acerta's reputation with the physician-scientists at the academic medical centers and potentially sink the entire effort. If they were coming from behind, these were the kinds of setbacks they couldn't tolerate—especially because their rival was not only well ahead, but partnered with a behemoth.

When it came time to chemically name the BTK inhibitor, Rothbaum called it acalabrutinib. The "cal" part of the name stood for Calistoga. Rothbaum saw Acerta as emerging out of the expertise— accomplishments and setbacks—accumulated at Pharmacyclics and Calistoga, the company he backed that developed the early B cell receptor CLL drug idelalisib. Rothbaum and Hamdy had hired several former Calistoga employees, like Roger Ulrich, who became chief science officer and also joined Acerta's board, and Dave Johnson, a mid-level medical affairs director at Calistoga. Acerta's connections to Pharmacyclics kept growing with the hiring of Jesse McGreivy, who had burned out at Pharmacyclics. Rothbaum's initials may not have been included in the Acerta corporate name, but his successes would be recognized.

/////////////

ON A SUMMER FRIDAY night, Wayne Rothbaum had just rolled into his Hamptons house in Quogue. He and his family had been stuck in three hours of traffic leaving New York City when Ahmed Hamdy called him. Hamdy said he wanted to discontinue escalating patient doses of acalabrutinib in Acerta's initial clinical trial.

The first-in-human trial of the drug had been set up as a dose-ranging study, first and foremost to evaluate the safety of the pill. The plan had been for the clinicians to get a better sense of what Acerta's drug was doing in the body as the doses increased. Another clear benefit was that effectiveness could be observed as well. Like most first-in-human studies, the idea was to find the biological optimal dose that would produce the most effectiveness with the least possible harm. But on this night, Hamdy told Rothbaum he wanted to discontinue the dose ranging and not go higher than the initial dose. He explained that the drug was almost completely blocking BTK, inhibiting its signal by 90 percent for more than four hours, and getting patient responses.

"I don't want to risk harming the baby," Hamdy said, adding that his experience at Pharmacyclics with Imbruvica was that blocking BTK's signal by 90 percent would be sufficient.

"Ahmed, we should be close to 100 percent," Rothbaum responded. "I don't give a shit about Pharmacyclics. We want to shut the target off 100 percent over twenty-four hours."

Hamdy had become anxious that the higher dose could spark a bad reaction in patients and potentially lead to adverse events that would harm the drug's reputation. Rothbaum disagreed, pointing out that the drug was much more selective than Imbruvica. Maybe shutting the target off completely could prevent future disease mutation and resistance to the drug? Such resistance had already emerged with Imbruvica and made the medicine stop working after a period of treatment. Maybe combining the drug at a higher dose with another therapy could lead to complete remission and disappearance of all signs of cancer, rather than the partial responses usually generated by Imbruvica?

The argument echoed the disagreement that had taken place a few years earlier around the dose escalation at Pharmacyclics of Imbruvica, when Duggan and Hamdy refused to follow Rothbaum's push toward dose escalation. Rothbaum again worried that a lot of the drug's effectiveness would be left on the table. He was keenly aware that any weakness in effectiveness would be measured head-to-head against Imbruvica. "Ahmed, six fucking patients," said Rothbaum. "You have no idea how safe our drug is."

But Rothbaum recognized that the debate wasn't about dosing. It was about power. Hamdy's impertinence threatened and concerned Rothbaum.

"Ahmed, you fucking argue with me one more time, I am firing you on the spot."

With Rothbaum owning about 47 percent of Acerta at the time, Hamdy was in no position to challenge him. Hamdy relented, and the dose escalation went ahead after being reviewed by an expert committee. But this episode shot off warning signals not only for Hamdy, but for Rothbaum as well. It occurred to Rothbaum there might be a problem with Hamdy being both the chief executive officer and the chief medical officer of Acerta. Rothbaum thought Hamdy had been acting as both judge and jury on important issues. In Rothbaum's mind, Hamdy was unilaterally making decisions and subverting institutional processes. To Hamdy, who had been trained to report everything to Rothbaum, the call felt more like a continuation of an ongoing conversation with the real decision-maker of the company. He found it surprising to see Rothbaum suddenly pulling rank.

Little flare-ups continued between Hamdy and Rothbaum. In the spring, Hamdy submitted an abstract of early preclinical results for acalabrutinib to the annual American Association for Cancer Research meeting. Rothbaum, who had put everyone under strict orders to remain in stealth mode, erupted. He did not want Acerta putting out data until it could show that its drug could potentially overtake Imbruvica. "What part of stealth mode didn't you understand?" Rothbaum asked. Hamdy pulled the abstract from the conference.

On another occasion, at around 4 p.m. on a Friday in California, Hamdy was driving his family to visit his father for his ninetieth birthday. They were bringing the cake and hoped to celebrate before Hamdy's father went to bed. He normally didn't make it much past 6 p.m. While still in the car, the phone rang.

"Wayne, you are on a speaker call. I'm in the car with my family. We're going to see my dad. It's my dad's birthday."

"What, you guys don't work in California? It's 4 o'clock and you're leaving work?" Rothbaum said before abruptly hanging up.

With so much at stake, Rothbaum continued to find deficiencies in Hamdy. Too often when Rothbaum called him, he caught Hamdy rowing on the water or playing tennis. Rothbaum's frustration became a running joke for Tom Turalski, who represented Joe Edelman's Perceptive hedge fund on Acerta's board and spent most of his time on Acerta-related issues. "Hold on," Turalski would say when Rothbaum called him. "I just need to finish this serve."

In part, this was a culture clash between the hard-charging New York hedge funders and the California biopharma executives. Hamdy believed he was working harder than he had ever worked in his life and bristled at Rothbaum's expectations for immediate responsiveness. He had lost track of how often each day Rothbaum called him. But Rothbaum ultimately controlled Hamdy's fate at Acerta. And Rothbaum's concerns were sincere and growing.

The escalating tensions exploded into an argument in 2014. Acerta was about to launch its small phase 2 study of acalabrutinib in relapsed mantle cell lymphoma patients. Dave Johnson, the former Calistoga medical affairs director who had been hired at Acerta, wanted to turn it into a large single-arm phase 2 registration trial that could lead to an accelerated FDA approval. He believed that Pharmacyclics had left the door open for such an end run.

When it came to chronic lymphocytic leukemia, the FDA had, in July 2014, upgraded Imbruvica's accelerated approval to a regular and full approval for previously treated CLL patients. The FDA also tacked on an additional approval for CLL patients with the 17p chromosomal abnormality deletion who had never received a prior treatment. Both these FDA approvals were based on the confirming results of the phase 3 RESONATE trial. It meant that acalabrutinib, which was the same class of drug as Imbruvica, would not be eligible to receive an accelerated approval for CLL. Acerta would need to conduct a full-blown randomized phase 3 trial to get any sort of approval from the FDA in the most common adult leukemia.

The state of play in mantle cell lymphoma was different. Even though it had launched a randomized controlled study in mantle cell lymphoma, Pharmacyclics had not yet been able to secure a full approval for Imbruvica in the rare blood cancer. As long as no such approval came, Acerta could apply for an accelerated approval for its BTK inhibitor in mantle cell lymphoma. Johnson thought Acerta could pull off a quick single-arm study that would meet the FDA's accelerated approval standards.

Hamdy did not like Johnson's plan and did not want to divert employees or resources to pursue it. He thought it would be difficult to enroll enough patients in a large mantle cell lymphoma study and worried that Pharmacyclics was too far ahead. The FDA could grant full approval for Imbruvica in mantle cell lymphoma before Acerta accumulated enough data for an accelerated approval. Around this time, Johnson flew to London on a business trip. When Rothbaum called him just to check in, he sensed Johnson's discontent. "What's bothering you?" Rothbaum asked.

"If you really want to know, we should be launching a registration trial and making this happen in mantle cell lymphoma right now,"

Johnson answered. "That is our fastest opportunity to get approved. You can keep treating all the CLL patients you want with this drug, but until you do a phase 3 in CLL this drug will not be on the market."

Rothbaum asked Johnson if he thought they could enroll enough patients, and Johnson assured Rothbaum that they could. Intrigued, Rothbaum set up a broad team call to discuss Johnson's idea. At Pharmacyclics, Hamdy had been early to push for a strategy that led to an initial accelerated approval in mantle cell lymphoma for Imbruvica. But this time around, Hamdy argued that the strategy would be too risky and waste time and other resources. On the call, however, a consensus emerged that Johnson was onto something.

As the discussion wrapped up, Rothbaum called for an amendment to the protocol of the existing mantle cell study. He wanted it to meet the FDA's registration requirements and increase to 120 patients. If the gambit didn't work, Rothbaum figured the worst outcome was that he would spend some extra money. On the flip side, Johnson could be right and this might be the quickest way to get acalabrutinib to market.

Four weeks later, Rothbaum woke up suddenly in the middle of night. "Where the fuck is the mantle cell amendment?" he asked himself. Rothbaum had not seen the important expansion of the study plan go through. He could not go back to sleep. Waiting until the sun had risen in California, Rothbaum called Raquel Izumi. "You need to check with Ahmed," Izumi said evasively.

Rothbaum took a deep breath and spoke slowly. He ordered Izumi to get the trial amendment for the mantle cell lymphoma study done the following week.

"I am a good foot soldier," Izumi said.

///////////////////////

JAMES TOPPER HAD HEARD about some of the clashes going on at Acerta. A partner at Frazier Healthcare Partners, Topper had been part of the small investment group that backed Acerta. He had gotten to know Wayne Rothbaum when both were investors in Calistoga, a company Topper cofounded. Topper had a lot more experience when it came to running private companies. While on vacation in Hawaii, he decided it might help to give Rothbaum some advice.

Walking along a pristine beach on the Pacific Ocean, Topper made a phone call to Rothbaum and suggested clearly that Rothbaum give management a bit more space and let them do their job. The conversation did not go well.

"I am management," Rothbaum exclaimed. "I've got a third of my net worth in this company. You have your investors' money and if it blows up, big deal, it doesn't change your life."

The disagreement was partly philosophical. The two had different approaches to business and investment. Topper had spent years as a buttoned-down private equity investor, who saw his role as empowering and strategically advising the management teams of the companies he backed. The day-to-day tactical decisions belonged to the executives.

Rothbaum didn't see things that way. He told Topper they were sitting on a potential multi-billion-dollar drug. Among the doctors participating in the clinical trial, the anecdotal early impression was that acalabrutinib had a better safety profile than Imbruvica and worked at least as well. They were enrolling patients so fast that Acerta, taken by surprise, had been having trouble providing enough of the drug to the medical sites—another issue Rothbaum kept fuming about and felt Hamdy had not properly managed. Rothbaum, who had taken the call while walking down a Manhattan street, told Topper Acerta would make him rich. "Back the fuck off," Rothbaum yelled, startling people nearby.

From the conversation with Izumi, Rothbaum assumed Hamdy had intentionally buried the protocol amendment for the mantle cell lymphoma study. And he assumed Hamdy had done so because the change had not been his idea. Hamdy claimed he had just not prioritized it. Nevertheless, to Rothbaum, the delay was part of a pattern. Rothbaum didn't think Hamdy should be CEO and CMO any longer. He called the directors individually. Some of them pushed for Hamdy to be fired outright. Rothbaum did not want that. He thought that Hamdy had done a good job bringing Acerta to its current position and had been, of course, integral to the founding of the company. But something needed to change. A general agreement emerged to remove Hamdy from the CEO position and have him focus on being CMO.

In the fall of 2014, Acerta's directors met in the Manhattan offices of Rothbaum's lawyers, just a block south of Grand Central Station, to discuss finding Hamdy's replacement. Hamdy had no idea the directors were discussing his fate. Rothbaum had been impressed with Dave Johnson's initiative and strategic thinking in mantle cell lymphoma and recommended him for the job. Some directors worried that Johnson had never run a company before and suggested maybe finding an experienced leader.

A search for a CEO from outside the organization could take six months, and finding someone with knowledge of BTK would be difficult. Rothbaum didn't think they had that kind of time and he certainly had no desire to share Acerta's secrets with external candidates, even if they signed a confidentiality agreement. Acerta had entered a crucially important time.

Rothbaum had been gearing up to lead the final part of the Series A financing to raise another $75 million for Acerta. It represented a new level of financial commitment and Rothbaum would be good for about half of it. The investment group had expanded to include OrbiMed Advisors, the New York hedge fund and private equity firm. Joe Edelman would not only be investing more cash belonging to his Perceptive hedge fund; he would also be investing more of his own personal money that he held outside the hedge fund. Seeing Rothbaum put up so much of his personal money emboldened the rest of the investment group.

The directors concluded that transitioning to a new CEO from outside the company could slow Acerta's momentum. They decided to name Johnson as CEO on an interim basis and see how things progressed. Rothbaum would become Acerta's executive chairman to oversee Johnson directly. He was pretty much doing the job of an executive chairman anyway.

When Rothbaum summoned Hamdy to Manhattan, Hamdy didn't think much of it. He didn't remember his seemingly routine walk into Duggan's office years before. Since he was going to be in New York, Hamdy set up a series of meetings around his appointment with Rothbaum. The two met in the conference room of Rothbaum's offices on Fifty-Seventh Street. When Hamdy got there, he saw that Tom Turalski was also in the room.

"It's not working," Rothbaum said.

Rothbaum walked Hamdy through the board meeting that had taken place and informed Hamdy he was being removed from the CEO position. From now on, Rothbaum said, Hamdy would concentrate solely on the CMO role. Rothbaum also told Hamdy he would be losing one million Acerta stock options that had been put aside to incentivize him as CEO that had not vested, a big chunk of the Acerta equity he received. Hamdy did not lose any of the common shares he received when he helped found the company.

For a brief moment, Hamdy started to tear up. This was the second time he had lost a big corporate role and been cut out of a significant amount of company equity. He then composed himself. He had no other choice but to accept the demotion. The only alternative would be to quit. He remembered what it felt like to be alone and afraid after his ouster by Duggan. And Hamdy didn't want to leave a company he had helped start. The A in Acerta stood for Ahmed. He would not just walk away.

Hamdy felt Rothbaum tended to cycle through people. The way Hamdy saw it, as he walked out onto the streets of Manhattan, was that his turn had come.

CHAPTER 16

Billions

Wayne Rothbaum felt like he had been kicked in the stomach. He had just arrived at Acerta's office in San Carlos when he received a letter from the FDA saying that the US regulator had rejected the company's plans for getting acalabrutinib approved for patients with relapsed chronic lymphocytic leukemia. Rothbaum was in Northern California attending the annual blood cancer meeting organized by the American Society of Hematology, taking place in December 2014 in San Francisco. He had come down to Acerta's offices to check in on his troops, and now he had a full-blown crisis on his hands.

The letter had broken a string of successes at Acerta. Nearly fifty relapsed CLL patients had been taking acalabrutinib for six months or more, and none of their cancers had progressed. But now, the FDA had told Acerta that the path to approval for acalabrutinib in its key market, CLL, would be more difficult. Each time Acerta had asked if the FDA approved of its testing protocols, the regulator had said "no." Acerta had told the FDA it intended to launch a phase 3 randomized registration trial that would pit acalabrutinib against ofatumumab, the monoclonal antibody drug. This had been the way Pharmacyclics had secured full regulatory approval for Imbruvica earlier in the summer.

For weeks, Acerta had been preparing to run the trial and set up several medical centers to do it.

The FDA had other ideas. The regulators knew that ofatumumab didn't work very well in CLL and made a poor control arm. Imbruvica, for example, worked much better. The FDA's letter told Acerta that it would need to compare acalabrutinib against another drug if it wanted to bring acalabrutinib to market.

Rothbaum quickly huddled the leaders of Acerta's clinical development team in a conference room. Ahmed Hamdy, Raquel Izumi, and the new CEO, Dave Johnson, were there. Jesse McGreivy, who had just been through this process at Pharmacyclics, also got pulled in. Their big fear was that the FDA would force Acerta to run a head-to-head trial of acalabrutinib against Imbruvica—and that could take a very long time. In such a trial, the endpoint, or measured outcome that could objectively determine whether acalabrutinib was a beneficial drug, would be its ability to roll back the cancer. The FDA would want to see significant improvement against Imbruvica, and even if acalabrutinib could demonstrate it, a trial like this could take a substantial amount of time and cost hundreds of millions of dollars. Imbruvica's ability to stave off CLL in patients was being measured in years. One patient had already been on the drug for half a decade and counting.

The Acerta team didn't know what to do. They brainstormed about using other drugs for the control arm, but there seemed to be significant barriers or stumbling blocks around every corner. After a while, Rothbaum could see that his team was exhausted. Acerta had booked a suite at the W Hotel in downtown San Francisco for the ASH conference and Rothbaum suggested the group take a break and reconvene there in the evening.

To everyone's surprise, Rothbaum showed up at the hotel with two bottles of expensive tequila and ordered a tremendous amount of food. As everyone loosened up, ideas started flowing. The group spent the night designing a complex and multipronged program to gain regulatory approval for acalabrutinib in CLL. First, they mapped out a phase 3 trial to test acalabrutinib as a first-line therapy in five hundred previously untreated patients. In the three-arm trial, some patients would get acalabrutinib alone, and some would take it in combination with a monoclonal antibody treatment. A third group of patients would receive the monoclonal antibody plus chemotherapy. Next, the Acerta team laid the foundation for another phase 3 trial of acalabrutinib against a control arm where the participating doctors could choose between two different combination therapies.

The intention was to gain regulatory approval in CLL through these two trials, but, as ever, Rothbaum was thinking big. They also drew up a head-to-head phase 3 trial of acalabrutinib against Imbruvica in relapsed CLL patients that aimed to show that acalabrutinib was a safer drug than Pharmacyclics' medicine. The study would be expensive, not only because of the amount of time it would take, but also because Acerta would need to acquire Imbruvica capsules. The head-to-head trial against Imbruvica, however, held the potential of differentiating acalabrutinib in the marketplace. And crowning the true victor.

Rothbaum would not let anyone leave the hotel suite until the strategy had been set. As the group revamped their entire clinical plan in CLL at the W Hotel, Bob Duggan was meeting with investment bankers across town. He had also been busy in San Francisco during the ASH conference, and the stakes of the battle that was brewing were about to rise even higher.

////////////////

THE IMBRUVICA BOOTH AT the 2014 ASH conference was gigantic. Illuminated arches soared over large glowing screens. Nobody at the meeting could miss the booth promoting the fastest-growing medicine blood specialists had ever seen. No longer the subject of curiosity, Bob Duggan had become the hottest CEO in the field after his fur-clad arrival at ASH in New Orleans five years before. A far cry from the sad lonely poster days there, Imbruvica data would now be featured in thirty-seven abstracts at the conference, and eight of those abstracts had been selected for oral presentation. Pharmacyclics was on the verge of securing Imbruvica's third FDA regulatory approval, this time in Waldenstrom macroglobulinemia, the first approved treatment specifically for the rare cancer.

The smashing success of Duggan's Pharmacyclics was embodied in his own Café Genius, opened at Pharmacyclics' offices in Sunnyvale. Duggan had grown way beyond standing at his storefront and handing out cookies, but he understood marketing. And there was satisfaction in seeing his people take a break with a cup of his branded coffee in their hands. In fact, Duggan had just opened his Sunnyvale doors to the first Pharmacyclics patient summit. For the patients who showed up, Duggan was like a rock star. They wanted to take their photos with Duggan and hug him. One patient, La Verne Harris, presented a large painting depicting her journey since being diagnosed with leukemia. In the painting, her broken heart soared because Imbruvica had given her life a second chance.

Back at the ASH conference, on day two, Duggan and Maky Zanganeh met with investment bankers from Centerview Partners, a boutique New York financial firm. The Wall Street bankers told Duggan and Zanganeh that multiple pharmaceutical companies had expressed interest in acquiring Pharmacyclics and its single drug, Imbruvica. Duggan and the bankers started to plan out timelines and strategies for getting those companies to bid aggressively against each other. The time to sell Pharmacyclics had come.

Duggan and Zanganeh also took time at the ASH conference to meet with Nina Mojas, head of oncology business development at AstraZeneca, the large British-Swedish pharmaceutical company. Duggan and Zanganeh had negotiated a deal to work together on combining Imbruvica with an experimental AstraZenenca therapy in solid tumors. The idea was to expand the potential of Imbruvica, at least in theory, and boost the market prospects of the drug just as Pharmacyclics was being put up for sale.

The day following the conclusion of the conference, Duggan and Zanganeh met with more investment bankers, this time from J.P. Morgan. The appetite in the market for Imbruvica was strong, and Duggan no longer had to knock on anyone's door. They were all coming to him. Duggan knew that the all-important J.P. Morgan Healthcare Conference was coming up in San Francisco and that there would be plenty more deal-hungry executives from pharmaceutical companies that would seek him out. Duggan was ready. He told executives at J&J, Pharmacyclics' Imbruvica partner, that he would be putting Pharmacyclics up for sale. Duggan owed J&J a shot at bidding, and J&J was the most logical candidate, since the conglomerate already owned half of Imbruvica. It didn't take long for J&J to put its hat in the ring.

On the first day of the J.P. Morgan Healthcare conference, Duggan showed up to the Westin St. Francis hotel in salesman mode. In a presentation he gave to conference attendees, Duggan injected some of his personal flair, describing Imbruvica as being a medicine that was "body harmonious," his own idea about how the body could be made to fix itself. But then he got down to business. "The success we've had in hematology, I truly believe that's just chapter one," he said. Imbruvica, he noted, had generated $185 million in the last three months of 2014. Over the summer, the FDA had fully approved the drug in relapsed CLL patients and even added an approval for patients with the troublesome genetic 17p abnormality who had never received treatment before. With all these approvals, Duggan announced, Pharmacyclics had forecast $1 billion in Imbruvica sales in 2015, conferring blockbuster status to the drug. He predicted that the FDA approval in Waldenstrom, the rare blood cancer, was imminent and that while the B cell cancer was diagnosed in only about fifteen hundred Americans annually, he expected that those patients would be on Imbruvica for between three and five years. Waldenstrom-related revenue would be three times larger than that for mantle cell lymphoma. "What it doesn't have in terms of quantity of patients, it makes up for in terms of years of therapy," Duggan declared.

These big financial projections would put some middle-class patients in a bind, even those with medical insurance. While Medicare and private insurance covered most of Imbruvica's immense price tag, patients often had to cough up some $7,000 annually out of pocket for the treatment. The drug companies funded nonprofit foundations to help patients out, but this aid often came with income limits. Patients who earned $80,000 or more often did not qualify and would have to make harrowing financial decisions. Some opted not to take Imbruvica and, as difficult as it was, instead went on a treatment more fully covered by their insurance, like chemotherapy.

Still, Imbruvica was making a difference. Government and drug company programs often made the drug available for poor patients. Under Duggan's watch, Pharmacyclics had supported more than fifty clinical trials that had already dosed 5,100 patients with Imbruvica. The CEO could rightly argue that his company had accomplished in five years what often would take a biopharma company a decade or more.

In his presentation, Duggan touted the relationship with J&J, which shared the high development costs and sold the drug outside the United States. Duggan announced positive results from new trials with previously untreated CLL patients, as well as the news that Imbruvica seemed to be working as a treatment for other diseases as well, such as graft-versus-host disease, which sometimes occurs after bone marrow or stem cell transplants. Going further, Duggan predicted that Imbruvica would eventually be used to treat rheumatoid arthritis and even solid tumors, an area Pharmacyclics had begun to explore with AstraZeneca.

After his talk, Duggan took this script to meetings with executives from pharmaceutical companies interested in buying Pharmacyclics. His first appointment was with J&J, but over the next few days of the conference, Duggan engaged in a carefully orchestrated dance, repeating the same talking points to other executive teams. At the same time, the investment bankers from J.P. Morgan, got to work lining up potential buyers and planning the sale. One of their most important calls was to a company in Chicago called AbbVie.

////////////////

RICHARD GONZALEZ HAD ALWAYS been a kind of wild card in
the pharmaceutical industry. For years, as he was climbing up the pharmaceutical industry ranks, he had falsely claimed to have received a
bachelor's degree in biochemistry from the University of Houston and
a master's degree in biochemistry from the University of Miami. In fact,
he had dropped out of the University of Houston in the early 1970s and
spent only four months at the University of Miami. He never earned a
degree of any kind.

By the time this lie was discovered, Gonzalez had become an
important and talented executive at Abbott Laboratories with decades
of experience in the pharmaceutical industry. Gonzalez spent much of
his career at the Chicago-area company, working his way up commercial, research, and manufacturing operations to the posts of chief operating officer and president.

In 2007, Gonzalez was diagnosed with throat cancer and retired.
The idea was to get healthy and play golf. The cancer went away, but
Gonzalez was miserable. "My golf game is lousy—it's not like I want to
spend four hours on the golf course," he would later say. He returned
to Abbott two years later, initially to run the company's venture portfolio. When he came back, Gonzalez informed the company that his
biography contained inaccurate information about obtaining academic
degrees, which Abbott corrected in his official biography. When *Crain's
Chicago Business* broke the news about Gonzalez's credentials, Abbott
initially said that the degrees were included in securities filings as a
result of an internal administrative error.

In 2013, Abbott, which specialized in medical devices and nutrition,
split itself up. The company spun out its biggest prescription drugs into
a new company called AbbVie, and Gonzalez was tapped to lead it as
CEO. He earned over $20 million a year and had a single big issue to
manage. AbbVie absolutely depended on Humira (adalimumab), the
anti-inflammatory treatment for rheumatoid arthritis, psoriasis, and

other conditions. It was not just AbbVie's best-selling drug. It would soon become the top-selling drug in the world. Period. In one year, it would generate nearly $20 billion, as much as 65 percent of AbbVie's total revenues. But Humira would soon start to lose its patent protection, allowing competitors to start manufacturing cheap generic versions of the drug, so Gonzalez had to find new revenue fast.

Unlike most biopharma CEOs, Gonzalez had a Bloomberg terminal, the ubiquitous Wall Street research tool, on his office desk. He was a dealmaker, and every investment banker from New York to San Francisco knew Gonzalez would be gunning for a large acquisition. The other big event Gonzalez was working on at the time was his upcoming wedding to Chantel Gia Poynton, a former *Playboy* model he had met while standing in line at a Starbucks.

No one was surprised when Gonzalez inserted himself into the feeding frenzy around a potential Pharmacyclics acquisition. He first met with Bob Duggan and Maky Zanganeh in late January 2015. In addition to J&J and AbbVie, Swiss pharmaceutical company Novartis and US giant Pfizer had also expressed keen interest.

By early February, Duggan and Zanganeh had started holding meetings with the top executives of the four potential buyers, each of which started conducting comprehensive due diligence and poring through Pharmacyclics' books and records.

Wall Street got wind of the wheeling and dealing in late February 2015, when Bloomberg News reported that Pharmacyclics had been engaged in deal talks that valued the company at between $17 billion and $18 billion. The news report sent Pharmacyclics' stock flying to $220; it had started the year trading for $123. The bidding war for Pharmacyclics became intense.

Back in Silicon Valley, on the first Monday of March 2015, Duggan and Zanganeh met with representatives from each of the final three bidders. Gonzalez made them the highest offer, saying AbbVie's board had authorized the company to pay $250 per share. It was an incredible offer, but Duggan wasn't ready to take it. He knew the power he had and could sense the desire and desperation of the bidders in front of him. Duggan had pitted J&J, Pfizer, and AbbVie against one another (Novartis had dropped out of the process) and thought he could get them to pay even more. With the support of Pharmacyclics' other directors, Duggan went back to the bidding companies the next day, saying he wanted to see one last round of proposals that included their best and final offers. In the early afternoon, Gonzalez came over the top again, with an offer of $261.25 per share, 58 percent in cash and the rest in AbbVie stock. The closest runner-up bid was $250 per share. An elated Duggan quickly conducted a meeting of Pharmacyclics' board. The directors decided to take the AbbVie deal.

The deal Gonzalez and Duggan struck shocked Wall Street and set the new high-water mark for success in the biotechnology industry. AbbVie had agreed to buy Pharmacyclics and its solitary drug, Imbruvica, for $21 billion.

It was almost impossible to comprehend the math because, in reality, AbbVie had only purchased about half of the drug. J&J still owned the rights to some 50 percent of Imbruvica's profits. Pablo Legorreta's Royalty Pharma had also hung onto the tiny slice of Imbruvica's income that stemmed from Celera Genomics, which he had bought at the bargain-basement price of $485 million.

Some on Wall Street thought that a desperate Gonzalez had panicked. There just were not too many drugs out there for sale that could replace Humira and reasonably be expected to become one of the world's top-selling medicines. Bank of Montreal's Alex Arfaei wrote a report suggesting that AbbVie "might be overpaying." Other analysts described the price tag as "staggering" and "astronomical." The *New York Times* ran a headline speculating about "why AbbVie may have overpaid" and concluded that "it's hard to see AbbVie coming out ahead."

After taking into account the profit split with J&J, the deal valued a single drug—Imbruvica—at more than $42 billion. That meant Imbruvica was worth more than the gross domestic profit of countries like Ghana, Jordan, and Bolivia. On paper, the drug was now worth nearly as much as all of Genentech, the foundational biotechnology company in South San Francisco that had been bought by Roche a few years earlier for $47 billion.

Still, for the CEO of a large pharmaceutical company, like Gonzalez, what mattered was that Imbruvica would materially increase AbbVie's earnings for years, the chief metric on which stock market investors evaluated the company. He did not need to make a sizable return on a $21 billion investment—like pocketing $30 billion from future Imbruvica sales—for the deal to be a success. As long as the drug performed reasonably well financially and AbbVie did not have to write-down a portion of the investment, buying a 50 percent stake in Imbruvica for $21 billion could be worth it. A large pharmaceutical company like AbbVie would rather overpay for a fully approved, sure-thing drug ("de-risked" in industry parlance) than invest in an experimental medicine that could fail.

Nevertheless, in an online interview, Adam Feuerstein, a popular biotech columnist, said the deal indicated that the biotechnology party had possibly raged on for too long. "You probably have been out to a bar, you are having a really good time, having a few drinks, it gets late, and you probably should go home, but your friend says to you 'hey, let's have another drink, let's keep the party going,'" Feuerstein analogized. "For biotech, this deal today, that's like that extra drink."

There were big financial winners throughout the organization. Maky Zanganeh's Pharmacyclics share holdings, mostly made up of granted stock options and incentive stock awards, were worth $200 million after accounting for option exercise prices as low as 75 cents per share. Felix and Julian Baker, who had bought heavily into the company via their Baker Brothers hedge fund, now held stock worth $2.4 billion. Baker Brothers had paid around $100 million or so for the position, and the trade helped fuel the growth of their hedge fund and turn it into a Wall Street giant. Felix and Julian Baker were well on their way to personally becoming billionaires. Peter Lebowitz and Paul Stoffels, the J&J executives who helped get the conglomerate to partner on Imbruvica, looked like geniuses. The decision helped fuel their careers and that of others who were involved. J&J's Janssen unit had purchased half of Imbruvica for $1 billion, and now the Pharmacyclics acquisition had conferred a value of some $21 billion on their stake in the drug.

Those who were shoved aside and forgotten had comparatively little to show financially from their time at Pharmacyclics. People like Richard Miller and Ahmed Hamdy were now nothing more than names that littered the corporate history.

With the final blockbuster sale of the company, the true value of the windfall Hamdy had missed by losing unvested shares and selling his vested shares had a concrete number: $86 million.

By selling a majority of his Pharmacyclics shares, Wayne Rothbaum lost out on $700 million.

The fortunes created and missed by Imbruvica would become a sore point for some who played a role in its success but did not financially profit from it—either in a big way or at all. The early Celera Genomics chemists behind the drug would wonder about a system that left them completely out of the big money. Zhengying Pan, who was fired from Celera after discovering the drug, had returned to China, where he became a researcher at Peking University. He didn't make any money on the deal. Doctors who worked on the Imbruvica trials as far away as Italy would darkly joke about the riches their labor created for others. They had never expected to participate in any financial success of Imbruvica and were in it for the patients and their passion for medicine. But, honestly, they never anticipated a drug they helped bring about could be worth $42 billion. The incentives seemed to be misplaced for those who were forgotten.

On the day the deal was announced, Gonzalez defended the high purchase price on a conference call with investors. He estimated that Imbruvica would eventually be good for $7.5 billion of annual revenues for AbbVie and that Pharmacyclics ran a competitive sales process with bids coming just under AbbVie's price.

"I've been through a lot of these and I'd say this was probably one of the most competitive ones I've seen," Gonzalez said. "There were multiple companies that were competing. There were multiple rounds for this asset. Three companies stayed in until the very end and bid against each other in this process, and we won."

On the morning of the deal announcement in Sunnyvale, Duggan gathered Pharmacyclics' employees at a ballroom of a local hotel. Breakfast and coffee were served. Duggan thanked everyone for all they had done to make this day happen. There was a lot of excitement. With Pharmacyclics shares at $261.25, a lot of people were doing the math on their stock options.

It turns out they would have another reason to stick around. As part of the negotiated transaction with AbbVie, Duggan had committed to retaining as many Pharmacyclics employees as possible during the transition. Standing in front of his employees, Duggan promised to personally buy a new Tesla Model S, much like the one he drove, for a few employees who stayed on. The winners' names would be drawn randomly and the lucky ones would get a new luxury car.

Bob Duggan could afford the perk. Among the sea of new millionaires, he was by far the biggest winner. He had never even previously worked in the biopharma industry. Over a nine-year period, Duggan had bet a $50 million fortune on a company that had initially tried to create a drug aimed at the cancer that took his son's life.

When the deal was complete, Duggan had made seventy times his initial investment.

His $3.5 billion payday made his bet on Pharmacyclics one of the greatest Wall Street trades ever—in any industry.

CHAPTER 17

The Whirlwind

Back at Acerta, Dave Johnson was learning how to run a company on the fly. He had never been an executive before, let alone a CEO. He had grown up in Indiana and Wisconsin, studying economics and chemistry at Indiana University before finding his way to a sales job in the biopharma industry. He lacked an MD or a PhD, but Johnson wiggled his way into clinical development through hard work and his down-to-earth midwestern personality. Now he was interim CEO at Acerta, having taken over from Ahmed Hamdy. He was grateful to Wayne Rothbaum for his big shot, but Johnson knew he needed help.

The upheaval at Acerta had only accelerated, and sometimes it went beyond the typical biotech start-up mayhem. The thing that kept the interim CEO awake at night was the company's continued inability to manufacture enough of its own drug. The way Johnson put it, the company was trying to thread a needle in a hurricane. So far, the precarious situation had been managed, but any unforeseen hiccup could bring the drug supply issue crashing down.

To accommodate the growing staff, nearing 150 employees, the company also needed to find a new Silicon Valley building. In San Carlos, the offices and cubicles were packed with up to four people in each. Acerta moved its main office 4 miles up Highway 101 to a larger space in Redwood City, near the cylinder-shaped buildings that made up the headquarters of software giant Oracle. With all the trials being launched under Rothbaum's aggressive plan, Raquel Izumi worried whether Acerta could even adequately oversee them all, as required by the regulators.

The unqualified success of Pharmacyclics was undeniable, and Rothbaum continued to ratchet up the pressure on his team. The unmitigated demands of Rothbaum were overwhelming. Those around him were subjected to a daily barrage of emails and phone calls. Like everyone else, Johnson found it difficult to end a phone call with Rothbaum. Sometimes he would mute his phone so he could get work done while the boss railed his frustrations on the other end of the line.

Johnson's smartest move may have been to hire Maria Fardis. Originally recruited by Bob Duggan, Fardis had led Pharmacyclics' clinical operations over its latest stretch, but she departed the company right before the sale to AbbVie. More than almost anyone, Fardis knew there was a need for a BTK inhibitor with fewer side effects. She clearly remembered the patients who showed up at Pharmacyclics headquarters for the patient summit, many of whom bore bruises on the back of their hands, a signature of the kind of issues Imbruvica could cause.

Fardis had acquired a reputation at Pharmacyclics for being incredibly tough and hardworking—and making sure things got done. Fardis said she drove harder because the patients were in the front of her mind. Others chalked it up to personal ambition. In any event, Johnson hired Fardis as Acerta's chief operating officer because she delivered results. Another Pharmacyclics refugee would fit right in. At first, however, Rothbaum worried that Fardis might be a secret agent sent over from Pharmacyclics to subvert progress at Acerta. But Fardis's abilities and no-nonsense approach quickly won Rothbaum over.

Some Acerta employees were unhappy with the hire. A few people who had worked with Fardis at Pharmacyclics did not want to deal with her demanding style again. But Fardis immediately made an impact.

She improved Acerta's forecasting process so the company could better anticipate how many patients it would enroll in its various trials, bolstering the entire clinical program. Together with McGreivy, Fardis also poured rocket fuel on the mantle cell lymphoma trial, helping to enroll a large number of patients.

///////////////////

STANDING IN FRONT OF Acerta's poster abstract at the American Association of Cancer Research's annual meeting, Wayne Rothbaum looked more like a member of the Praetorian Guard than the chairman of a biotechnology company. With his athletic build, Rothbaum's stance was imposing, and he remained focused and alert, carefully eyeing anyone who approached. The L-shaped Pennsylvania Convention Center occupied four city blocks in downtown Philadelphia. It had attracted 18,500 doctors, scientists, clinicians, and investors to discuss advances in cancer science. Rothbaum thought the time had come to give the industry a little taste of acalabrutinib by revealing a smidgen of data about what it could do. But he was going to be very careful about it. Rothbaum had placed a sign in front of the poster that said "No Photos."

Rothbaum was right to worry. At one point during the poster presentation, Rothbaum spotted two attendees lurking nearby. They were hiding cameras under their jackets, trying to surreptitiously take photos of Acerta's poster. To Rothbaum, it seemed like amateur hour. Their conference badges identified them as employees of BeiGene, a China-based biotechnology company that had been developing a BTK inhibitor called zanubrutinib. Rothbaum told them to get lost.

Plenty of other doctors and industry professionals stopped by without hidden cameras. One of those people was Chris Sheldon. Sheldon worked at the British-Swedish pharmaceutical conglomerate AstraZeneca, where he evaluated oncology developments taking place in the biotechnology industry and looked for potential partnerships. After chatting for a while and exchanging business cards, Sheldon asked Rothbaum to follow up on their meeting by sending a more detailed presentation on acalabrutinib. "I am not sending you anything," Rothbaum told him.

Despite Rothbaum's standoffishness, pharmaceutical companies soon started to take notice of Acerta. The tiny company had become incredibly active. Working seven days a week, Raquel Izumi had been churning out study protocol after study protocol, and the company was on its way to launching more than twenty clinical trials. Those studies had popped up on the public registry maintained by the National Institutes of Health and caught the attention of some pharmaceutical researchers. They wondered what was going on at this obscure company officially headquartered in the Netherlands.

In addition to the phase 3 trials for chronic lymphocytic leukemia, there were studies testing the drug for everything from blood cancers like mantle cell lymphoma and Waldenstrom macroglobulinemia to solid tumor cancers like ovarian, head and neck, and bladder cancer. For the solid tumor cancers, Rothbaum had a theory about combining the BTK inhibitor with Keytruda (pembrolizumab), Merck's blockbuster drug that had originated in the same Dutch building as acalabrutinib. There were trials in rheumatoid arthritis, and Izumi had even written up a protocol for a trial testing acalabrutinib in patients with glioblastoma, the brain cancer that caused Demian Duggan's death. Maria Fardis, Jesse McGreivy, and Izumi had also gone to White Oak, Maryland, and sold the FDA on the clinical studies it thought should lead to regulatory approval of the drug in CLL.

Rothbaum was all in. He funded all these activities and continued to devote his resources to achieving success. There was not a clinical stone that Rothbaum left unturned in his search. The company was on track to spend $180 million in 2015. Acerta's spending had become so rapid that the company almost ran out of money in the spring of 2015. At one point, Dave Johnson called up Rothbaum and told him the company coffers had only six weeks of cash left. Rothbaum raged over the company's inability to accurately budget. He had been told a few weeks earlier that Acerta had enough cash to get through the year. Now it was almost bankrupt. Rothbaum was forced to accelerate Acerta's next phase of fundraising, a Series B round planned for the late summer. In less than three weeks, Rothbaum pulled it off, and Acerta had raised $375 million.

The investors included some new faces, like John Paulson, the New York hedge fund billionaire; a corporate investment from Amgen; and some investment funds, like one managed by Behzad Aghazadeh at VenBio; in addition to the original Acerta investment group. It brought Acerta's total funds raised from inception to $500 million. Rothbaum remained the biggest single investor and shareholder, having put $80 million of his own money, a third of his net worth, into Acerta.

One of the big funding needs was for the initial acalabrutinib trial in CLL. John Byrd and the other participating doctors had been enrolling boatloads of patients. The study had been expanded to include 440 patients in March 2015, including some who had never been treated previously and were taking acalabrutinib as a first-line treatment. In a new portion of the trial, patients were receiving two doses per day of acalabrutinib instead of one. This was known as b.i.d. dosing, an acronym for the Latin "*bis in die*," meaning twice a day.

It was Rothbaum who pushed for the twice-a-day dosing. He believed that b.i.d. dosing would further shut down BTK, potentially distinguishing acalabrutinib from its big competitor, Imbruvica. Byrd, the trial's principal investigator, thought Rothbaum was smart to want to put more pressure on BTK and agreed the drug's short half-life and selectivity would allow for it. This theory couldn't be tested in a preclinical study. But Byrd agreed with the inference that shutting down the target for longer could correlate with better outcomes. Johnson worried that patients might forget to take the pill twice each day, but he was willing to give it a shot.

With the CLL patients taking acalabrutinib experiencing a very high response rate, the early indications looked extremely promising.

It had also become obvious to the physician-scientists, like Byrd, that patients tolerated acalabrutinib better than Imbruvica. The patients were not experiencing problematic cardiovascular side effects (such as atrial fibrillation) that had become associated in a limited way with Imbruvica and had started referring to acalabrutinib as a "sugar pill."

Not everyone felt so good about acalabrutinib's progress. Executives at J&J and AbbVie worried about putting acalabrutinib in a head-to-head trial against Imbruvica, their financially lucrative blockbuster drug. The US specialty pharmacy companies that often provide medicines for clinical trials refused to sell Imbruvica capsules to Acerta, and some suspected that was a result of AbbVie and J&J influence.

At first, Johnson called up Peter Lebowitz at J&J and had a good conversation about obtaining a supply of Imbruvica. But each time Acerta requested Imbruvica capsules directly from AbbVie and J&J, the big companies always asked for more information about how Acerta's clinical trial had been structured. At one point, the pharmaceutical companies demanded to see an unredacted version of the protocol for the head-to-head trial. Acerta refused, arguing that providing such proprietary information was not conventionally shared.

Finally, Johnson wrote a letter to J&J's Janssen unit and AbbVie's Pharmacyclics in July 2015. Izumi had put together most of the letter's language, which accused the companies of deviating "from a well-accepted and collaborative practice in the pharmaceutical industry to supply approved drug product for clinical trials and to effectively refuse access to Imbruvica."

J&J and AbbVie wrote back rejecting that they had denied Acerta access to Imbruvica, but continued to insist on seeing the full protocol and demanding that Acerta make changes to it before they supplied Acerta with their drug. "Pharmacyclics and Janssen are willing to provide ibrutinib for a price to parties for clinical studies that meet our requirement of advancing patient care, designed with scientific rigor, and patient safety," two executives representing both companies wrote.

In the end, Fardis came up with the solution of having Acerta buy

Imbruvica capsules directly from networks of contract research organizations in Europe, where the supply of Imbruvica was less tightly controlled. Fardis knew which networks to tap. But Acerta had to pay the high wholesale market price for the drug instead of buying Imbruvica at the much lower cost of its production as Acerta had hoped.

The rivalry between the companies behind Imbruvica and acalabrutinib had become intense.

///////////////

TO SOME, IT LOOKED like Pascal Soriot had accepted a suicide mission. When the fifty-three-year-old Soriot became CEO of Astra-Zeneca in 2012, the company had lost its sense of purpose. The product of a 1999 merger between Swedish Astra and British Zeneca Group, the corporation faced the twin challenges of its key drugs coming off patent and a development pipeline in disarray. To solve the problem, management had pursued the shortsighted route of channeling money toward stock buybacks rather than pursuing new science. Soriot had surprised his colleagues by taking the top job. But Soriot had a vision of pivoting AstraZeneca toward innovation, especially with cancer drugs. One of his goals was to build a hematology franchise.

The son of a tax collector, Soriot grew up in a troubled banlieue, one of the suburbs packed with high-rise buildings north of Paris. With gang violence a feature of the neighborhood, Soriot learned to fight with his fists in local turf battles. He found an escape through his love of horses and became a veterinarian. When Soriot was twenty, his father died of a heart attack, and Soriot spent three years supporting his mother and three younger brothers. He then got his MBA at HEC Paris before joining the French pharmaceutical firm Roussel Uclaf. His work at the company took Soriot to Australia, which he adopted as his home. Soriot shed all traces of the banlieue streets, speaking softly in a French accent, wearing expensive jackets, and keeping his dark hair short and carefully combed.

Fiercely determined, Soriot spent decades climbing the pharmaceutical ladder, with stops in Japan and the United States, until he reached Roche, becoming the marketing chief of the well-regarded Swiss pharmaceutical conglomerate. A few years after he got there, in 2009, Roche spent $47 billion to purchase Genentech, the foundational biotechnology company in South San Francisco. Soriot was put in charge as CEO of Genentech and tasked with integrating the spirited Northern California company with its more conservative new Swiss parent—one of his main jobs was keeping the entrepreneurial Genentech staffers happy in the more buttoned-down culture of Roche. Soriot performed flawlessly and rose to become chief operating officer of Roche's pharmaceutical division before leaving for the United Kingdom to run AstraZeneca. Once he got there, he had to fight off a $118 billion takeover attempt from Pfizer just to keep AstraZeneca an independent company.

A strong strategic thinker willing to take big risks, Soriot's success was grounded in his hands-on approach to navigating corporate bureaucracies. On any project, he would identify the lowest employees on the totem pole and call them to figure out what was really going on. At AstraZeneca, everybody got to know Soriot, and many wanted to produce results for him. The man in the trenches on the hematology project was Chris Sheldon, who had first met Rothbaum in Philadelphia.

For all the tens of thousands of people who work at a big pharmaceutical company, nothing happens at these institutions unless a project has an internal senior champion. In Soriot, Sheldon and his boss, Nina Mojas, were backed by the guy at the top. Mojas knew the BTK inhibitor space well, having struck a collaboration deal a year earlier with Bob Duggan and Maky Zanganeh to explore Imbruvica's potential in solid tumors. Mojas and Sheldon researched acalabrutinib and concluded it was one of the most important hematology assets in early development that could be obtainable. They signed a confidentiality agreement with Acerta to get some data from Rothbaum, pushing their case forward with Soriot by showing him the world's most boring chart. It contained a simple, flat horizontal line. But that line represented how long patients on acalabrutinib had been able to halt their chronic lymphocytic leukemia. Soriot spoke to the key investigators, like John Byrd and Susan O'Brien, who reported to Soriot that acalabrutinib was not causing the kind of side effects that forced some of their patients to stop taking Imbruvica. As he often did, Soriot wanted to know what the absolute upside was of the drug, as opposed to the worst-case scenario. Mojas and Sheldon figured the drug could generate as much as $5 billion annually.

At first, Rothbaum didn't see Sheldon and Mojas as serious contenders if he decided to sell Acerta. The investor had been getting serious attention from other pharmaceutical companies. Nearly a year earlier, at a lunch at Midtown Manhattan's Benjamin Steakhouse, executives from Merck & Co. had floated the idea of buying Acerta for nearly $1 billion. Rothbaum had brushed them off by telling them, as Acerta's biggest shareholder, he was not afraid of risk. They should value the drug as if it had already been proven to work and been approved by regulators. Rothbaum spoke loudly, so his voice could be heard in the high-ceilinged dining room. He had access to capital and this was a once-in-a-lifetime opportunity. If Merck wanted to buy him out, they would have to pay for the regulatory and clinical trial risks that Rothbaum was willing to take. It quickly became clear the Merck executives could not go much higher. After all, it was Merck that had sold acalabrutinib two years earlier—for $1,000. Buying it back for $1 billion would literally mean they had paid a million-percent markup. Paying *more* than that would be hard to explain to the company's board.

Rothbaum had also conducted discussions with Pfizer. The American pharmaceutical giant had considered partnering with Acerta on acalabrutinib, but the talks had not gone smoothly. At one point, Rothbaum found himself in a Pfizer war room in the belly of its Manhattan headquarters. The conference room blocked all wireless communication, rendering cell phones useless. It also did not have an Apple USB wire that could plug into the Acerta computer containing Rothbaum's presentation. Rothbaum had put the presentation on a small flash drive and used a computer belonging to one of the Pfizer executives that connected to the conference room's projector. During the presentation, the Pfizer executive's computer started receiving emails that popped onto the big screen. Those emails made clear that Pfizer had also been negotiating to license a different BTK inhibitor being developed by Germany's Merck Serono (not to be confused with Merck & Co). Rothbaum later canceled a dinner with Pfizer executives that had been on the calendar for weeks because his son was pitching in a baseball game out in Long Island's Baseball Heaven complex. Ultimately, Rothbaum was not too interested in a partnership and the message from him was clear.

At the end of August 2015, Rothbaum was driving to Cooperstown, New York, where his son's baseball team would be playing in a tournament near the National Baseball Hall of Fame. He got a phone call from AstraZeneca's Sheldon. Pascal Soriot would be in Manhattan over Labor Day weekend. Would Rothbaum have time for a meeting?

On the first Friday of September 2015, Rothbaum and Soriot met at the lavish and medieval-looking coffee bar of the Parker Meridien hotel in Midtown Manhattan. At around 2 p.m., they sat in large armchairs and started drinking espressos that were placed on a low table. It turned out that Soriot had not randomly found himself in New York over Labor Day weekend. He had flown in just for this meeting. Downing multiple cups of coffee, the two hit it off and spoke for hours.

Soriot told Rothbaum about his early years in the banlieue and becoming a veterinarian. Rothbaum told Soriot about how he had treated Simba, his miniature pinscher who suffered from head and neck cancer, with acalabrutinib, which had improved the dog's condition for about a year. Rothbaum also described how he had ended up on Wall Street. As they talked about acalabrutinib, Rothbaum repeated to Soriot what he had told the Merck executives about his willingness to take on risk. He then walked Soriot through Acerta's strategy and the ways acalabrutinib could differentiate itself from Imbruvica. Leaving the door open, Rothbaum did admit that Acerta was nearing an inflection point where it would need to invest in a sales force and start thinking about commercialization. Soriot got the message.

Soriot left New York knowing it would take a rich deal to pry aca-labrutinib from Rothbaum. Soriot recognized Rothbaum's hedge fund roots and ambitious personality, and his salesmanship was not subtle. That might make some suspicious. But Soriot's impression was that Rothbaum was someone he could trust.

The meeting had gone extremely well. In the days that followed, Rothbaum continued communicating with AstraZeneca's Chris Shel-don. Rothbaum and Sheldon got to know each other, and Sheldon learned about Rothbaum's large collection of stained glass Louis Tiffany lamps. In one of the subsequent phone calls, Sheldon told Rothbaum he could expect to get a letter soon. "You will be able to buy all the lamps you want," Sheldon said.

On the last Friday of September 2015, Rothbaum was in his Man-hattan apartment when he got an email from Soriot with a letter attached. Rothbaum started to read the letter on his phone.

When Rothbaum got to the second page of the letter, his jaw dropped, his hands started to shake, and Rothbaum fell to the floor.

"We propose to purchase Acerta for a single upfront payment of $7B," Soriot wrote.

////////////////////

RAQUEL IZUMI LOOKED AT Wayne Rothbaum and urged him to take AstraZeneca's deal. She was emphatic about it. Izumi could no lon-ger keep up the grueling pace and felt, in many ways, that Acerta had started to come apart at the seams. Rothbaum knew Izumi was right, and he himself had been waking up with stress pains in his stomach for the first time in his life.

Rothbaum had flown to Northern California with Tom Turalski to meet with the top Acerta executives and see if they were ready to sell. If the management team wanted to keep going, Rothaum was prepared to support them. He met with Dave Johnson, Maria Fardis, and Jesse McGreivy. They all wanted to sell the company.

It had taken them everything they had to get acalabrutinib to this point. The drug was in phase 3 registration trials that could lead to FDA approval in two blood cancers, and a head-to-head study against Imbruvica, the incumbent BTK inhibitor that had first been approved two years earlier.

The drug manufacturing problems remained difficult to resolve. Building up Acerta to prepare for commercialization did not appeal to any of them. Johnson likened Acerta to manufacturing a car while driving it at Ferrari-like speeds. He strongly believed acalabrutinib would be the best BTK inhibitor in the race. The only drug that had ever worried him was Ono's BTK inhibitor, but the Japanese firm had licensed its drug to Gilead, the big California biotech, and its development had gone completely sideways.

"Are you kidding me?" said Fardis. "It is not even a question." Fardis had quickly emerged as an executive Rothbaum listened to closely and trusted. Her ability to deliver results time and time again had a convincing way of building confidence around her. For her part, Fardis learned how to manage Rothbaum. She appreciated Rothbaum's ability to make decisions and knew how to work with such a strong personality. One time, in the middle of a call with Rothbaum that had gone on too long, Fardis simply got up and left her office to attend her next meeting. Rothbaum had continued ranting over the speaker phone, his voice carrying through the paper-thin walls of Acerta's offices. On this matter, when it came to the current inflection point, she wasn't going to leave the room without being heard. Fardis said that hiring two hundred people to launch a commercialization program to compete with AbbVie and J&J would break Acerta.

The only senior employee who had reservations about the deal was Ahmed Hamdy. His talk with Rothbaum had been tense. The relationship between them had deteriorated further with Rothbaum removing more of Hamdy's responsibilities and handing them to McGreivy. Imbruvica had effectively been sold at a valuation of $42 billion and Hamdy, so often one of the more prudent or conservative movers in a sea of sharks, thought the offer for Acerta may actually be too low. Joe Edelman, the hedge fund manager and Acerta's second-biggest shareholder, had wondered the same thing. Nevertheless, while both expressed their doubts to Rothbaum, they came around to Rothbaum's perspective and ultimately supported trying to make a deal.

It was far from a certainty. AstraZeneca's offer was nonbinding and contingent on due diligence, verifying everything was in proper order, and there were several issues Rothbaum had to resolve. A small Astra-Zeneca army descended on Acerta's office in Redwood City, California, to examine its data and files, and Rothbaum wanted to make sure the people AstraZeneca sent were in a good frame of mind. He organized a fleet of black SUVs outside the office to be ready to whisk any one of them to the destination of their choosing and ordered Johnson to have the bathrooms cleaned and stocked with new toothbrushes, toothpaste, and other items. "Two-ply toilet paper," Rothbaum demanded. Giant cookies from Levain Bakery in New York were flown in. The British pharma team called them cookie-scones.

The financial investors and employees of Acerta also owed it to themselves to see if they could get a better deal elsewhere. Rothbaum had returned to New York with a mandate to sell Acerta, but the deal was itself not without stumbling blocks. In his letter, Soriot had mandated that Acerta own the global rights to acalabrutinib in all diseases. Dating back to the founding of Acerta, Merck had retained the rights to the development of acalabrutinib for rheumatoid arthritis patients. Some fancy footwork on Rothbaum's part and a cash payment of $10 million managed to convince Merck to let those rights go.

The last hurdle Rothbaum had to navigate would prove tougher. Two months into the diligence work, AstraZeneca's lawyers found new and broad patents that had just been assigned to Pharmacyclics by the US Patent and Trademark Office in July and September of 2015. The new expansive patents seemed to cover part of acalabrutinib's structure. AstraZeneca's lawyers thought it could be a deal killer. AstraZeneca was a big pharmaceutical company, like AbbVie, that was willing to pay top dollar for a promising drug. But large companies with powerful boards and major stockholders hate taking risks. If a corporation is going to pay top dollar, they want it to be "de-risked," made less risky and unlikely to produce a major financial loss. Pascal Soriot knew he would have to de-risk acalabrutinib to push the transaction forward internally.

One evening in November 2015, Pascal Soriot called up Rothbaum and told him the intellectual property concerns had created opposition at AstraZeneca that could derail the deal. Rothbaum brought up a creative alternative and Soriot was open to pursuing it: breaking up the $7 billion purchase price in two parts—$4 billion at the outset, and $3 billion could be held back until the resolution of any patent issues. AstraZeneca could deduct any patent-related costs from the $3 billion back-end payment, which was a big number. In the worst-case scenario, AstraZeneca would not get too badly burned.

Rothbaum's lawyers had assured him that Acerta could beat back any patent assault from AbbVie and Pharmacyclics. Their confidence stemmed from the patent Acerta had purchased for some $250,000 from OSI Pharmaceuticals that was issued in 2008, well before any of the Imbruvica patents. It covered molecules that inhibited several kinases, including BTK. Rothbaum called it "the nuclear button" because it potentially could challenge Imbruvica. If AbbVie ever argued that acalabrutinib fell into an extension of some of the original Pharmacyclics patents, Acerta could argue that Imbruvica fell within the domain of the OSI patent. Like a military deterrence strategy, Acerta could threaten AbbVie's multi-billion-dollar franchise if AbbVie took a shot at Acerta's drug.

Rothbaum considered his options. Did he really have the courage of his convictions or was he full of idle talk? Just saying "trust me" on the patent issue would not cut it. He needed to put his own money on the line that Acerta would be able to fend off a serious patent challenge.

Rothbaum and Soriot agreed to the new structure that split the $7 billion payment. The deal was on.

CHAPTER 18

A Biotech Odyssey

The 12-foot black slab had been modeled after the monolith from Stanley Kubrick's classic movie *2001: A Space Odyssey*. The floor around the slab was made up of white square panels, just like in the movie. The digital screens on the front and back sides of the flat slab showcased animation that took viewers at the Orange County Convention Center through a new blood cancer drug's mechanism of action. "Acalabrutinib, also known as ACP-196, is a potent second-generation BTK inhibitor that was rationally designed to be highly selective," the monolith blared.

For years, Wayne Rothbaum protected acalabrutinib as a carefully guarded secret, known only to people on the inside of Acerta's efforts. Now, he was finally ready to share it with the world. The annual American Association of Hematology meeting in Orlando, Florida, would be acalabrutinib's coming-out party, with the monolith rising up in the middle of the exhibit hall to proclaim the potential future that acalabrutinib could reveal. Rothbaum was not only introducing his long-sought-after success to the world, but was making it clear that the promise of acalabrutinib was part of the evolution of how humans fight to survive cancer. He insisted on designing the monolith and digital animation himself.

The monolith was part of Acerta's carefully coordinated release of the first comprehensive data presentation for acalabrutinib. On the third day of the blood cancer summit, the *New England Journal of Medicine* published the results of the initial trial of acalabrutinib in sixty-one patients with relapsed chronic lymphocytic leukemia. Raquel Izumi had written much of the article, together with John Byrd and Rothbaum, and she would be listed as one of its authors, together with Ahmed Hamdy.

After starting her biotech career as a medical writer fifteen years earlier, this would be the first time Izumi's name would appear on top of an article published in the prestigious medical journal. She was extremely proud. The fact that she shared the byline with Rothbaum, a financier with no formal scientific training, indicated how far Rothbaum had inserted himself into the operations of Acerta.

The data detailed in the article revealed that acalabrutinib achieved a very impressive overall response rate of 95 percent in relapsed CLL patients. The paper described acalabrutinib as a more selective BTK inhibitor designed to improve on the safety of Imbruvica. For the patients in the trial, the most common problems were low-grade headaches, diarrhea, and weight gain. None of the patients experienced major bleeding or atrial fibrillation, side effects that sometimes happened with Imbruvica. There also had not been any cases of Richter's transformation, a worrisome condition that occurs when CLL evolves into large-cell lymphoma.

Izumi watched as John Byrd, the lead author of the paper, presented the data in an auditorium, reporting how well patients tolerated acalabrutinib. Sitting in the audience, Izumi remembered the last time she sat listening to Byrd give an oral presentation on a study she helped design and launch. The pain and regret welled inside her. But this time, she sat taller. Izumi did not have to sneak into the conference or rely on the grace of others to catch a glimpse of the product of her work. This time, Izumi wore a conference badge with her own name on it.

The next day, the American Society of Hematology presented Byrd with the William Dameshek Prize, recognizing outstanding achievement in hematology. Brian Koffman, the CLL patient who had flown home with capsules of Imbruvica that Byrd had given him in his pocket, interviewed Byrd on the last day of the conference. Koffman had expanded his popular patient blog into the CLL Society, a nonprofit that focused on patient education. "Who would have thought that with ibrutinib (Imbruvica), a great drug, we could do better?" Byrd said. "The uniqueness of this drug . . . potentially is going to allow us to take a step forward particularly for high risk patients where we can dose the drug twice a day, put better pressure on the target, BTK."

///////////////////

WAYNE ROTHBAUM HAD ARRIVED in Orlando with a lot on his plate. In addition to managing Acerta's big data presentation, he also had a deal to negotiate. After Pascal Soriot had offered to buy Acerta for $7 billion, Rothbaum had initiated a limited sales process offering a small number of potential buyers the chance to bid on the company. Merck and Pfizer both passed. But Amgen, the nation's second-biggest biotech company, wanted in on the bidding. Its new CEO, Robert Bradway, was a former Wall Street banker itching to do deals, and Amgen had the resources to compete with a big pharmaceutical company like AstraZeneca.

Amgen already had links to Acerta, having invested in the company and licensed a drug to it that had been combined with acalabrutinib in a trial. David Piacquad, Amgen's deal chief, had previously worked at Schering-Plough and helped pioneer the deal in which the New Jersey company purchased Organon and its research facility at Oss, where acalabrutinib had originated. He knew about the talent that once resided there. Amgen was a more natural fit.

Rothbaum flew to Thousand Oaks, California, to meet with Bradway. There he learned something interesting: lawyers at Amgen were perfectly comfortable with Acerta's patent position. Both AstraZeneca and Amgen shared a keen interest in Acerta's Dutch innovation tax treatment and figured the low tax rate into their valuation of acalabrutinib. Amgen loosely offered to buy Acerta for about $5 billion up front, without any additional strings attached around potential patent litigation with AbbVie and Imbruvica.

Amgen's offer was compelling. Keeping the deal clean and easy appealed to Rothbaum and his fellow Acerta shareholders. The $2 billion haircut in purchase price was offset by getting paid out entirely up front and not having to worry about any contingent liabilities popping up down the road. No matter how good Acerta's lawyers felt about their patent position, not having to worry about what may or may not come to pass in the future was liberating. AstraZeneca's price tag came with strings attached and muddied waters. But Amgen also had an issue to manage. Amgen had just bought Onyx Pharmaceuticals to beef up its drug development pipeline. The clinical trials Amgen acquired in the Onyx deal had boosted expenses on Amgen's income statement and depressed its earnings. Absorbing Acerta's expensive clinical program would dent Amgen's earnings even more—increasing costs without providing any offsetting revenues until acalabrutinib got approved. That could sour Wall Street on Amgen's stock.

To deal with the earnings problem, Piacquad came up with a smart work-around. Amgen had negotiated a synthetic royalty deal with a large sovereign wealth fund in Asia that would fund acalabrutinib's clinical trial costs in a way that allowed Amgen to avoid showing all of Acerta's losses on its books. This kind of financial engineering had just started to become popular in the biopharma industry. But with the New Year holiday approaching, the sovereign wealth fund had shut down for the year and its officials would not be back at work to authorize the transaction until January. At the same time, Soriot and his surrogates had been pressing Rothbaum to sign a term sheet agreement with exclusivity if he wanted to move the AstraZeneca deal forward.

At the ASH conference in Orlando, Rotbaum assembled Acerta's board late at night at the Ritz-Carlton Hotel to make a decision.

Most of the directors sat around the table together with Rothbaum in Orlando, and a few joined by phone. Dave Johnson and Ahmed Hamdy also attended. Rothbaum wanted their perspectives as well. Either the board could decide to take AstraZeneca's $7 billion deal— $4 billion up front and $3 billion when and if the patent issues had been resolved—or they could wait until January on Amgen and risk losing the deal AstraZeneca had been offering. Rothbaum believed in unanimous board decisions, especially in a situation like this. After protracted discussions, the decision boiled down to risk. Going with AstraZeneca meant taking a risk that $3 billion of the purchase might never materialize if the patent situation went south. Going with Amgen put the entire deal at risk, since no one knew what the new year would bring or how an Asian sovereign wealth fund would ultimately react. Soon the answer became clear. Rothbaum and all the other directors voted to sign AstraZeneca's term sheet. Now a final deal needed to be hammered out.

Together in Orlando, Rothbaum, Chris Sheldon, and a few others from AstraZeneca got on Rothbaum's Gulfstream IV jet and flew to New York to negotiate the transaction at the Midtown offices of AstraZeneca's lawyers. Two days into the negotiation, the *Wall Street Journal* reported on the potential deal. The AstraZeneca group accused the Acerta side of leaking the story to hold their feet to the fire. Rothbaum denied it, but the negotiations became tense. Next, AstraZeneca insisted that it be allowed to terminate the deal if certain adverse events came up in the acalabrutinib trials prior to the transaction closing. The issue had become a sticking point.

Late one night, Rothbaum got a call from Nina Mojas, AstraZeneca's head of oncology business development. She told Rothbaum that Soriot had a tough meeting with AstraZeneca's board. Soriot's job would be on the line if the Acerta acquisition turned into a fiasco.

"I need to know, is there anything I am not aware of at this company?" Mojas asked. "Pascal is sticking his neck out for this transaction."

"Everything you know is everything I know," Rothbaum assured her, adding he had no intention of doing anything to hurt Soriot. "I have shared everything. There is nothing untoward going on in this company."

Rothbaum's words seemed to break the logjam. AstraZeneca gave up on their deal-closing condition linked to clinical trial adverse events. Everything was starting to fall into place. Acerta and AstraZeneca began constructing the infrastructure to bind their companies.

But as the deal came together, Rothbaum realized that there had been a significant miscalculation, and it was going to create havoc with the staff. Rothbaum himself had misunderstood how much the Acerta employees would actually receive in the deal, and leadership had raised employee expectations to a degree that could not be met. Rothbaum feared the issue was explosive enough to blow the bridges connecting all of the elements of the transaction.

Typically, new start-up companies are put together in a way to protect the venture capitalists and other financial investors who back them. The investors buy preferred shares in the company, as opposed to common shares, meaning they get preferential treatment. At minimum, they get paid first in the event of a liquidation event (such as the sale of a distressed company) until they recoup their investment, often through a contractual feature known as a liquidation preference. This only comes into play when start-ups are not successful. But many start-ups issue investors participating preferred shares, meaning that in the event of a successful sale the investors recoup all of their investment before their preferred shares convert to common shares, diluting the stake held by the common shareholders—which often include employees and founders. Only after the big investors are paid out does the remaining money get split among the common shareholders.

Acerta had been incorporated in the Netherlands by the company's Dutch founders and structured to issue participating preferred shares. The dilution would be extreme, cutting the payout to employees by about half. Rothbaum had not previously realized how much the dilution would reduce the employees' payday. He felt that the dilution to the Acerta employees would be unfair. He decided the financial investors should give up $140 million of their windfall and create what he thought of as a "make-whole" pool that would cushion the blow from the share dilution for employees. This amount wouldn't get the Acerta employees to the payout level they had anticipated, but it was a considerable cushion. Rothbaum would be contributing $60 million of his own gains as part of this process. The rest of the investors went along with Rothbaum's plan, which would reinstate 43 cents on the dollar for each employee-owned common share on the first $4 billion payment of the AstraZeneca deal. That would mean that each employee would get 93 cents on the dollar for their shares on the first payment. An employee entitled to a $1 million payout under the first payment before the dilution, for example, would get $930,000. On the entire $7 billion deal, the employee shares would be diluted by about a quarter, which fell in line with a standard share dilution in the sale of a Silicon Valley start-up.

To put his "make-whole" plan into action, Rothbaum needed to structure it in the deal documents and get AstraZeneca to sign off on it. The big pharma was willing to go along—up to a point. AstraZeneca understood the predicament that Rothbaum was in. The big pharma was also contending with its own employee concerns. AstraZeneca needed the Acerta workforce and was searching for a way to incentivize them to stay on staff and keep working hard. Acalabrutinib had not yet received its critical FDA approvals, and without the Acerta scientists and developers those goals would be harder to reach. AstraZeneca found the answer to its employee incentive problem by spending Rothbaum's money. It wanted to turn the $140 million pool into an employee retention fund. To earn the retention bonus, Acerta employees would have to remain at AstraZeneca for three years or until acalabrutinib received an FDA approval, whichever came first. If AstraZeneca determined that any Acerta employees should leave the company, Rothbaum had the right to decide whether those employees would receive their cut from the pool. Any money that did not get paid out would go to

Rothbaum and the other Acerta investors. But if anyone quit before the milestones were reached, they lost their future payout from the $140 million pool altogether. For the employee entitled to $1 million before any dilution on the first payment, this retention bonus would be worth $430,000. In other words, the $1 million payout would come down to $500,000 without it. Selling this construct to the team at Acerta would not be easy and, if handled incorrectly, could lead to mass upheaval.

In the middle of December 2015, AstraZeneca announced it had struck a deal to buy Acerta, a company few people had ever heard of, and its one promising drug, acalabrutinib, for $7 billion. The deal was slated to close in the winter of 2016. For the deal's press release, John Byrd, the expert CLL doctor, noted that "the BTK inhibitor class has been transformational in the management of B-cell cancers but a portion of patients treated with ibrutinib (the first generation BTK inhibitor), can't tolerate the side effects and sadly discontinue their treatment."

Byrd's focus was on the fact that CLL patients would soon have more options, but it was impossible to ignore the allusion to the rivalry that now lay ahead between AbbVie and J&J's Imbruvica and the drug AstraZeneca was acquiring.

///////////////

THE CLOCK HAD STRUCK midnight in San Francisco and Wayne Rothbaum was feeling good. He had started off the day by having breakfast with AstraZeneca CEO Pascal Soriot and one of his trusted lieutenants, Nina Mojas. The rest of the day had flashed by quickly. Rothbaum had just left a celebratory dinner with executives from AstraZeneca and started making his way to the Exploratorium, a science and technology museum along a shoreline promenade that doubled as a corporate party space. A biotech investment relations firm, LifeSci Advisors, had thrown a party at the Exploratorium for those attending the annual J.P. Morgan Healthcare conference, and a hedge fund friend, Kevin Tang, had texted Rothbaum to join him there.

By the time Rothbaum got to the museum, the party had begun to wind down. As he walked around the event space, Rothbaum noticed several young beautiful women, wearing tight, short black dresses, mingling with the remaining healthcare industry professionals, who were decidedly older and less attractive. If this was a biotech event, it was the strangest one Rothbaum had ever seen. Something wasn't right. Finally, Rothbaum found Tang, who pressed Rothbaum to have a drink. "Dude, I got to get out of here," Rothbaum said. "I don't know where I am."

Tang said he wanted to celebrate Rothbaum's Acerta success. Moments later, Tang had three black SUVs spring Rothbaum and the rest of his group from the museum. Bloomberg News would go on to report about the party at the Exploratorium, highlighting that LifeSci Advisors had hired models to escort J.P. Morgan Healthcare conference attendees, who were overwhelmingly male, to the party and entertain them. The party quickly became a scandal highlighting the lack of diversity in the biotechnology industry. LifeSci Advisors apologized amid a barrage of criticism. The firm had hired the women from a modeling agency Tang owned.

Tang kept the night going at a different San Francisco bar. Rothbaum got back to his hotel around 4 a.m. He needed to leave three hours later to get to Redwood City for a sensitive town hall meeting with Acerta's employees. In the world of megadeals, it's hard to keep anything quiet for long, and many of the Acerta employees already had heard rumors that their shareholding in Acerta had been significantly diluted. Some were upset and frustrated. The feeling that Rothbaum had deceived them started at the top and included Dave Johnson, the interim CEO of the company.

A bleary-eyed Rothbaum showed up at the Pullman Hotel San Francisco Bay in bad shape. The bumper-to-bumper morning traffic down to Redwood City made him feel even worse. A hotel conference room had been booked, and Acerta's employees were waiting to hear from him. Once in the room, Rothbaum tried to describe the retention bonus pool he had set up with AstraZeneca. He explained that the dilution that came with the participating preferred shares was more drastic than normal because of the way Acerta had been initially formed and structured under Dutch law. Rothbaum described how Acerta's investors had set up the bonus pool to make the employees nearly whole on the first $4 billion AstraZeneca payment. Tension in the room was high, and at the end of his presentation it was clear that a lot of questions were left unanswered.

Afterward, Rothbaum had a second meeting only with Acerta's top executives and founders. It was telecast so that those from the group who were in Acerta's offices in both Seattle and the Netherlands could participate. Executives had submitted questions anonymously that Rothbaum started reading out loud. One question asked if Acerta's lawyers really worked primarily for Rothbaum or the company. "Are you stealing money?" another question asked. Next up, there was a demand for an audit into the relationship between Rothbaum's Quogue Capital vehicle and Acerta. "We want to know if employees are being screwed."

"No!" Rothbaum replied emphatically. His magical conviction had gotten AstraZeneca across the line in hammering out their transaction. The executive group at Acerta was less impressed. This was a dollars-and-cents issue for them, and they were keenly aware that millions of dollars were flowing, in their minds, the wrong way.

To Rothbaum, the questions were hostile and misguided. He thought they were fueled by the inexperience of many of Acerta's founders and executives, who were not generally aware of the common use of participating preferred shares when it came to start-up companies. Most of them had only worked for publicly traded companies or big pharma. It seemed to Rothbaum that some of the Acerta employees were upset about the concept of any share dilution, which was going to happen at a start-up like Acerta one way or the other. Rothbaum tried to explain again that the Dutch nature of the participating preferred shares, which had been set up by the Dutch founders and their lawyers, made the dilution more severe and he had only discovered the issue in the last few weeks. Once he learned about it, Rothbaum said, he had rallied the other major investors to come up with the make-whole program and fund it out of their own pockets.

Some at Acerta, especially Johnson, did not buy Rothbaum's explanation. Johnson thought that not enough of the Acerta financial gains had been shared with him and other employees. He was particularly frustrated with the idea of having to stay on at AstraZeneca for years. Johnson shared his opinions liberally and often. Others, like Maria Fardis, accepted Rothbaum's explanation. To be sure, there were some employees who were thrilled with their Acerta payday, but the dissension at the top of the company spread through the ranks.

The top execs knew the math. Rothbaum and the other investors would take the lion's share of the Acerta windfall.

Rothbaum alone stood to make $3 billion.

For his part, Ahmed Hamdy was insulted and felt robbed once again. He had recovered after being fired by Bob Duggan and missing out on Pharmacyclics' financial bonanza, lending his name and efforts to build up an entirely new and incredibly successful company. Having his hard-earned proceeds diverted into golden handcuffs pressing him into service at AstaZeneca was an insult he could not ignore. If Astra-Zeneca wanted to incentivize him to stay, Hamdy believed it should set up a new retention incentive plan.

The structure of the payout could not have more clearly highlighted the divide between the operators and the financial investors. It was Hamdy's blood, sweat, and tears, it was Izumi's garage, vision, and drafting, it was the constant devotion and work of so many unsung heroes that helped create acalabrutinib. Hamdy recognized the role of Rothbaum and his group of financial investors. They clearly were essential, but the reward seemed misallocated. While the financial investors spent their time manufacturing equity instruments that allowed them to be paid first and most, those in the trenches spent their time manufacturing medicines and had no idea about potential payouts or how to protect themselves. Hamdy and Izumi felt history repeating itself.

They felt wildly aggrieved and underappreciated. Any way they sliced it, their commitment to the company and their naivete had translated into financial losses.

For all the talk of helping cancer patients, the success of Acerta was now being overshadowed by bitterness over money. Rothbaum became frustrated that what he viewed as an incredibly positive outcome had been turned into something nasty and negative. Rothbaum thought he had treated the employees fairly and that they simply did not appreciate all the facts. They were irate over the idea that the capital had reaped most of the gains, but Rothbaum and his investors had risked a lot of their money and that was how capitalism functioned. Acerta had paid generous wages and bonuses, and before each equity funding round he had given employees the opportunity to invest alongside the other investors. With the exception of the first equity rounds, the employees largely declined. Truly, Rothbaum believed he had done nothing wrong and had tried to protect the employees.

Now, for the Acerta employees, Rothbaum had become the villain from New York. After the meetings at the Pullman Hotel, Rothbaum tried to explain things further to people like Jesse McGreivy, who refused to listen. "You gave me something, then you took half of it away, and then you told me to get some of it back I have to work another three years," McGreivy said. "That's not right."

Rothbaum's relationship with Johnson became especially fraught. As the deal headed toward closing in February 2016, AstraZenca executives grew tired of the complaints they were hearing from Johnson and other Acerta people over the retention pool. It was not lost on those at Astra-Zeneca that even with the haircut and discounting the retention pool, some of the loudest complaints from Acerta were coming from those who, like Johnson, stood to make as much as $30 million, more than many AstraZeneca employees could hope to earn over a lifetime. It was hard to empathize too much with people who themselves were multimillionaires.

But the main contingent of the Acerta team felt cheated, that they deserved more and had done more and that the fat cats were taking home an outsized portion of the wins created by what they had done.

These feelings were confusing but tied to the harsh reality of the biotechnology revolution. Even in cancer drug development, most of the financial gains often went to capital and not to labor.

As time went on, Rothbaum came to believe that Johnson had betrayed him by fomenting the animosity at Acerta. He never forgave him for it.

The bad feelings were mutual. And the two never spoke to each other again.

CHAPTER 19

Graduation Day

Raquel Izumi sat on an outdoor stage staring at a sea of college kids clad in caps and gowns. She had been invited to be the commencement speaker for the mathematical, life and physical sciences division at the University of California, Santa Barbara, the school from which she had collected her college degree.

"We are honored to have Dr. Raquel Izumi joining us today, a leader in cancer drug research," Pierre Wiltzius, the dean of science, said before giving the lectern to Izumi.

"I used to believe all I had to do was work really hard and be very good at my job and as such I would be justly rewarded. It turns out life doesn't always work that way," Izumi told the graduating class of 2017. "Imagine being incredibly passionate about what you do so you work tirelessly and devotedly and make many personal sacrifices. One day the CEO personally acknowledges your hard work and effort . . . and gives you the biggest raise of your career."

Izumi then told the graduates about being fired by that same CEO weeks later, never mentioning Bob Duggan's name or the fact that he was a trustee of the UC Santa Barbara Foundation.

Eight years earlier, it had been Duggan on this same stage giving a commencement speech. Now, it was Izumi's turn. She described "the mortification" of being summoned in front of Duggan and being told she was no longer needed.

"Life is 10 percent what happens to you and 90 percent how you react to it," Izumi intoned. "Being fired for doing some of the best work of my career was the catalyst that made me start my own biotech company."

In October 2017, just four months after Izumi gave her speech, the FDA approved acalabrutinib for previously treated mantle cell lymphoma patients. Dave Johnson had been right. Acerta had squeezed through an approval in the rare blood cancer before AbbVie and J&J could close the accelerated approval pathway by getting a full approval for Imbruvica in mantle cell lymphoma.

AstraZeneca decided the brand name of acalabrutinib should be Calquence. It was one of fourteen new cancer drugs launched in 2017. Over the course of the decade, the FDA would approve nearly one hundred oncology treatments in the United States, more than three times the number of cancer drugs approved during the previous decade. The gobs of money flowing into cancer drug development coupled with the FDA's more accommodating regulatory posture had resulted in a flood of new oncology treatments. Many of these new products were targeted small-molecule drugs that inhibited tyrosine kinases, much like Imbruvica and Calquence.

Still, Richard Gonzalez and AbbVie were not going to take this sitting down. AbbVie's Pharmacyclics immediately sued AstraZeneca's Acerta unit for patent infringement in Delaware's federal court, claiming that Calquence infringed on three of its patents that had been issued in 2015 and 2017. The litigation surprised nobody. Whenever a second-in-class drug comes to market, the incumbent drug's company often sues the newcomer if it can find a reasonable way to do so. In this case, lawyers did not have to search hard, as the newly issued patents did cover portions of Calquence's structure. The fact that both drugs were developed by some of the same people enhanced the case further.

Still, AbbVie had to overcome the niggling fact that Allard Kaptein and Tjeerd Barf conceived of Calquence in the Netherlands before they ever met Izumi and Ahmed Hamdy. Also, the patents AbbVie claimed were infringed upon had been issued after Calquence was already in clinical development and itself had been issued a patent. But the big problem for AbbVie was that AstraZeneca owned Rothbaum's nuclear button patent that had been purchased from OSI Pharmaceuticals. To make sure its deterrent strategy was clear, AstraZeneca turned around and had Acerta sue Pharmacyclics back, asserting that the use of the active ingredient of Imbruvica infringed on its patent, purchased from OSI. J&J also got involved in the litigation and confronted AstraZeneca.

A colossal fight had begun. AbbVie together with J&J seemed headed toward a battle with AstraZeneca both in the courtroom and in the marketplace. But before flipping into war mode, AstraZeneca rallied its troops and held a small party at its offices in South San Francisco to celebrate its first regulatory approval. Izumi and Hamdy attended, but they felt a bit like outsiders. AstraZeneca had taken them off Calquence and put them in charge of developing some early-stage assets, five of which Hamdy and Izumi put in clinical trials. Hamdy likened the situation to an open adoption, in which he could watch others raise his baby, but not have any say in how they were doing it.

For Hamdy, working at AstraZeneca had become something of a grind. He loathed the long commute he had to make each day from Santa Cruz to South San Francisco. Battling through the traffic, it sometimes took him two hours just to get to work. As he started out on his commute, driving through the peaks and valleys of the Santa Cruz mountains, Hamdy had plenty of time to reflect on the ups and downs of the last few years. On the way, Hamdy would pass Holy City, a California ghost town founded in 1918 by a cult leader who built a commune that promoted white supremacy. For some unknown reason, Bob Duggan had recently purchased it for $6 million. His plans for it remained a mystery. Later, Hamdy's drive would take him within a few miles of Pharmacyclics' headquarters and the two original Acerta offices in San Carlos and Redwood City. At least Hamdy had been able to purchase a new Tesla; owning one was table stakes for those who wanted to demonstrate their place among Silicon Valley success stories. The car came with the added privilege of allowing the driver to motor alone in the carpool lane and skip the worst traffic lines on Highway 101. When he found some open road, Hamdy enjoyed driving his Tesla at blazing speeds.

Nevertheless, with the sale to AstraZeneca, Hamdy had made less money than the other Acerta founders. When he had been fired from Pharmacyclics, Hamdy had sold his vested Pharmacyclics stock for some $1 million to finance his life, and he deferred paying capital gains taxes on the stock sale. To pay the taxes he owed, Hamdy had later privately sold some of his Acerta stock to an investor. He had lost another one million stock options when he had been demoted from the CEO position—which were essentially transferred to Dave Johnson. The amount of money Hamdy had lost through these moves was enormous. Two hours alone in his Tesla afforded Hamdy plenty of time to count the dollars he had missed.

It was easy math that kept Hamdy at AstraZeneca. He wanted to secure the full amount from the retention pool, together with the paycheck and benefits he would receive over three years at the new company. But both Hamdy and Izumi bristled under the big pharma bureaucracy and were terrible at playing office politics. Together, they started searching for a new project.

Most of the people who had revolutionized the treatment of chronic lymphocytic leukemia with BTK inhibitors were trying to move on to new chapters. Duggan left his home in Clearwater, Florida, divorced his longtime wife, Patricia Duggan, and moved to Costa Rica. By funding different drug development projects, he intended to prove the naysayers wrong again and show that his big biotech success was more than luck and could be repeated. He also continued to fund the Church of Scientology. Duggan's contributions to the Church exceeded $360 million and included financing Freewinds, a 440-foot cruise ship that provides parishioners with a distraction-free study environment, and the construction of L. Ron Hubbard Hall, a 3,600-seat auditorium close to the Church of Scientology's spiritual headquarters in Clearwater. He openly credited the teachings of L. Ron Hubbard for his business success.

"Companies I started have generated value of over $100 billion," Duggan said in a November 2019 interview. "I don't remember doing that before (Scientology). . . . It's there to help the able become more able. For me it worked."

Wayne Rothbaum struggled with what to do after Acerta. Despite having made one of the biggest fortunes ever derived from the biotechnology industry, Rothbaum became despondent. He was physically and emotionally exhausted from the experience, and the backlash from the Acerta employees over the stock options had wounded him. To try something different, his wife convinced Rothbaum, a lifelong New Yorker, to relocate to Florida, where he bought a $27 million mansion.

Behzad Aghazadeh, a partner at a biotech investment firm, tried to convince Rothbaum to join him in an investor attack against the management of Immunomedics, a publicly traded company developing a promising triple-negative breast cancer treatment. The move would resemble Bob Duggan's takeover of Pharmacyclics. But Rothbaum had no interest in being an active stock market participant anymore, pushing and trading paper around. Aghazadeh went ahead, took control of Immunomedics, got its medicine approved, and sold it to Gilead for $22 billion in 2020.

Rothbaum thought about going into the baseball business, coming close to buying the Miami Marlins, at one point in partnership with Derek Jeter and Jeb Bush. Fixing a struggling baseball operation appealed to Rothbaum, and he thought he could use what he had learned in the life sciences business and apply those lessons to a sports team. When hedge fund manager Joe Edelman, Rothbaum's close friend, heard about this partnership, he laughed. Edelman looked forward to the day when Rothbaum would tell Jeter he knew more about baseball than one of the greatest shortstops ever. In the end, Rothbaum became disenchanted with the idea.

Even John Byrd, the expert CLL doctor at Ohio State University who had been the principal investigator for some of the key trials of both Imbruvica and Calquence, was finding it harder than he anticipated to travel a new path. With his role in the development of BTK inhibitors, Byrd had helped transform the treatment of CLL, establishing the drugs as a way to truly control the disease and stave off its progression. Byrd received no financial reward for his work, unlike those who owned equity in Pharmacyclics and Acerta. But without his efforts, neither company would have seen the success it achieved, and the lives of hundreds of thousands of patients would have suffered. Stepping past his success in treating CLL, Byrd turned his attention to acute myeloid leukemia, a deadly blood cancer where there had been far less therapeutic success. He quickly realized that progress would be slow and difficult.

The science for treating CLL advanced more swiftly. Another class of drug, venetoclax, started to show serious promise in CLL, especially when combined with BTK inhibitors. Venetoclax held out the ability for shorter fixed-duration treatment, as opposed to the chronic treatment of BTK inhibitors that went on for years. Eli Lilly, the Indianapolis pharmaceutical company, had been developing a noncovalent, or reversible, BTK inhibitor, and its clinical trials suggested it could be a good alternative, particularly for blood cancer patients who can no longer tolerate Imbruvica or with disease that had mutated and become resistant to it.

Patients now had good choices. They were surviving and living a high quality of life, and chemotherapy for CLL patients had become a much more infrequent tool. It was reserved largely for some fit and previously untreated younger patients who could tolerate it and might not want to pop pills for many years.

//////////////////

THE APPROVAL OF CALQUENCE in mantle cell lymphoma was a win, but at AstraZeneca, Pascal Soriot was still waiting for the approval in CLL. He knew it would come through. And so did his board and shareholders. His turnaround of AstraZeneca was a raging success. Soriot had revived a shelved experimental therapy for ovarian cancer, Lynparza (olaparib), and nurtured it into a winner. He pushed Tagrisso (osimertinib) through an aggressive development strategy that would make the lung cancer treatment the company's top seller. Soriot was also blazing a new path for AstraZeneca in China. Once Calquence would come online for CLL, he and the company would be in incredible shape.

However, the integration of an entrepreneurially minded small biotech, like Acerta, into a large pharmaceutical corporation is never simple. After a rocky start, Susan Galbraith, AstraZeneca's senior vice president of early oncology, rushed from London to South San Francisco, where she camped out for three months righting the ship. The drug manufacturing issues that Rothbaum could never conquer had to be solved, and the personnel issues needed to be fixed. Galbraith and Dave Johnson agreed it was time for him to go. A few of Acerta's other senior executives, like Jesse McGreivy, just quit, either because of the way the retention pool had been handled or due to frustration from becoming mid-level cogs at a huge organization.

More than a few of AstraZeneca's drug researchers did not know what to make of all the trials Acerta had launched in different diseases. Glioblastoma? Head and neck cancer? A combination with a PI3K delta inhibitor? To the buttoned-down big pharma crew, some of these ideas seemed far-fetched. For the Acerta employees, this kind of skepticism reflected why small biotech companies were producing more innovation than the pharmaceutical behemoths.

Still, it became clear to AstraZeneca that some things at Acerta had truly gone out of control. AstraZeneca researchers uncovered an abstract

Acerta had submitted to the peer-reviewed journal *Cancer Research* that contained some preclinical Calquence data that had been falsified by an Acerta employee. The falsified data had distorted the therapeutic benefit of Calquence in mice with pancreatic cancer. The discovery rang alarm bells at AstraZeneca, causing concern that something could be rotten in the Calquence data in blood cancers and harm the entire franchise. After a careful investigation, AstraZeneca found that the falsified data had no impact on any work done outside of the laboratory and did not involve any of the blood cancer programs. The employee who falsified the data left AstraZeneca, but the incident provided a scare.

Nevertheless, the strategic thinking behind the Acerta acquisition remained sound. In early November 2019, AbbVie, together with J&J, decided not to take their patent litigation with AstraZeneca to trial. The companies agreed to settle the fight. As part of the settlement, Astra-Zeneca agreed to make a payment of about $550 million to AbbVie, but it was not the kind of royalty that often accompanies such patent settlements. AstraZeneca would continue to own all of Calquence, except for the small royalty that belonged to Merck. Rothbaum's nuclear button patent from OSI seemed to have deterred the threat.

Urte Gayko had stayed on at Pharmacyclics after it had been swallowed by AbbVie, and she had rung her office bell several more times, as Imbruvica racked up a total of eleven FDA approvals, including treatment of graft-versus-host disease. More than two hundred thousand people suffering from cancer had already been treated with Imbruvica around the world, including CLL patients who had never previously received prior medicine. In the United States, the FDA had approved Imbruvica as a first-line CLL therapy based on the strong results of the RESONATE-2 study—the same study some CLL doctors had objected to years earlier because it included a control group receiving chemotherapy. Increasingly, CLL patients were taking Imbruvica as a first-line treatment.

This was a drug that truly made an impact for blood cancers. For all the money that had been poured into drug development for other cancers, excruciatingly familiar methods like surgery, chemotherapy, radiation, and bone marrow transplants remained common. Doctors were stuck prescribing many cancer drugs simply because they were better than any alternative therapy, not because of their spectacular effectiveness. Some of the new cancer drugs just were not very good. But BTK inhibitors had become a game changer for certain blood cancers.

Imbruvica was well on its way to generating $5.7 billion of sales in 2019, and forecasts from the research firm Evaluate Pharma predicted it would produce $10 billion annually by 2024 and become the fifth best-selling drug in the world. In the United States, most annual prescriptions of Imbruvica cost $160,000, and more patients kept going on the drug and staying on the treatment for years. AbbVie and J&J increased the price of Imbruvica each year and split the profits. Pablo Legorreta's Royalty Pharma had been collecting as much as $349 million a year of income from the small slice of the drug it had purchased for $485 million. The vast majority of Imbruvica's sales had come from the treatment of CLL, a condition Calquence had not yet even been approved to treat. AstraZeneca appeared to be way behind.

The money used to settle the litigation with AbbVie and J&J came out of the pockets of the Acerta shareholders. The settlement cleared the way for AstraZeneca to make the second half of its payment to them. After accounting for the associated costs, Acerta would end up being sold for a total of $6.6 billion. AstraZeneca and Rothbaum agreed to break up the $2.6 billion back-end payment into three installments that stretched out to 2024.

For those who had backed a drug originally acquired from Merck for $1,000, the final financial returns were gigantic. Together, the investors had put about $500 million into Acerta and generated a return of thirteen times their money. By virtue of how much and when they invested, some, naturally, profited much more than others.

Wayne Rothbaum, who had invested $80 million of his own money in Acerta, would make $2.8 billion, thirty-five times his investment.

Acerta elevated his wealth to a whole new dimension, for which some Acerta employees could not forgive him.

Joe Edelman got the second-biggest payday. He and his Perceptive hedge fund operation turned an investment of $43 million into more than $1 billion. Putting money into Acerta, a private start-up company, became the best investment Edelman ever made, far outpacing his returns on any single publicly traded stock. He had made a significant personal investment in Acerta separate from the position held by his hedge fund, and as the biggest single investor in his hedge fund, Edelman benefited both from the compounding of his own capital plus the 25 percent of profits he charged his clients. In total, Edelman made about $700 million from Acerta. The investment transformed him from being merely rich into being a billionaire. It also helped his hedge fund's returns stand out against just about any hedge fund on the planet. Edelman's hedge fund, Perceptive Life Sciences, generated 29 percent annualized net returns from its inception in 1999 through the end of 2019. That made Edelman the best-performing hedge fund manager in the world during the period—at least when judged against human beings. His returns were better than the biggest names in the business. Only a very few computer-driven quantitative trading firms had outperformed him.

Sven Borho's OrbiMed Advisors, which had also missed out on most of the Pharmacyclics windfall by selling its stake in the company, made close to the same amount of money on Acerta as Edelman and Perceptive. But OrbiMed's entire investment had been made out of OrbiMed's venture fund.

Still, a kind of mixed feeling came over many of the people who had helped build Acerta. Even with a financial bonanza, many believed they had not received their fair share of the recognition or the financial reward. The path to success for both Pharmacyclics and Aceta was littered with forgotten scientists and entrepreneurs. It was not unusual for successful biotechnology stories to end this way, without elation or euphoria.

For her part, Raquel Izumi ended up suing Acerta and AstraZeneca, claiming she had been stripped of stock option rewards that she had earned. Without the options, Izumi still stood to make nearly $20 million on the sale of the company. The options, however, represented many millions more in proceeds. She settled her lawsuit with AstraZeneca for an undisclosed sum and continued working for the company.

Izumi watched as the development of the drug Acerta produced steadily moved forward. In November 2019, the FDA approved Calquence for the treatment of CLL. This was the big win for AstraZeneca. The approval was based on the studies Acerta had put together through the night in the W Hotel San Francisco suite. In the years since, 845 CLL patients had participated in the two randomized controlled trials. The trials showed patients treated with Calquence experiencing significantly longer progression-free survival than those who received other treatments, like chemotherapy and monoclonal antibody drugs.

Work on the head-to-head trial of Calquence against Imbruvica continued. On the surface, the position of Imbruvica seemed unassailable. As more people took the drug, the data showed that 83 percent of patients whose CLL had first been treated with Imbruvica remained alive five years later. When it came to CLL patients who had first failed a previous therapy and then started swallowing Imbruvica pills, slightly more than half of them were still alive seven years later. This survivability data kept extending as the years rolled by.

But doctors treating CLL remained intrigued with Calquence, the more selective BTK inhibitor. As the clinical trials of Imbruvica matured, the wonder drug had shown some problematic side effects, particularly cardiovascular issues like a significant increase in incidence over time of atrial fibrillation. A pooled analysis of fifteen hundred CLL and mantle cell lymphoma patients treated with Imbruvica in clinical trials showed that 10.4 percent of them reported atrial fibrillation after thirty-six months of treatment. For many of those patients, the atrial fibrillation remained manageable. But they often required blood-thinning medications to stay on Imbruvica. In addition to this side effect, there were sometimes issues with hypertension and rare reports of Imbruvica patients suffering arrhythmias and, on very seldom occasions, sudden death from cardiac causes.

At AstraZeneca and among CLL doctors, the hope was that the head-to-head trial would determine whether Calquence worked safer, or maybe even better, than its multi-billion-dollar rival. Calquence also induced side effects, like hypertension. Low-grade headaches were a side effect specific to Calquence that made it hard for some patients when they started on the drug. But the clinical trials suggested that its overall problems were more limited compared with Imbruvica, especially when it came to atrial fibrillation. As a new decade began, AstraZeneca plugged Calquence into its sales and marketing machine, trying to get it to as many CLL patients as possible. The company sold the lifesaving cancer drug for $170,000 per year. In 2019, the drug had generated $164 million, mostly in the United States, with only mantle cell lymphoma on its label.

"We now will see larger contributions from products like Calquence in CLL," Pascal Soriot, AstraZeneca's CEO, predicted on an investor call in the middle of February 2020.

EPILOGUE

Head-to-Head

Ahmed Hamdy stood in the stables at Jade's Ranch, a Santa Cruz horse farm perched on a hill with a breathtaking view of the Pacific Ocean. He had gone to visit Porsche, an aptly named fast filly he kept there, on the last Friday afternoon of March 2020. Hamdy had been around horses his entire life, going back to his childhood in Egypt, and tried to fence off time regularly to be with his pony. But on this visit, Hamdy's head was elsewhere.

Earlier in the day, Hamdy had received a call from Wyndham Wilson, the lymphoma guru at the National Cancer Institute. Over the years, Hamdy had developed a close personal relationship with Wilson. Now Wilson wanted to run an idea by him. Wilson had been conferring with his colleague, the eminent scientist Louis Staudt, and they thought that BTK inhibitors could save lives that were being lost in the nightmare COVID-19 pandemic that was now raging.

Wilson shared his reasoning that the BTK enzyme seemed to play a key role in the out-of-control immune response that caused some COVID-19 patients to become critically ill or die. Shutting down BTK in these extremely sick patients might tamp down the cytokine molecules and macrophage cells triggering this lung-damaging immune system storm.

Initially, Hamdy did not devote much time to this discussion and kept his conversation with Wilson short. He had a busy day planned and needed to get through a lot quickly to ensure he had time to get to his pony as scheduled. But now at the ranch, in the quiet moments as he groomed Porsche, Hamdy was able to pause and reflect. BTK inhibitors really did decrease inflammatory responses for some key cytokines, like interleukin-6 and interleukin-1, that seemed to drive the overzealous and destructive immune response in COVID-19 patients. His mind started to race. Hamdy called Wilson back.

"We got to do a study right away," Hamdy said.

"Hold your horses," Wilson replied.

"I am holding my horse," Hamdy shot back. "I am literally holding my horse!"

Hamdy returned home and in the evening opened a bottle of wine. Many existing therapeutic drugs were already being repurposed for possible use against the infectious virus. The entire biopharma industry had mobilized to combat this new plague, and thanks to the prior decade of financial growth, they were exceptionally well-capitalized to do so. Two highly funded biotechnology companies, BioNTech and Moderna Therapeutics, were well on their way to applying the experimental technology they had worked on for a decade to create the first two vaccines. Pascal Soriot, the CEO of AstraZeneca, would partner with the University of Oxford to develop one of the other early vaccines, and Paul Stoeffels, who had helped acquire half of Imbruvica and risen to the position of chief scientific officer at Johnson & Johnson, was leading another crucial vaccine effort at the company's Janssen unit.

As he sipped from his glass, Hamdy became emboldened. He marched to his home office, sat at his computer, and started writing an email to Soriot, laying out the potential of BTK inhibitors to help severely ill COVID-19 patients and the interest of Wilson and Staudt. The fact that Hamdy had been relegated to a supporting role in Astra-

Zeneca's operations and had no direct contact with Soriot did not slow his fingers as they typed out Soriot's email address.

"Acalabrutinib may be the drug of choice to do a randomized trial to show the benefits of BTK inhibition in the prevention of acute respiratory distress syndrome in COVID-19," Hamdy wrote.

Minutes later, Soriot replied. "Thanks, Ahmed. Fantastic idea."

Over the weekend, Staudt and Wilson had arranged for a few sick COVID-19 patients to be treated with Calquence and been encouraged by the results—a small number of patients with severe lung disease had the condition improve after taking the drug. AstraZeneca created a task force to rush the drug into a clinical trial. Hamdy and Raquel Izumi designed a study with Staudt and Wilson as the lead investigators. Izumi spent her fifty-first birthday and two straight nights whipping up a trial plan.

But over the next few days, as more AstraZeneca executives and scientists got involved in what became a high-profile project, Hamdy and Izumi started to get shoved aside. Hamdy stopped being copied on important emails and was no longer invited to key meetings. Izumi's study protocol got taken over by others and changed in ways she opposed. She was not asked to help answer the FDA's questions about the proposed trial. Izumi had successfully written the previous seven Investigational New Drug Applications for Calquence. Nobody knew BTK inhibitors better than Izumi and Hamdy—they had spent the last decade of their lives developing them and shepherding them through to blockbuster results, though the duo was time and again pushed off to the side. Izumi and Hamdy saw the same story unfolding in front of them yet again. The politics of big pharma made no sense to either of them. Together, Hamdy and Izumi unceremoniously quit their jobs at AstraZeneca.

AstraZeneca motored ahead without them, putting Calquence in two phase 2 studies of 225 hospitalized COVID-19 patients. But the patients who received Calquence did not remain free from respiratory failure at a greater rate than patients in the study's control arm. Ultimately, the trials failed.

While Calquence would not be coming to the rescue of those suffering from COVID-19, the drug quickly became popular with those it was approved for—blood cancer patients. Calquence performed extremely well in the marketplace as doctors increasingly recommended the drug to their chronic lymphocytic leukemia patients. After its first year on the US market, Calquence already represented 45 percent of all new BTK inhibitor prescriptions in CLL and about half of new prescriptions in mantle cell lymphoma, exceeding the rosiest internal forecasts AstraZeneca had put together when Soriot had first decided to buy Acerta. In 2020, Calquence generated $511 million of sales in the United States alone, with new approvals coming from Europe and Japan.

Imbruvica, however, still remained the king of the BTK inhibitor space. AbbVie and J&J recorded $6.6 billion in revenues for Imbruvica in 2020. No doctor would take patients already being successfully treated with Imbruvica off the drug and switch them to another medicine like Calquence. But Imbruvica's reign was being seriously challenged by its rival.

In January 2021, the primary results of Calquence's head-to-head trial against Imbruvica came in—the trial for which Acerta had initially struggled to obtain a supply of Imbruvica. For AstraZeneca, the outcome was a home run, if not a grand slam. The initial analysis of the trial showed that Calquence was safer than Imbruvica, causing fewer incidents of atrial fibrillation in high-risk previously treated patients, while being just as effective at staving off progression of CLL. As a result, it was easier for patients in the trial receiving Calquence to keep taking the drug, while a greater number of patients on Imbruvica had to stop treatment. After a relatively short forty months of follow-up, there were signs that patients on Calquence were living longer than patients who took Imbruvica—but the statistical significance was insufficient to determine that Calquence conferred a survival benefit over Imbruvica.

AstraZeneca used these results to convince more patients in need of a treatment for their CLL to choose Calquence. Some patients who could no longer tolerate treatment with Imbruvica were also making the switch. On Wall Street, analysts started to realize that Imbruvica's status as the market leader was not impenetrable. Indeed, by the second half of 2021, Calquence was beating Imbruvica when it came to new CLL patients. More than 50 percent of patients who started to initially treat CLL by taking a BTK inhibitor were choosing to take Calquence over Imbruvica. It had become the drug of choice for CLL patients starting treatment. In 2021, Calquence became a blockbuster drug, generating $1.2 billion in revenue. For its part, Imbruvica produced $6.9 billion in revenue in 2021.

Executives at AbbVie, who for years had insisted to Wall Street that Calquence was no threat to them, publicly acknowledged feeling the heat. AbbVie's top-selling cancer drug, Imbruvica, saw its US sales drop by 22 percent between April and June of 2022. It was clear that most of those sales had instead gone to AstraZeneca's Calquence, which generated $903 million in sales in the first half of 2022.

"Acalabrutinib (Calquence) in the market right now is doing so well. On a new patient grab basis it's over 50 percent over ibrutinib (Imbruvica)," marveled Umer Raffat, one of the most widely followed biopharma research analysts on Wall Street. "It's quite something." AbbVie responded by launching a television advertising campaign for Imbruvica.

"I think it is going to be one of our best transactions," Soriot would say about AstraZeneca's purchase of Acerta. "You have a huge pool of patients who have been on [Imbruvica] for a long time, but you have to look at new patient initiations and in that goal we are doing very well."

///////////////

FOR HIS SECOND ACT in biotechnology, Bob Duggan wanted to develop cutting-edge antibiotic treatments to fight bacteria. He invested in Achaogen, a company working on an antibiotic for urinary tract infections, and became its biggest shareholder. The FDA approved the antibiotic, but Achaogen wound up in bankruptcy court regardless and collapsed. Over its history, the company had sunk more than $350 million on research and development, but hospitals refused to buy large quantities of an antibiotic that cost as much as $14,000 for a course of treatment.

In choosing to back new antibiotics, Duggan had ventured into an area that most biopharma players carefully avoid. It was seen as a bad bet. Antibiotics can lose effectiveness and, unlike cancer therapies, usually can't command a high price.

Still, the biopharma industry's preference for backing the development of drugs that treat cancer or rare diseases has created a serious public health problem. In the United States, the Centers for Disease Control and Prevention became increasingly concerned about the rising rates of infections that are resistant to traditional antibiotic treatments, 2.8 million annually causing 35,000 deaths. The emergence of superbugs could potentially turn seemingly mundane sicknesses, like strep throat, into life-threatening events. But the lack of financial incentives for investors meant that biopharma was not working on solutions.

Duggan was not deterred by his experience with Achaogen and believed he was investing in the right space. He just needed to modify his approach. After the Achaogen defeat, Duggan invested $75 million into Summit Therapeutics, a British company working on an antibiotic for *Clostridioides difficile* infection. The contagious bacteria can grow during the course of antibiotic treatment, causing 223,900 infections and 12,800 deaths in the United States each year. At the age of seventy-six, Duggan became CEO of Summit in 2020, his first biotech executive role since Pharmacyclics. Maky Zanganeh joined Duggan in his quest, purchasing about 10 percent of Summit and becoming chief operating officer of the company, the same role she held at Pharmacyclics.

"I have lost some money in anti-infectives," Duggan said in one interview. "I believe it is a game that we can win and a game that should be played by somebody." Nevertheless, Summit's antibiotic failed its phase 3 trial.

Duggan and Zanganeh were not unique. Many of the financiers, scientists, chemists, and doctors who had helped bring Imbruvica and Calquence to blood cancer patients were channeling their efforts into finding new medicines and treatments. Part of the legacy of Pharmacyclics and Acerta would be several new biotechnology companies targeting a wide variety of medical conditions. But these companies would be facing a much harsher biotechnology environment, at least in the financial markets. The sales of Pharmacyclics and Acerta represented a high point for the great biotechnology decade of the 2010s. The bull market for biotech stocks came to an end right after investor enthusiasm around the COVID-19 vaccines faded. It could reasonably be argued that Imbruvica, half of which had been sold for $21 billion, was a financial peak of the boom.

By 2021, investors had lost their appetite for the risk of biotechnology stocks, which crashed down to earth. Joe Edelman's main Perceptive hedge fund suffered big losses, as did a fund managed by OrbiMed. With interest rates rising, financial speculators started to take a less favorable view of biotechnology companies as a new decade got underway. While it was clear that incredible progress was being made in understanding cancer and other diseases, it was less clear that new treatments would command the gigantic valuations of Imbruvica and Calquence and, in turn, whether speculative capital would continue to fund a feverish pace of drug development.

Dave Johnson managed to be one of the last guys to ring the register on the biotechnology boom of the last decade. Acerta's former interim CEO got right to work after he left AstraZeneca and founded VelosBio to develop a cancer treatment targeting the tyrosine kinase ROR1 (a pursuit Hamdy had eyed at the start of Acerta). Johnson raised nearly $200 million and put the experimental drug in promising clinical trials targeting conditions ranging from lymphoma to breast cancer before selling VelosBio to Merck for $2.75 billion in 2020.

At least there were signs that the more challenging financial environment was not dissuading those who were hooked on finding new therapies and treatments for cancer. Wayne Rothbaum expected that biotechnology investors and entrepreneurs were in for an extremely scary and bumpy ride in financial markets. But that didn't mean he wanted to sit on the sidelines. Slowly, he started to find his way once again.

Rothbaum donated at least $300 million in anonymous philanthropic contributions to Ohio State University and the State University of New York at Binghamton. With John Byrd and his patients at Ohio State who had agreed to go on the experimental Calquence trials in mind, Rothbaum earmarked some of the money to build a new apartment hotel consisting of some one hundred units. Those hotel apartments would be subsidized for cancer patients traveling to The James hospital to participate in future clinical trials. He also planned to set up a not-for-profit outfit, Simba Biologics, to work with Ohio State's veterinary medical center to repurpose human prescription drugs for dogs. At Binghamton, Rothbaum directed the money to a new sports complex, scholarships, and the launch of a synthetic biology department. As always, Rothbaum got in the weeds on these projects, and the impact they could have excited him.

When Amgen approached Rothbaum about licensing one of its experimental drugs, known as an MDM2 inhibitor, it sparked an all-too-familiar feeling in him. Amgen had been unsuccessfully shopping the drug that blocks a protein in a way that switches on a tumor suppressor gene, p53, also known as the "guardian of the genome." The idea had previously created a lot of hype in life sciences, but many of the programs had been abandoned because of the seeming lack of effectiveness and the side effects associated with the approach. The more Rothbaum looked into it, the more he thought people had prematurely given up on a promising target. The body was a biomechanical machine, and for Rothbaum, p53 was an app with a job to repair or kill damaged cells. He licensed the drug from Amgen and formed a company, Kartos Therapeutics, to figure it out.

To run Kartos, Maria Fardis suggested that Rothbaum recruit Jesse McGreivy. "He hates me, he won't speak to me," Rothbaum told her. But Fardis got the two on the phone and they reconciled, putting the fight over the stock option dilution at Acerta behind them. With McGreivy as CEO, Kartos launched trials of the drug in patients with Merkel cell carcinoma, a terrible skin cancer, and myelofibrosis, a rare blood cancer. As the work progressed, Rothbaum saw something that reminded him about the way CLL patients reacted to BTK inhibitor treatment, and it led him to a revelation.

Rothbaum started to believe that the real story of BTK inhibitors might not only be as a single-agent treatment for CLL, mantle cell lymphoma, or Waldenstrom macroglobulinemia, but as a medicine that was meant to be administered with other cell-killing drugs. BTK inhibitors were game changers by themselves in cancers like CLL. But Rothbaum thought that BTK inhibitors could play a crucial role in treating other cancers by disrupting the protective tumor microenvironment—the surrounding blood vessels, immune cells, fibroblasts, and signaling molecules—and releasing the malignant cells and making them vulnerable to a second drug that could kill them. To Rothbaum, blood cancer cells and solid tumors reside in a cavernous hell that BTK inhibitors might be able to open up, allowing angels to start slaying the cancerous demons.

Rothbaum licensed an irreversible BTK inhibitor from Merck Serono (the German company)—the same BTK inhibitor that had flashed on the screen during Rothbaum's ill-fated meeting at Pfizer's headquarters—and put the drug in a new company he called Telios Pharma. McGreivy became CEO of Telios as well, and the company launched clinical trials to test out Rothbaum's theory, combining the BTK inhibitor with Kartos' MDM2 inhibitor in diseases like myelofibrosis and acute myeloid leukemia. Telios also experimented with the BTK inhibitor alone in myelofibrosis and ophthalmology applications. Rothbaum had strong convictions about the drug in ophthalmology. John Byrd signed on to the effort by getting involved in some of the studies. As he turned fifty-three, Rothbaum backed both Kartos and Telios with a $300 million investment. Nobody seemed to believe in BTK inhibitors more than Rothbaum.

Ahmed Hamdy and Raquel Izumi had been among the first to witness the potential of BTK inhibitor drugs. They had played a major role in the development of both Imbruvica and Calquence—Izumi had written the clinical trial protocols that led to many of their regulatory approvals. But the experience had not been easy for either of them. In Duggan and Rothbaum, they had worked for two enormous and hard-charging personalities. Hamdy barely made it through intact, but he still had more to give.

At age fifty-six, he teamed up again with Izumi to start Vincerx Pharma, acquiring three drug candidates targeting different cancers. John Byrd joined them, this time not as an investigator but as a corporate cofounder. Byrd would advise on strategy and not be directly involved in any clinical trials. He was their partner.

As CEO, Hamdy merged his new company into a publicly traded special acquisition company, resulting in $60 million of financing to pursue his ideas. Hamdy and Izumi committed themselves to learn from experience and not commit any of the mistakes of the past.

"We'll make new mistakes," Hamdy told Izumi.

ACKNOWLEDGMENTS AND
A NOTE ON SOURCES

This book emerged from reporting I started while working at *Forbes*, where I became intrigued about a mystery biotech billionaire named Wayne Rothbaum. He wouldn't return my phone calls or emails, so I went searching for people who had worked with him. One of the first people I reached out to was Ahmed Hamdy. I explained to Ahmed that I wanted to tell Rothbaum's story. But after our talk I became obsessed with telling the full story of BTK inhibitors and the people who created Imbruvica and Calquence.

I flew out to California and met with Hamdy in a cafe in Santa Cruz. He had been through a lot and was hesitant to get involved in the reporting project I proposed. We spent two days together, and gradually he warmed to the idea. Ahmed introduced me to Raquel Izumi. The talks I had with them got me going on this book, and I am grateful for the many hours they spent speaking with me in the years since we first met.

This book would not have been possible without the dozens of former Pharmacyclics and Acerta employees who agreed to speak with me. They were incredibly generous with their time and reflections on events that, in many cases, had occurred years earlier. The dialogue that appears in this book comes from the recollections of people who said or heard what was spoken and in some cases from video recordings and transcripts of court proceedings or earnings presentations. I have tried to corroborate the dialogue with others.

I would also never have been able to write this book without the assistance of some of the physician-scientists who participated in the key BTK inhibitor trials, especially John Byrd and Jeff Sharman. Even though he did not fully cooperate with this project, I am very appreciative of the time Bob Duggan spent talking with me.

Wayne Rothbaum finally did return my phone calls and overcame his lifetime habit of avoiding reporters. I am deeply thankful for the many conversations we had over the course of years and for his respect for journalism principles and practices.

When writing a book about biotechnology, it is helpful to have one of the nation's top biotech journalists as a friend. I was fortunate to be able to bounce ideas off Matt Herper and receive his guidance.

To make a book like this happen, you need a champion, and mine was Eric Lupfer, my agent at Fletcher & Company. Eric believed in this project, and his confidence and enthusiasm were sometimes the only things that kept moving it forward when I encountered setbacks along the way. My editors at W. W. Norton, Tom Mayer and Nneoma Amadi-obi, spent a tremendous amount of time on this book. Their efforts made it a much better read.

Writing a book in the middle of a pandemic can be challenging. Lucky for me, I had my loving parents, Gideon and Tsipora, cheering me on as they always do. My children, Rachel and Jonah, were always supportive and excited about this project, even on weekends when I focused on this book instead of them. My wife, Carolyn, is the bravest person I know. She greets every obstacle with a determined smile and willed me to finish writing this book when I was ready to move on. Carolyn read and edited the manuscript several times and kept our lives filled with laughter and purpose. This book is a testament to her love and strength.

NOTES

CHAPTER 1: THE SURFING SCIENTOLOGIST

4   **median survival time:** Wenya Linda Bi and Rameen Beroukhim, "Beating the Odds: Extreme Long-Term Survival with Glioblastoma," *Neuro-Oncology* 16, no. 9 (September 2014): 1159–1160, https://academic.oup.com/neuro-oncology/article/16/9/1159/2509249.

5   **Scientologists believe:** Scientology.org, "What Is Scientology?" Scientology.org, accessed February 8, 2021, https://www.scientology.org/what-is-scientology/.

8   **Ralph Nader:** John D. Morris, "Cereal Monopoly by 4 Top Makers Charged by F.T.C.," *New York Times*, January 25, 1972, https://www.nytimes.com/1972/01/25/archives/cereal-monopoly-by-4-top-makers-charged-by-ftc-price-inflation-is-a.html.

8   **The complaint accused:** *Federal Trade Commission Decisions* 99 (January–June 1982): 1–151, https://www.ftc.gov/sites/default/files/documents/commission_decision_volumes/volume-99/ftc_volume_decision_99_january_-_june_1982pages_1-151_including_part_1_of_the_kellogg_case.pdf.

10   **focused on Alfred Barrios:** Self-Programmed Control Center, About Us, Spccenter.com, accessed February 2, 2021, http://www.spccenter.com/aboutus.php.

10   **hypnosis to heal cancer:** Alfred A. Barrios, "Curing Cancer through the Mind," Spccenter.com, accessed February 2, 2021, http://www.spccenter.com/cancercure.php.

10   **issued an executive directive:** L. Ron Hubbard, Genius, Executive Directive, Central Office of LRH ED 821, July 21, 1980, wiseoldgoat.com, https://www.wiseoldgoat.com/papers-scientology/popup-windows/scn_colrhed_821_800721_genius.html.

12   **$24 million of annual revenues:** Computer Motion, Inc., Form 10-K Annual Report 2002, EDGAR, Securities and Exchange Commission, March 28, 2003, https://www.sec.gov/Archives/edgar/data/906829/000089161803001500/f88391orei0vk.txt.

12   **Computer Motion lost money:** Ibid.

12   **Intuitive Surgical bought:** Intuitive Surgical, Inc., Form 10-K Annual Report 2003,

p. 3, EDGAR, Securities and Exchange Commission, March 12, 2004, https://www
.sec.gov/Archives/edgar/data/1035267/000119312504040493/d10k.htm.

12   **most important financial donor:** Brendan Coffey, "Scientology Donor Becomes
a Billionaire with Cancer Drug," Bloomberg News, January 29, 2013, https://www
.bloomberg.com/news/articles/2013-01-29/scientology-donor-becomes-a-billionaire
-with-cancer-drug.

CHAPTER 2: MAN OF SCIENCE

15   **state of Pharmacyclics' clinical trials:** Pharmacyclics, Inc., Form 10-K Annual
Report 2004, EDGAR, Securities and Exchange Commission, August 30, 2004,
https://www.sec.gov/Archives/edgar/data/949699/000094969904000030/
body10k.htm.

15   **By September 2004:** Robert W. Duggan, Form Schedule 13G, EDGAR, Securities
and Exchange Commission, September 22, 2004, https://www.sec.gov/Archives/
edgar/data/949699/000130342204000001/pc13g.txt.

16   **Idec would produce:** Charles McCoy, "New Cancer Drug, Rituxan, is Approved
by FDA Panel," *Wall Street Journal*, July 28, 1997, https://www.wsj.com/articles/
SB870048334363881500.

18   **By 2000, Pharmacyclics:** Pharmacyclics, Inc,. Form 10-K405 Annual Report
2000, pg. 2 and pg. 29, EDGAR, Securities and Exchange Commission, September
27, 2000, https://www.sec.gov/Archives/edgar/data/949699/000109581100003607/
f65849e10-k405.txt.

18   **Xcytrin failed:** Pharmacyclics, Inc., "Pharmacyclics Announces Results From Phase
3 Smart Trial of Xcytrin for Lung Cancer Brain Metastases," EDGAR, Securities and
Exchange Commission, December 19, 2005, https://www.sec.gov/Archives/edgar/
data/949699/000095013405023363/f15590exv99w1.htm.

18   **he had famously stood:** "How Diplomacy Helped to End the Race to Sequence the
Human Genome," *Nature* 582 (June 24, 2020), https://www.nature.com/articles/
d41586-020-01849-w.

18   **could be mined:** David Stipp, "Celera, the Genome, and the Fruit-Fly Lady,"
Fortune, July 10, 2000, https://archive.fortune.com/magazines/fortune/fortune_
archive/2000/07/10/283762/index.htm.

18   **To get into the drug business:** Scott Hensley, "Celera to Buy Axys for $174 Million;
Move Bolsters Drug-Production Plans," *Wall Street Journal*, June 14, 2001, https://
www.wsj.com/articles/SB992451561739433508.

19   **The industry had blossomed:** Rory J. O'Connor, "Choosing South City," Gene.
com, April 7, 2016, https://www.gene.com/stories/choosing-south-city.

19   **Genentech led the way:** Jonathan Smith, "Humble Beginnings: The Origin Story of
Modern Biotechnology," Labiotech.eu, December, 23, 2020, https://www.labiotech
.eu/synbio/history-biotechnology-genentech/.

19   **Celera would figure:** Robert Langreth, "Gene Jockeys," *Forbes*, June 22, 2001,
https://www.forbes.com/forbes/2001/0723/052.html?sh=112372d61f06.

20 **One group of these enzymes:** Manash K. Paul and Anup K. Mukhopadhyay, "Tyrosine Kinase—Role and Significance in Cancer," *International Journal of Medical Sciences* 1, no. 2 (2004): 101–115, https://www.medsci.org/v01p0101.htm.

21 **Pan had come:** Zhengying Pan, LinkedIn profile, Linkedin.com, accessed February 3, 2021, https://www.linkedin.com/in/zhengying-pan-b099151/.

25 **Miller negotiated:** Pharmacyclics, Inc., Form 10-K Annual Report 2006, EDGAR, Securities and Exchange Commission, September 12, 2006, https://www.sec.gov/Archives/edgar/data/949699/000094969906000054/body10k.htm.

CHAPTER 3: THE TAKEOVER

26 **had a reputation:** Gardiner Harris, "Where Cancer Progress Is Rare, One Man Says No," *New York Times*, September 15, 2009, https://www.nytimes.com/2009/09/16/health/policy/16cancer.html.

26 **Miller sketched out:** Richard Miller, "Drug Disaster," *Wall Street Journal*, May 10, 2007, https://www.wsj.com/articles/SB117876417452298064.

27 **A few months earlier:** Adam Feuerstein, "Pharmacyclics Needs a Fair Shake," TheStreet.com, April 26, 2007, https://www.thestreet.com/investing/stocks/pharmacyclics-needs-a-fair-shake-10353101.

27 **he wrote a second:** Richard Miller, "Cancer Regression," *Wall Street Journal*, August 1, 2007, https://www.wsj.com/articles/SB118593325021784255.

27 **Miller wrote a third:** Richard Miller, "The Biotech Bottleneck," *Wall Street Journal*, December 28, 2007, https://www.wsj.com/articles/SB119880414063654409.

28 **Duggan owned 3.9 million:** Robert W. Duggan, Form Schedule 13D, EDGAR, Securities and Exchange Commission, July 30, 2007, https://www.sec.gov/Archives/edgar/data/949699/000092189507001628/sc13d00322pha_04272007.htm.

28 **Duggan hopped onto:** Pharmacyclics, Inc., "Pharmacyclics Announces Addition of Robert W. Duggan to Board of Directors," EDGAR, Securities and Exchange Commission, September 19, 2007, https://www.sec.gov/Archives/edgar/data/949699/000094969907000035/exh99-1.htm.

28 **Three months after:** Pharmacyclics, Inc., "Pharmacyclics Receives Non-Approvable Letter from the FDA For Xcytrin For the Treatment of Lung Cancer Brain Metastases," EDGAR, Securities and Exchange Commission, December 21, 2007, https://www.sec.gov/Archives/edgar/data/949699/000094969907000046/exh99-1.htm.

28 **corporate realignment:** Pharmacyclics, Inc., "Pharmacyclics Realigns to Focus on Advancing Expanded Pipeline of Promising Product Candidates," EDGAR, Securities and Exchange Commission, February 28, 2008, https://www.sec.gov/Archives/edgar/data/949699/000094969908000008/exh99-1.htm.

32 **Investigational New Drug Application:** Nicole Verdun, Clinical Review for Application Number 205552 Original-2, Center for Drug Evaluation and Research, Food and Drug Administration, February 10, 2014, p. 18, https://www.accessdata.fda.gov/drugsatfda_docs/nda/2014/205552Orig2s000MedR.pdf.

32 **stock had now dipped:** Pharmacyclics, Inc., "Pharmacyclics Announces It Received Nasdaq Notification," EDGAR, Securities and Exchange Commission, April 21, 2008, https://www.sec.gov/Archives/edgar/data/949699/0000949699 08000015/exh99-1.pdf.

33 **To push Pharmacyclics:** RWD Acquisition I LLC, Form Schedule TO-T Tender Offer Statement, EDGAR, Securities and Exchange Commission, May 1, 2008, https://www.sec.gov/Archives/edgar/data/949699/000092189508001300/exa1itot06922002_05012008.htm.

33 **Through the tender:** Robert W. Duggan, Form Schedule 13D/A, EDGAR, Securities and Exchange Commission, June 5, 2008, https://www.sec.gov/Archives/edgar/data/949699/000092189508001683/sc13da206922002_05302008.htm.

33 **Born in Iran:** FierceBiotech, "Maky Zanganeh, Pharmacyclics," FierceBiotech, November 26, 2013, https://www.fiercebiotech.com/special-report/maky-zanganeh-pharmacyclics.

35 **now owned 29 percent:** Robert W. Duggan, Form Schedule 13D/A, EDGAR, Securities and Exchange Commission, September 17, 2008, https://www.sec.gov/Archives/edgar/data/949699/000092189508002385/sc13da406922002_08212008.htm.

35 **$322 million of operating losses:** Ramses Erdtmann and Tom Butler, "Pharmacyclics: Transformation of a Biotech Company," p. 8., Duggan Investments, 2020.

CHAPTER 4: STARTING FRESH

38 **He loaned Pharmacyclics:** Pharmacyclics, Inc., Form 10-K Annual Report 2009, EDGAR, Securities and Exchange Commission, September 22, 2009, p. 57, https://www.sec.gov/Archives/edgar/data/949699/000113626109000278/body10k.htm.

38 **Duggan found purpose:** Pharmacyclics, Inc., "Pharmacyclics Secures $5.0 Million in Debt Financing," EDGAR, Securities and Exchange Commission, January 6, 2009, https://www.sec.gov/Archives/edgar/data/949699/000113626109000005/exh99-1.htm.

40 **In February 2009:** Pharmacyclics, Inc., "Pharmacyclics Reports Second Quarter Fiscal 2009 Financial Results," EDGAR, Securities and Exchange Commission, February 13, 2009, https://www.sec.gov/Archives/edgar/data/949699/000094969909000008/exh99-1.htm.

41 **The job paid:** Pharmacyclics, Inc., Form 10-Q Exhibit 10–6, EDGAR, Securities and Exchange Commission, May 12, 2009, https://www.sec.gov/Archives/edgar/data/949699/000113626109000169/exhibit10-6.pdf.

43 **forty-six employees:** Pharmacyclics, Inc., Form 10-K 2009 Annual Report, EDGAR, Securities and Exchange Commission, September 22, 2009, p. 24, https://www.sec.gov/Archives/edgar/data/949699/000113626109000278/body10k.htm.

43 **eleven thousand people:** Genentech, Inc., Form 10-K Annual Report 2008, EDGAR, Securities and Exchange Commission, February 20, 2009, p. 10, https://

www.sec.gov/Archives/edgar/data/318771/000031877109000003/form10-k_2008
.htm.

45 **Staudt revealed the mysteries:** Francis Collins, G. Burroughs Mider Lecture Introduction, February 2017, YouTube, February 2, 2017, https://www.youtube .com/watch?v=2RwMvWiEyTg&t=401s.

46 **Pharmacyclics tried to create:** Pharmacyclics, Inc., "Pharmacyclics Initiates Phase 1 Clinical Trial of Novel Oral Btk Inhibitor for Refractory B-cell Non-Hodgkin's Lymphoma," EDGAR, Securities and Exchange Commission, April 14, 2009, https://www.sec.gov/Archives/edgar/data/949699/000113626109000138/exh99 -1.htm.

46 **one out of four dogs:** Lee Honigberg, et al., "Abstract #3740: A Clinical Trial of the Bruton's Tyrosine Kinase (Btk) Inhibitor PCI-32765 in Naturally Occurring Canine Lymphoma," *American Association for Cancer Research* 69, no. 9 (May 2009), Supplement, https://cancerres.aacrjournals.org/content/69/9_ Supplement/3740.

47 **bought the non-US rights:** Pharmacyclics, Inc., "Pharmacyclics Announces Global Strategic Alliance with Les Laboratoires Servier Pharmacyclics to Maintain All US Rights," April 22, 2009, https://www.sec.gov/Archives/edgar/ data/949699/000094969909000017/exh99-1.htm.

CHAPTER 5: WALL STREET

48 **Duggan planned on:** Pharmacyclics, Inc,. Form S-3 Registration Statement, EDGAR, Securities and Exchange Commission, June 1, 2009, https://www.sec.gov/ Archives/edgar/data/949699/000092189509001529/s307380_05282009.htm.

54 **improperly shorting:** Securities and Exchange Commission, "SEC Files Settled Action against Quogue Capital LLC and Wayne P. Rothbaum," SEC.gov, May 8, 2008, https://www.sec.gov/litigation/litreleases/2008/lr20561.htm.

54 **At $1.28 a share:** Pharmacyclics, Inc., "Pharmacyclics, Inc. Rights Offering Oversubscribed," EDGAR, Securities and Exchange Commission, August 5, 2009, https://www.sec.gov/Archives/edgar/data/949699/000092189509002201/ ex991to8k07380_08052009.htm.

54 **Duggan raised $28.8 million:** Ibid.

55 **CLL is diagnosed:** National Cancer Institute, "Cancer Stat Facts: Leukemia— Chronic Lymphocytic Leukemia (CLL)," Surveillance, Epidemiology, and End Results, accessed February 2, 2021, https://seer.cancer.gov/statfacts/html/clyl .html.

55 **186,000 Americans:** National Cancer Institute, "Cancer Stat Facts: Leukemia— Chronic Lymphocytic Leukemia (CLL)," Surveillance, Epidemiology, and End Results, accessed February 2, 2021, https://seer.cancer.gov/statfacts/html/clyl.html.

55 **The median age:** Julio Delgado and Neus Villamor, "Chronic Lymphocytic Leukemia in Young Individuals Revisited," *Haematologica* 99, no. 1 (January 2014): 4–5 , https://haematologica.org/article/view/6902.

CHAPTER 6: THE BIG EASY

59   **one of twenty-one thousand:** Walter Alexander, "American Society of Hematology, 51st Annual Meeting and Exposition," *Pharmacy and Therapeutics* 35, no. 2 (February 2010), https://www.ncbi.nlm.nih.gov/pmc/articles/PMC2827916/.

60   **The white and red poster:** Daniel A. Pollyea, et al., "A Phase I Dose Escalation Study of the Btk Inhibitor PCI-32765 in Relapsed and Refractory B Cell Non-Hodgkin Lymphoma," Poster Board III-649, American Society of Hematology, 51st Annual Meeting and Exposition, New Orleans, Louisiana, December 7, 2009.

62   **changed hands for $2.35:** PCYC stock data, Historicalstockprice.com, accessed February 5, 2021.

62   **a morning press release:** Pharmacyclics, Inc., "Pharmacyclics, Inc. Announces Presentation of Interim Results from Phase I Trial of Its First-In-Human BTK Inhibitor PCI-32765," EDGAR, Securities and Exchange Commission, December 8, 2009, https://www.sec.gov/Archives/edgar/data/949699/000092189509002866/ex992to8k07380_12062009.htm.

63   **over one million shares changed hands:** Ibid.

63   **At $37 million:** Ramses Erdtmann and Tom Butler, "Pharmacyclics: Transformation of a Biotech Company," p. 15, Duggan Investments, 2020.

66   **Duggan told the graduating class:** Robert Duggan, UCSB Commencement Exercises, Mathematical, Life, and Physical Sciences, June 2009, YouTube, May 8, 2015, https://www.youtube.com/watch?v=HZ5TofPexnA&t=392s.

66   **As he delivered:** Ibid.

66   **Staudt's team finally published:** R. Eric Davis et al., "Chronic Active B-Cell-Receptor Signalling in Diffuse Large B-Cell Lymphoma," *Nature* 463, no. 7277 (January 2010): 88–92, https://doi.org/10.1038/nature08638.

CHAPTER 7: THE NEXT PHASE

72   **"I believe 32765 is a rare":** Wayne Rothbaum, letter to Robert Duggan, February 7, 2010.

72   **Once the call began:** Pharmacyclics, Inc., "FQ2 2010 Earnings Call Transcripts," S&P Global Market Intelligence, February 11, 2010.

76   **Burger had analyzed:** Maite P. Quiroga, "B-Cell Antigen Receptor Signaling Enhances Chronic Lymphocytic Leukemia Cell Migration and Survival: Specific Targeting with a Novel Spleen Tyrosine Kinase Inhibitor, R406," *Blood* 114, no. 5 (July 20, 2009): 1029–37, https://ashpublications.org/blood/article/114/5/1029/103730/B -cell-antigen-receptor-signaling-enhances-chronic.

81   **the average clinical trial:** Mary Jo Lamberti et al., "Assessing Study Start-Up Practices, Performance, and Perceptions among Sponsors and Contract Research Organizations," *Therapeutic Innovation and Regulatory Science* 52, no. 5 (January 11, 2018): 572–578, https://journals.sagepub.com/doi/abs/10.1177/2168479017751403?jo urnalCode=dijc&.

82   **In June 2010, the company:** Pharmacyclics, Inc., Form 10-K Annual Report

2010, EDGAR, Securities and Exchange Commission, September 13, 2010, p. 60, https://www.sec.gov/Archives/edgar/data/949699/000092189510001360/form10k07380_06302010.htm.

82   **he held a 5 percent stake:** Pharmacyclics, Inc., Form DEF 14A Proxy Statement, EDGAR, Securities and Exchange Commission, November 12, 2010, p. 28, https://www.sec.gov/Archives/edgar/data/949699/000092189510001663/def14a07380_12092010.htm.

82   **leading a $40 million financing:** Calistoga Pharmaceuticals, Inc., "Calistoga Pharmaceuticals Raises $40 million In Series C Financing," BusinessWire, June 30, 2010, https://www.fiercebiotech.com/biotech/calistoga-pharmaceuticals-raises-40-million-series-c-financing.

82   **It now showed that eight:** Pharmacyclics, Inc., "Pharmacyclics Announces Presentation of Results from Phase I Trial of Its First-in-Human Btk Inhibitor: PCI-32765," EDGAR, Securities and Exchange Commission, June 7, 2010, https://www.sec.gov/Archives/edgar/data/949699/000092189510000941/ex991to8k07380_06062010.htm.

CHAPTER 8: FIRED

84   **Robert Azopardi made the short trip:** Amy Crawford, "Improving the Odds," Weill Cornell Medicine, January 6, 2016, https://news.weill.cornell.edu/news/2016/01/improving-the-odds.

84   **About four weeks:** Weill Cornell Medicine Office of External Affairs, "Taking Steps Toward the Future: Bob's Story," Weill Cornell Medicine, February 16, 2018, https://news.weill.cornell.edu/news/2018/02/taking-steps-toward-the-future-bob's-story.

86   **This time around:** Pharmacyclics, Inc. "Pharmacyclics Reports Recent Developments and Financial Results for Fiscal First Quarter 2011," EDGAR, Securities and Exchange Commission, November 8, 2010, https://www.sec.gov/Archives/edgar/data/949699/000092189510001637/ex991to8k07380_11082010.htm.

87   **The company pooled:** Pharmacyclics, Inc., "Pharmacyclics Reports CLL Results from Preclinical and Clinical Studies of its Btk Inhibitor PCI-32765," EDGAR, Securities and Exchange Commission, December 6, 2010, https://www.sec.gov/Archives/edgar/data/949699/000092189510001790/ex991to8k07380_12052010.htm.

87   **There was one catch:** Ibid.

87   **With his PhD in immunology:** IGM Biosciences, Inc., Form 8-K, EDGAR, Securities and Exchange Commission, January 28, 2021, https://www.sec.gov/Archives/edgar/data/1496323/000119312521020891/d42263d8k.htm.

87   **Baker Brothers Advisors start:** Baker Bros. Advisors, LLC, Form-13F-HR, EDGAR, Securities and Exchange Commission, February 14, 2011, https://www.sec.gov/Archives/edgar/data/1263508/000114420411008502/v210979_13fhr.txt.

87   **hovering around $6:** PCYC stock data, https//historicalstockprice.com, accessed February 8, 2021.

88   **sold most of their:** Quogue Capital, LLC, FORM SC 13G/A, EDGAR, Securities

and Exchange Commission, February 14, 2011, https://www.sec.gov/Archives/edgar/
data/949699/000110465911007299/a11-5946_3sc13ga.htm.

89   **Fewer than three thousand Americans:** Lymphoma Research Foundation, "Mantle
Cell Lymphoma Consortium Scientific Workshop," EurekAlert!, June 24, 2009,
https://www.eurekalert.org/pub_releases/2009–06/lrf-mcl062309.php.

90   **Peter Lebowitz had been:** Jonathan D. Rockoff, "Pharmaceutical Scouts Seek New
Star Drugs for Cancer, Diabetes," *Wall Street Journal*, March 9, 2014, https://www
.wsj.com/articles/SB10001424052702304703804579384871050414310.

91   **Lebowitz spent three days:** Ibid.

92   **published in *Blood*:** Sarah E. M. Herman et al., "Bruton's Tyrosine Kinase
Represents a Promising Therapeutic Target for Treatment of Chronic Lymphocytic
Leukemia and Is Effectively Targeted by PCI-32765," *Blood* 117, no. 23 (June 9, 2011):
6287–96,   https://ashpublications.org/blood/article/117/23/6287/22260/Bruton
-tyrosine-kinase-represents-a-promising.

94   **The letter of employment:** Pharmacyclics, Inc., Form 10-Q Exhibit 10–6, EDGAR,
Securities and Exchange Commission, May 12, 2009, https://www.sec.gov/Archives/
edgar/data/949699/000113626109000169/exhibit10-6.pdf.

95   **The letter added:** Ibid.

CHAPTER 9: PARTNERS

97   **The interim results of the phase 1B/2:** Pharmacyclics, Inc., "Pharmacyclics Reports
Recent Developments from Clinical Studies of Its Btk Inhibitor PCI-32765,"
EDGAR, Securities and Exchange Commission, June 6, 2011, https://www.sec.gov/
Archives/edgar/data/949699/000092189511001238/ex991t08k07380_06062011.htm.

97   **Her name was on the abstract:** J. C. Byrd, et al., "Activity and Tolerability of
the Bruton's Tyrosine Kinase (Btk) Inhibitor PCI-32765 in Patients with Chronic
Lymphocytic Leukemia/Small Cell Lymphocytic Lymphoma (CLL/SLL): Interim
Results of a Phase IB/II Study," *Journal of Clinical Oncology*, 29, no. 15 (May 2011):
suppl 6508, https://ascopubs.org/doi/10.1200/jco.2011.29.15_suppl.6508.

99   **Pharmacyclics' second-biggest shareholder:** Pharmacyclics, Inc., Form DEF 14A
Proxy Statement, EDGAR, Securities and Exchange Commission, November 14,
2011, p. 34, https://www.sec.gov/Archives/edgar/data/949699/000092189511002183/
def14a07380_12152011.htm.

100   **Zanganeh's child:** Genius, Inc., "Self-made Billionaire Bob Duggan is the Winning
Bidder Kobe Bryant Rookie Jersey," GlobeNewswire, May 26, 2021. https://www
.globenewswire.com/news-release/2021/05/26/2236641/0/en/Self-made-Billionaire-
Bob-Duggan-is-the-Winning-Bidder-Kobe-Bryant-Rookie-Jersey.html.

102   **still quite modest at $11:** Pharmacyclics, Inc., Form 10-K Annual Report 2012,
EDGAR, Securities and Exchange Commission, September 5, 2012, p. 43, https://
www.sec.gov/Archives/edgar/data/949699/000092189512001806/form10k07380
_06302012.htm.

104   **J&J bought half the future worldwide profits:** Pharmacyclics, Inc., "Pharmacyclics
Forms Pact to Develop and Commercialize PCI-32765 for Hematologic Cancers with

Janssen Biotech, Inc.," EDGAR, Securities and Exchange Commission, December 14, 2011, https://www.sec.gov/Archives/edgar/data/949699/000092189511002340/ex991t08k07380_12082011.htm.

CHAPTER 10: GOING DUTCH

108 **395 drug companies:** Meg Tirrell, Ryan Flinn, and Jeffrey McCracken, "Pharma Acquisitions Expected: J.P. Morgan Healthcare Conference for Drugmakers," Bloomberg News, January 8, 2012.

109 **Akzo Nobel sold:** Schering-Plough Corp., "Schering-Plough to Acquire Organon BioSciences," EDGAR, Securities and Exchange Commission, March 7, 2007, https://www.sec.gov/Archives/edgar/data/310158/000095012307003971/y32059exv99w1.htm.

110 **Merck did the deal:** Natasha Singer, "Merck to Buy Schering-Plough for $41.1 Billion," *New York Times*, March 9, 2009, https://www.nytimes.com/2009/03/10/business/10drug.html.

CHAPTER 11: GENIUS

116 **"I was stuck":** Robert Duggan, Robert Duggan Presentation of the 24 Characteristics of Geniuses, YouTube, February 1, 2019, https://www.youtube.com/watch?v=SCIh1Xkzh00&t=32s.

118 **counterculture roots:** Lawrence Wright, *Going Clear: Scientology, Hollywood, and the Prison of Belief* (New York: Vintage Books, 2013), p. 13.

118 **heaps of news coverage:** Richard Behar, "The Thriving Cult of Greed and Power," *Time*, June 24, 2001, http://content.time.com/time/magazine/article/0,9171,156952,00.html.

118 **mistreated its members:** Laurie Goodstein, "Defectors Say Church of Scientology Hides Abuses," *New York Times*, March 6, 2010, https://www.nytimes.com/2010/03/07/us/07scientology.html.

120 **Joshua Brumm, vice president:** Pharmacyclics, Inc., Form 8-K, EDGAR, Securities and Exchange Commission, August 20, 2013, https://www.sec.gov/Archives/edgar/data/949699/000092189513001784/form8k07380_08202013.htm.

120 **Cindy Anderson had been hired:** Cindy Anderson, LinkedIn profile, Linkedin.com, accessed February 8, 2021, https://www.linkedin.com/in/cindy-anderson-21269818/.

120 **Rebecca D'Acquisto got hired:** Rebecca D'Acquisto, LinkedIn profile, Linkedin.com, accessed February 8, 2021, https://www.linkedin.com/in/rdacquisto/.

121 **Duggan called Kunkel:** Matthew Herper, "A Lucky Drug Made Pharmacyclics' Robert Duggan a Billionaire. Will Long-Term Success Follow?" *Forbes*, May 5, 2014, https://www.forbes.com/sites/matthewherper/2014/04/16/a-lucky-drug-made-pharmacyclics-robert-duggan-a-billionaire-will-long-term-success-follow/?sh=4b62e3875cf6.

123 **designed RESONATE:** Pharmacyclics, Inc., "A Phase 3 Study of Ibrutinib versus Ofatumumab in Patients with Relapsed or Refractory Chronic Lymphocytic Leukemia (RESONATE)," ClinicalTrials.gov, US National Library of Medicine, April, 13, 2012, https://clinicaltrials.gov/ct2/show/NCT01578707.

123   **patients with 17p deletion:** Pharmacyclics, Inc., "A Multicenter Phase 2 Study of Ibrutinib in Patients with Relapsed or Refractory Chronic Lymphocytic Leukemia (CLL) or Small Lymphocytic Lymphoma (SLL) with 17p Deletion," ClinicalTrials.gov, US National Library of Medicine, December 7, 2012, https://clinicaltrials.gov/ct2/show/NCT01744691.

123   **Duggan skillfully raised:** Pharmacyclics, Inc., Form 10-Q Quarterly Report, EDGAR, Securities and Exchange Commission, May 7, 2013, p. 8, https://www.sec.gov/Archives/edgar/data/949699/000144530513001176/pcyc2013033110-q.htm.

124   **"the disposition effect":** Hersh Shefrin and Meir Statman, "The Disposition to Sell Winners Too Early and Ride Losers Too Long: Theory and Evidence," *Journal of Finance*, 40, no. 3 (July 1985): 777–90, https://onlinelibrary.wiley.com/doi/abs/10.1111/j.1540-6261.1985.tb05002.x.

CHAPTER 12: TRUFFLE PIG

129   **protest Merck's decision:** Phil Taylor, "Merck Says Sale of Oss Facility Would Be Too Expensive," Pharmafile, August 3, 2011, http://www.pharmafile.com/news/150362/merck-sale-oss-research-manufacturing-facility.

130   **generating $14.4 billion:** Merck & Co., Inc., Form 10-K Annual Report 2020, EDGAR, Securities and Exchange Commission, February 25, 2021, p. 2, https://www.sec.gov/ix?doc=/Archives/edgar/data/310158/000031015821000004/mrk-20201231.htm.

137   **The study's resulting 25 percent:** Bonnie K. Harrington et al., "Preclinical Evaluation of the Novel BTK Inhibitor Acalabrutinib in Canine Models of B-Cell Non-Hodgkin Lymphoma," *PLOS One* 11, no. 7 (July 19, 2016), https://journals.plos.org/plosone/article?id=10.1371/journal.pone.0159607.

CHAPTER 13: MASTER SWITCH

140   **O'Brien published:** Susan O'Brien, "Ibrutinib CLL Trial: Where Is the Equipoise?" *ASCO Post*, May 1, 2013, https://ascopost.com/issues/may-1-2013/ibrutinib-cll-trial-where-is-the-equipoise/.

140   **issued a response:** R. Angelo de Claro et al., "FDA on CLL Drug Approval and Expanded Access," *ASCO Post*, September 15, 2013, https://ascopost.com/issues/september-15–2013/fda-on-cll-drug-approval-and-expanded-access/.

140   **a second big RESONATE:** Pharmacyclics, Inc., "Open-Label Phase 3 BTK Inhibitor Ibrutinib vs Chlorambucil Patients 65 Years or Older with Treatment-Naive CLL or SLL," ClinicalTrials.gov, US National Library of Medicine, November 6, 2012, https://clinicaltrials.gov/ct2/show/NCT01722487.

141   **the *New England Journal of Medicine* published:** John C. Byrd et al., "Targeting BTK with Ibrutinib in Relapsed Chronic Lymphocytic Leukemia," *New England Journal of Medicine* 369 (July 4, 2013): 32–42, https://www.nejm.org/doi/full/10.1056/nejmoa1215637.

142   **soared to $123:** PCYC stock data, https//historicalstockprice.com, accessed February 9, 2021.

142   **had purchased Celera:** Krishnakali Sengupta and Rajarshi Basu, "Quest Diagnostics to Buy Celera for $657 million," Reuters, March 18, 2011, https://www.reuters .com/article/celera/update-2-quest-diagnostics-to-buy-celera-for-657-million -idUSL3E7EI1DQ20110318.

143   **Royalty Pharma, swooped in:** Quest Diagnostics, Inc., "Quest Diagnostics Sells Ibrutinib Royalty Rights to Royalty Pharma for $485 million in Cash," PR Newswire, July 18, 2013, https://www.prnewswire.com/news-releases/quest-diagnostics-sells -ibrutinib-royalty-rights-to-royalty-pharma-for-485-million-in-cash-215969291.html.

143   **The *NEJM* paper listed:** Byrd et al., "Targeting BTK with Ibrutinib in Relapsed Chronic Lymphocytic Leukemia."

143   **the final paper of the study:** Ranjana H. Advani et al., "Bruton Tyrosine Kinase inhibitor Ibrutinib (PCI-32765) Has Significant Activity in Patients with Relapsed/ Refractory B-Cell Malignancies," *Journal of Clinical Oncology* 31, no. 1 (2013): 88–94, https://ascopubs.org/doi/10.1200/JCO.2012.42.7906.

143   ***NEJM* published the promising results:** Michael L. Wang et al., "Targeting BTK with Ibrutinib in Relapsed or Refractory Mantle-Cell Lymphoma," *New England Journal of Medicine* 369 (August 8, 2013): 507–516, https://www.nejm.org/doi/full/10 .1056/nejmoa1306220.

143   **Hamdy had exercised:** Pharmacyclics, Inc., Form DEF 14A Proxy Statement, EDGAR, Securities and Exchange Commission, November 14, 2011, p. 47, https://www.sec.gov/Archives/edgar/data/949699/000092189511002183/ def14a07380_12152011.htm.

CHAPTER 14: APPROVED

150   **Pazdur's wife:** Gardiner Harris, "F.D.A. Regulator, Widowed by Cancer, Helps Speed Drug Approval," *New York Times*, January 2, 2016, https://www.nytimes .com/2016/01/03/us/politics/fda-regulator-widowed-by-cancer-helps-speed-drug -approval.html.

150   **biopharma companies would soon:** Evaluate Ltd., EvaluatePharma data, November 2020.

150   **During the meeting:** Center for Drug Evaluation and Research, "Application Number: 205552Orig2s000, Administrative and Correspondence Documents," Center for Drug Evaluation and Research, Food and Drug Administration, February 12, 2014, p. 75, https://www.accessdata.fda.gov/drugsatfda_docs/nda/2014/205552Or ig2s000AdminCorres.pdf.

151   **"In the end, the FDA":** Richard Pazdur, "How the Changing Landscape of Oncology Drug Development and Approval Will Affect Advanced Practice," transcript from JADPRO Live at Advanced Practitioner Society for Hematology and Oncology, Houston, Texas, November 2–5, 2017, https://jadproce.com/media/1090/keynote -transcript.pdf.

153   **They had arrived at a price:** Andrew Pollack, "Imbruvica, Drug to Treat Blood
      Cancer, Gains F.D.A. Approval," *New York Times*, November 13, 2013, https://www
      .nytimes.com/2013/11/14/business/drug-to-treat-blood-cancer-gains-fda-approval
      .html.

153   **granted Imbruvica accelerated approval:** Pharmacyclics, Inc., "U.S. Food and Drug
      Administration Approves IMBRUVICA (ibrutinib) as a Single Agent for Patients
      with Mantle Cell Lymphoma Who Have Received at Least One Prior Therapy,"
      EDGAR, Securities and Exchange Commission, November 13, 2013, https://www
      .sec.gov/Archives/edgar/data/949699/000092189513002233/ex991t08k07380_11132013
      .htm.

153   **$131,000 annual price tag:** Andrew Pollack, Imbruvica, Drug to Treat Blood
      Cancer, Gains F.D.A. Approval," *New York Times*, November 13, 2013, https://www
      .nytimes.com/2013/11/14/business/drug-to-treat-blood-cancer-gains-fda-approval
      .html.

154   **He expected $42 million:** The Superior Court of California, County of Santa
      Clara, *Michael Crum v. Pharmacyclics, Inc.*, Case no. 114cv262815, Complaint for
      Damages and Injunctive Relief, March 26, 2014, p. 3.

154   **Michael Crum, vice president:** Ibid., pp. 2–3.

154   **Ali ran an analysis:** The Superior Court of California, County of Santa Clara, *Yasser
      Ali v. Pharmacyclics, Inc.*, Case no. 114cv263241, Complaint for Damages, April 3,
      2014, p. 4.

154   **Crum, Ali's boss, argued:** The Superior Court of California, County of Santa Clara,
      Michael Crum v. Pharmacyclics, Inc., Case no. 114cv262815, Complaint for Damages
      and Injunctive Relief, March 26, 2014, p. 3.

154   **According to a lawsuit he:** Ibid., p. 4.

154   **Ali reported the situation:** The Superior Court of California, County of Santa
      Clara, *Yasser Ali v. Pharmacyclics, Inc.*, Case no. 114cv263241, Complaint for
      Damages, April 3, 2014, p. 4.

155   **On Monday morning:** The Superior Court of California, County of Santa Clara,
      Michael Crum v. Pharmacyclics, Inc., Case no. 114cv262815, Complaint for Damages
      and Injunctive Relief, March 26, 2014, pp. 4–5.

155   **According to a lawsuit Ali:** The Superior Court of California, County of Santa
      Clara, *Yasser Ali v. Pharmacyclics, Inc.*, Case no. 114cv263241, Complaint for
      Damages, April 3, 2014, pp. 4–5.

155   **While he was at home:** The Superior Court of California, County of Santa Clara,
      Michael Crum v. Pharmacyclics, Inc., Case no. 114cv262815, Complaint for Damages
      and Injunctive Relief, March 26, 2014, p. 5.

155   **Pharmacyclics generated $13.6 million:** Pharmacyclics, Inc., "Pharmacyclics
      Reports Fourth Quarter and Full Year 2013 Results," EDGAR, Securities and
      Exchange Commission, February 20, 2014, https://www.sec.gov/Archives/edgar/
      data/949699/000092189514000394/ex991t08k07380_02202014.htm.

155   **Early on in 2014:** Pharmacyclics, Inc., "Independent Data Monitoring
      Committee Recommends Phase III Study of Imbruvica (ibrutinib) versus

Ofatumumab be Stopped Early Based on Statistically Significant Improvement in Progression Free Survival and Overall Survival," EDGAR, Securities and Exchange Commission, January 7, 2014, https://www.sec.gov/Archives/edgar/data/949699/000092189514000027/form8k07380_01072014.htm.

156 **Ohio State's John Byrd:** Pharmacyclics, Inc., "U.S. Food and Drug Administration Approves Imbruvica (ibrutinib) as a Single Agent for Patients with Chronic Lymphocytic Leukemia Who Have Received at Least One Prior Therapy," EDGAR, Securities and Exchange Commission, February 12, 2014, https://www.sec.gov/Archives/edgar/data/949699/000092189514000199/ex99ıto8k07380_02122014.htm.

157 **When a *Forbes* article weighed:** Matthew Herper, "A Lucky Drug Made Pharmacyclics' Robert Duggan a Billionaire. Will Long-Term Success Follow?" *Forbes*, May 5, 2014, https://www.forbes.com/sites/matthewherper/2014/04/16/a-lucky-drug-made-pharmacyclics-robert-duggan-a-billionaire-will-long-term-success-follow/?sh=4b62e3875cf6.

157 **Duggan was approached:** Pharmacyclics, Inc., Schedule 14D-9A Solicitation Statement, EDGAR, Securities and Exchange Commission, April 17, 2015, https://www.sec.gov/Archives/edgar/data/949699/000119312515136090/d910279dsc14d9a.htm.

CHAPTER 15: DEMOTED

170 **upgraded Imbruvica's accelerated approval:** Pharmacyclics, Inc., "U.S. FDA Grants Regular (Full) Approval for Imbruvica for Two Indications," EDGAR, Securities and Exchange Commission, July 28, 2014, https://www.sec.gov/Archives/edgar/data/949699/000092189514001642/ex992to8k07380004_07282014.htm.

CHAPTER 16: BILLIONS

177 **Imbruvica data would now be featured:** Pharmacyclics, Inc., "Imbruvica (ibrutinib) Data to be Presented Across Multiple Histologies, including in Eight Oral Presentations, at 2014 American Society of Hematology (ASH) Annual Meeting," Securities and Exchange Commission, November 6, 2014, https://www.sec.gov/Archives/edgar/data/949699/000092189514002311/ex99ıto8k07380004b_11062014.htm.

178 **Café Genius:** Ramses Erdtmann and Tom Butler, "Pharmacyclics: Transformation of a Biotech Company," p. 96, Duggan Investments, 2020.

178 **La Verne Harris:** Ibid., p. 92.

178 **Back at the ASH conference:** Pharmacyclics, Inc., Schedule 14D-9A Solicitation Statement, EDGAR, Securities and Exchange Commission, April 17, 2015, https://www.sec.gov/Archives/edgar/data/949699/000119312515136090/d910279dsc14d9a.htm.

179 **The day following the conclusion:** Ibid.

179 **In a presentation he gave:** Pharmacyclics, Inc., "Pharmacyclics LLC, Company Conference Presentation," S&P Global Market Intelligence, January 12, 2015.

180 **patients often had to cough:** Joseph Walker, "Patients Struggle with High Drug

Prices," *Wall Street Journal*, December 31, 2015, https://www.wsj.com/articles/ patients-struggle-with-high-drug-prices-1451557981.

180 **In his presentation:** Pharmacyclics, Inc., "Pharmacyclics LLC, Company Conference Presentation," S&P Global Market Intelligence, January 12, 2015.

180 **Duggan took this script:** Pharmacyclics, Inc., Schedule 14D-9A Solicitation Statement, EDGAR, Securities and Exchange Commission, April 17, 2015, https:// www.sec.gov/Archives/edgar/data/949699/000119312515136090/d910279dsc14d9a .htm.

181 **he had falsely claimed:** Andrew L. Wang, "Abbott Spinoff CEO Lacks Claimed Degrees," *Crain's Chicago Business*, September 27, 2012, https://www.chicagobusiness .com/article/20120927/NEWS03/120929788/abbott-spinoff-ceo-to-be-gonzalez -lacks-claimed-university-degrees.

181 **spent only four months:** Andrew L. Wang, "AbbVie Chief Gonzalez Only Briefly Attended School That Supposedly Issued Master's," *Crain's Chicago Business*, October 2, 2012, https://www.chicagobusiness.com/article/20121002/ NEWS03/121009946/abbvie-chief-gonzalez-only-briefly-attended-school-that -supposedly-issued-master-s.

181 **Gonzalez was diagnosed:** Cynthia Koons, "Bored by Golf and Cancer Cured, AbbVie CEO Came Back to Work," Bloomberg News, March 5, 2015, https:// www.bloomberg.com/news/articles/2015-03-05/bored-by-golf-and-cured-of-cancer -abbvie-ceo-came-back-for-more.

181 **Gonzalez informed the company:** Wang, "AbbVie Chief Gonzalez Only Briefly Attended School that Supposedly Issued Master's."

181 **Abbott initially said:** Wang, "Abbott Spinoff CEO Lacks Claimed Degrees."

181 **He earned over $20 million:** AbbVie, Inc., Form DEF 14A Proxy Statement, EDGAR, Securities and Exchange Commission, March 20, 2015, p. 33, https://www .sec.gov/Archives/edgar/data/1551152/000104746915002548/a2222986zdef14a.htm.

182 **In one year:** AbbVie, Inc., Form 10-K Annual Report, EDGAR, Securities and Exchange Commission, February 16, 2018, https://www.sec.gov/Archives/edgar/ data/1551152/000155115218000014/abbv-20171231x10k.htm.

182 **upcoming wedding:** "Dear Spotlight Chantel Gia," *Modern Luxury*, June 2014, http://digital.modernluxury.com/publication/?i=211841&article_id=1725631&view= articleBrowser&ver=html5.

182 **He first met with Bob Duggan:** Pharmacyclics, Inc., Schedule 14D-9A Solicitation Statement, EDGAR, Securities and Exchange Commission, April 17, 2015, https:// www.sec.gov/Archives/edgar/data/949699/000119312515136090/d910279dsc14d9a.htm.

182 **Bloomberg News reported that Pharmacyclics:** Manuel Baigorri, Dinesh Nair, and Ed Hammond, "Pharmacyclics Weighs Sale of $15 Billion U.S. Drugmaker," Bloomberg News, February 15, 2015, https://www.bloomberg.com/news/ articles/2015-02-25/pharmacyclics-said-to-weigh-sale-of-15-billion-u-s-drugmaker.

182 **Back in Silicon Valley:** Pharmacyclics, Inc., Schedule 14D-9A Solicitation Statement, EDGAR, Securities and Exchange Commission, April 17, 2015, https://www.sec.gov/ Archives/edgar/data/949699/000119312515136090/d910279dsc14d9a.htm.

183   **AbbVie had agreed to buy:** Abbvie, Inc., "AbbVie to Acquire Pharmacyclics, including Its Blockbuster Product Imbruvica, Creating an Industry Leading Hematological Oncology Franchise," PR Newswire, March 4, 2015, https://www.prnewswire.com/news-releases/abbvie-to-acquire-pharmacyclics-including-its-blockbuster-product-imbruvica-creating-an-industry-leading-hematological-oncology-franchise-300045951.html.

183   **Bank of Montreal's Alex Arfaei:** Tracy Staton, "AbbVie Paid a 'Lofty,' 'Staggering,' 'Astronomical' Price for Pharmacyclics. But Was It Too Much?" FiercePharma, March 6, 2015, https://www.fiercepharma.com/financials/abbvie-paid-a-lofty-staggering-astronomical-price-for-pharmacyclics-but-was-it-too-much.

183   *New York Times* **ran a headline:** Robert Cyran, "Why AbbVie May Have Overpaid for Cancer Drug Maker," *New York Times*, March, 6, 2015, https://www.nytimes.com/2015/03/06/business/dealbook/why-abbvie-may-have-overpaid.html.

184   **Adam Feuerstein, a popular:** Adam Feuerstein, "AbbVie Spending Historic Amount of Cash to Buy Half of a Cancer Drug," TheStreet.com, March 5, 2015, https://www.thestreet.com/investing/stocks/abbvie-spending-historic-amount-of-cash-to-buy-half-of-a-cancer-drug-13068252.

184   **Maky Zanganeh's Pharmacyclics share:** Pharmacyclics, Inc., Form DEF 14A Proxy Statement, EDGAR, Securities and Exchange Commission, April 8, 2014, https://www.sec.gov/Archives/edgar/data/949699/000119312514135670/d692301ddef14a.htm.

184   **Baker Brothers hedge fund:** Baker Bros. Advisors, LLC, Form-13F-HR, EDGAR, Securities and Exchange Commission, May 15, 2015, https://www.sec.gov/Archives/edgar/data/1263508/000114420415031569/xslForm13F_X01/infotable.xml.

185   **Gonzalez defended:** AbbVie, Inc., "AbbVie to Acquire Pharmacyclics Conference Call," Thomson Reuters StreetEvents, March 5, 2015.

186   **Duggan had bet:** Robert W. Duggan, Form Schedule 13D/A, EDGAR, Securities and Exchange Commission, March 9, 2015, https://www.sec.gov/Archives/edgar/data/949699/000092189515000567/sc13da807380004_03042015.htm.

CHAPTER 17: THE WHIRLWIND

191   **The study had been expanded:** Acerta Pharma, BV, "ACP-196 (Acalabrutinib), a Novel Bruton Tyrosine Kinase (Btk) Inhibitor, for Treatment of Chronic Lymphocytic Leukemia," ClinicalTrials.gov, US National Library of Medicine, January 8, 2014, https://clinicaltrials.gov/ct2/show/NCT02029443.

192   **Johnson wrote a letter:** David Johnson, letter to Peter Aurup and Craig Tendler, July 14, 2015.

192   **J&J and AbbVie wrote back:** Peter Aurup and Craig Tendler, letter to David Johnson, July 30, 2015.

193   **The son of a tax collector:** Andrew Ward, "Pascal Soriot on His Rise To Become CEO of AstraZeneca," *Financial Times*, January 21, 2016, https://www.ft.com/content/39020eb0-b627-11e5-b147-e5e5bba42e51.

199   **patents that had just been assigned:** Lee Honigberg, Erik J. Verner, et al., Granted

July 14, 2015, *Inhibitors of Bruton's Tyrosine Kinase*, US Patent 9,079,908, US Patent and Trademark Office, https://patents.google.com/patent/US9079908B2/en.

199 **July and September of 2015:** Lee Honigberg, Erik J. Verner, et al., Granted September 22, 2015, *Inhibitors of Bruton's Tyrosine Kinase*, US Patent 9,139,591, US Patent and Trademark Office, https://patents.google.com/patent/US9139591B2/en.

CHAPTER 18: A BIOTECH ODYSSEY

202 **published the results:** John C. Byrd et al., "Acalabrutinib (ACP-196) in Relapsed Chronic Lymphocytic Leukemia," *New England Journal of Medicine* 374 (January 28, 2016): 323–32, https://www.nejm.org/doi/full/10.1056/nejmoa1509981.

203 **"Who would have thought":** Brian Koffman, "2015 ASH: Dr. John Byrd Discusses ACP 196 or Acalabrutinib, a New BTK Inhibitor," CLL Society, June 6, 2016, https://cllsociety.org/2016/06/2015-ash-dr-john-byrd-discusses-acp-196-acalabrutinib-new-btk-inhibitor/.

205 **Two days into the negotiation:** Dana Mattioli, Jonathan D. Rockoff, and Dana Cimilluca, "AstraZeneca in Talks to Buy Cancer Drug Developer Acerta Pharma," *Wall Street Journal*, December 11, 2015, https://www.wsj.com/articles/astrazeneca-in-talks-to-buy-cancer-drug-developer-acerta-pharma-1449856603.

208 **AstraZeneca announced it had struck:** AstraZeneca PLC., "AstraZeneca Enhances Long-Term Growth through Oncology Investment in Acerta Pharma," AstraZeneca.com, December 17, 2015, https://www.astrazeneca.com/media-centre/press-releases/2015/AstraZeneca-enhances-long-term-growth-through-Oncology-investment-in-Acerta-Pharma.html.

209 **the party at the Exploratorium:** Sasha Damouni, Doni Bloomfield, and Caroline Chen, "At Biotech Party, Gender Diversity Means Cocktail Waitresses," Bloomberg News, January 13, 2016, https://www.bloomberg.com/news/articles/2016-01-13/at-biotech-party-gender-diversity-means-cocktail-waitresses.

CHAPTER 19: GRADUATION DAY

214 **"I used to believe":** Raquel Izumi, UCSB Commencement Exercises, Mathematical, Life, and Physical Sciences, June 2017, YouTube, September 8, 2017, https://www.youtube.com/watch?v=90WcAWxl2bM.

215 **the FDA approved acalabrutinib:** Food and Drug Administration, "FDA Grants Accelerated Approval to Acalabrutinib for Mantle Cell Lymphoma," FDA.gov, October 31, 2017, https://www.fda.gov/drugs/resources-information-approved-drugs/fda-grants-accelerated-approval-acalabrutinib-mantle-cell-lymphoma.

215 **It was one of fourteen:** Evaluate Ltd., EvaluatePharma data, November 2020.

215 **AbbVie's Pharmacyclics immediately sued:** The US District Court for the District of Delaware, *Pharmacyclics LLC v. Acerta Pharma B.V., et al.*, Case no. 1:17-cv-01582, Complaint for Patent Infringement, November 3, 2017.

216 **Acerta sue Pharmacyclics:** The US District Court for the District of Delaware, *Acerta Pharma B.V., et al., v. Pharmacyclics LLC, and AbbVie, Inc.*, Case no. 1:18-cv-00581, Complaint for Patent Infringement, April 18, 2018.

216 **Bob Duggan had recently purchased:** Nathan Donato-Weinstein, "Exclusive: Holy City, a 142-Acre Ghost Town Near Los Gatos, is sold to Billionaire Couple," *Silicon Valley Business Journal,* August 8, 2016, https://www.bizjournals .com/sanjose/news/2016/08/08/exclusiveholy-city-a-142-acre-ghost-town-near -los.html.

217 **Duggan's contributions:** Tracey McManus, "The Man Who Gave Scientology $360 Million Actually Answered the Phone," *Tampa Bay Times,* November 22, 2019, https://www.tampabay.com/news/business/2019/11/22/the-man-who-gave -scientology-360-million-actually-answered-the-phone/.

220 **AstraZeneca researchers uncovered:** Retraction Watch, "Early Data on Potential Anti-Cancer Compound Now in Human Trials Was Falsified, Company Admits," *Retraction Watch,* October 5, 2017, https://retractionwatch.com/2017/10/05/early -data-potential-anti-cancer-compound-now-human-trials-falsified-company -admits/.

221 **eleven FDA approvals:** AbbVie, Inc., "Imbruvica (Ibrutinib) Receives 11th FDA Approval," AbbVie.com, April 21, 2020, https://news.abbvie.com/news/press -releases/imbruvica-ibrutinib-receives-11th-fda-approval.htm.

221 **More than two hundred thousand:** AbbVie, Inc., "Imbruvica (Ibrutinib) U.S. Prescribing Information Updated to Include Long-Term Data for Waldenstrom's Macroglobulinemia (WM)," AbbVie.com, December 23, 2020, https://news.abbvie .com/news/press-releases/imbruvica-ibrutinib-us-prescribing-information-updated -to-include-long-term-data-for-waldenstrms-macroglobulinemia-wm.htm.

221 **as a first-line CLL therapy:** AbbVie, Inc., "Imbruvica (Ibrutinib) Approved by U.S. FDA for First-Line Treatment of Chronic Lymphocytic Leukemia," AbbVie. com, March 4, 2016, https://news.abbvie.com/news/imbruvica-ibrutinib-approved -by-us-fda-for-first-line-treatment-chronic-lymphocytic-leukemia.htm.

222 **Evaluate Pharma predicted:** Karen Pomeranz, Karen Sirlwardana, and Freya Davies, "Orphan Drug Report 2020," EvaluatePharma, 2020, p. 4.

222 **Pablo Legorreta's Royalty Pharma:** Royalty Pharma Plc., Form 424B4 Prospectus, EDGAR, Securities and Exchange Commission, June 17, 2020, p. 100, https:// www.sec.gov/Archives/edgar/data/1802768/000119312520171165/d862976d424b4 .htm.

224 **the FDA approved Calquence:** AstraZeneca, Plc., "Calquence Approved in the US for Adult Patients with Chronic Lymphocytic Leukaemia," AstraZeneca.com, November 21, 2019, https://www.astrazeneca.com/media-centre/press-releases/2019/ calquence-approved-in-the-us-for-adult-patients-with-chronic-lymphocytic -leukaemia-21112019.html.

224 **As more people took the drug:** Jan A. Burger, "Treatment of Chronic Lymphocytic Leukemia," *New England Journal of Medicine* 383 (July 30, 2020): 460–73, https:// www.nejm.org/doi/full/10.1056/NEJMra1908213.

224 **A pooled analysis:** Jennifer R. Brown, "Characterization of Atrial Fibrillation Adverse Events Reported in Ibrutinib Randomized Controlled Registration Trials," *Haematologica* 102 (October 2017): 1796–1805, https://haematologica.org/article/view/8228.

224 **there were sometimes issues:** Burger, "Treatment of Chronic Lymphocytic Leukemia."

225 **the drug had generated:** AstraZeneca, Plc., "AstraZeneca PLC (AZN) Q4 2019 Earnings Call Transcripts," *The Motley Fool*, February 14, 2020, https://www.fool .com/earnings/call-transcripts/2020/02/14/astrazeneca-plc-azn-q4-2019-earnings -call-transcri.aspx.

EPILOGUE: HEAD-TO-HEAD

229 **the patients who received:** AstraZeneca, Plc., "Update on CALAVI Phase II Trials for Calquence in Patients Hospitalised with Respiratory Symptoms of Covid-19," AstraZeneca.com, November 12, 2020, p. 13, https://www.astrazeneca.com/ media-centre/press-releases/2020/update-on-calavi-phase-ii-trials-for-calquence-in -patients-hospitalised-with-respiratory-symptoms-of-covid-19.html.

230 **Calquence already represented:** AstraZeneca, Plc., "H1 2021 Results," AstraZeneca. com, July 21, 2021, https://www.astrazeneca.com/content/dam/az/PDF/2021/h1 -2021/H1_2021_results_presentation.pdf.

230 **$6.6 billion in revenues:** Royalty Pharma Plc, Form 10-K Annual Report, EDGAR, Securities and Exchange Commission, February 24, 2021, https://www.sec.gov/ ix?doc=/Archives/edgar/data/1802768/000180276821000006/rprx-20201231.htm.

230 **The initial analysis of the trial:** AstraZeneca, Plc., "Calquence Met Primary Efficacy Endpoint in Head-to-Head Trial against Ibrutinib in Chronic Lymphocytic Leukemia," AstraZeneca.com, January 25, 2021, https://www.astrazeneca.com/ media-centre/press-releases/2021/calquence-met-primary-endpoint-against -ibrutinib.html.

231 **On Wall Street, analysts started:** Angus Liu, "AstraZeneca Touts Calquence Safety Win against Imbruvica in Leukemia Trial Showdown," FiercePharma, January 25, 2021, https://www.fiercepharma.com/marketing/astrazeneca-touts-safer-calquence -against-imbruvica-leukemia-trial-showdown.

231 **More than 50 percent of patients:** AstraZeneca, Plc., "Year to date and Q3 2021 Results," AstraZeneca.com, November 12, 2021, https://www.astrazeneca.com/ content/dam/az/PDF/2021/q3/Year-to-date_and_Q3_2021_results_presentation .pdf.

231 **$1.2 billion in revenue:** AstraZeneca, Plc, "Full-Year and Q4 2021 Results," AstraZeneca.com, February 10, 2022, https://www.astrazeneca.com/content/dam/ az/PDF/2021/full-year/Full-year-2021-results-presentation.pdf.

231 **$6.9 billion in revenue:** Royalty Pharma Plc, Form 10-K Annual Report, EDGAR, Securities and Exchange Commission, February 15, 2022, https://www.sec.gov/ ix?doc=/Archives/edgar/data/1802768/000180276822000011/rprx-20211231.htm.

231 **Executives at AbbVie:** Ned Pagliarulo, "AbbVie Cancer Drug Sales Fall as AstraZeneca Competitor Gains Ground," BioPharma Dive, July 29, 2022, https:// www.biopharmadive.com/news/astrazeneca-abbvie-imbruvica-calquence-cll- market-sales/628442/.

231   **For his second act:** Nathan Vardi, "Billionaire Robert Duggan's New Biotech
       Chapter: An Antibiotics Quest," *Forbes*, February 27, 2020, https://www.forbes
       .com/sites/nathanvardi/2020/02/27/billionaire-robert-duggans-new-biotech
       -chapter-an-antibiotics-quest/?sh=3db30cfa161c.

232   **the Centers for Disease Control:** Centers for Disease Control and Prevention,
       "Antibiotic/Antimicrobial Resistance (AR/AMR)," CDC.gov, accessed February 22,
       2021, https://www.cdc.gov/drugresistance/index.html.

232   **After the Achaogen defeat:** Vardi, "Billionaire Robert Duggan's New Biotech
       Chapter: An Antibiotics Quest."

233   **VelosBio to Merck:** Merck & Co., Inc., "Merck to Acquire VelosBio," Merck.com,
       November 5, 2020, https://www.merck.com/news/merck-to-acquire-velosbio/.

236   **Hamdy merged his new company:** Vincera Pharma, Inc., "Vincera Pharma
       Announces Completion of Business Combination and Listing on Nasdaq,"
       Global Newswire, January 5, 2021, https://www.globenewswire.com/news
       -release/2020/12/23/2150106/0/en/Vincera-Pharma-Announces-Completion-of
       -Business-Combination-and-Listing-on-Nasdaq.html.

INDEX

Rothbaum, Wayne (*continued*)
 philanthropic donations by, 233–34
 profits from sale of Acerta, 222–23
 receives letter from FDA, 175
 Salva and, 112–13, 126
 sells Pharmacyclics shares, 88
 spooked by Pharmacyclics' data, 87–88
 Telios Pharma and, 235
 Topper and, 171–72
 translational science and, 52–53
 Van Wezel and, 114–15
Roussel Uclaf, 193
Royalty Pharma, 143, 221

Salva, Francisco, 37, 39, 48, 49, 93, 106,
 107–8, 112–13, 126, 131, 133, 134,
 162–63
ScH 2046835, 110. *See also* ACP-196
 (Aspire Covalution Pharma-196)
Schering-Plough, 109, 110
Scientology, 4, 5, 9–10, 32, 39, 116,
 117–20, 148, 217–18. *See also*
 Church of Scientology
Securities and Exchange Commission
 (SEC), 54
self-actualization, 10
serious adverse events, 159–60
Sessler, Jonathan, 17–18
Sharman, Jeff, 56–58, 60–61, 75, 76,
 85–86, 87, 88–90, 143
Sheldon, Chris, 189, 194, 195, 196, 205
Silicon Valley, ix–x, 130–31
Simba Biologics, 234
solid tumor cancers, 190, 194, 235
Soriot, Pascal, 193–97, 199–200, 203,
 205–6, 208, 219, 225, 228–29, 231
Sprengeler, Paul, 21–22
Stanford Medical Center, 16–17, 22–23,
 30, 39, 44
start-ups, 130–31
 biotech start-ups, 108, 131
 preferred shares vs. common shares,
 206–7

venture capitalist funding and, 206–7
State University of New York at Bingham-
 ton, 234
Staudt, Louis "Lou," 45–46, 66–67, 92,
 227, 229
sticky covalent compounds, 29–30. *See
 also* covalent compounds
Stoffels, Paul, 90–91, 103–4, 184–85,
 228
Summit Therapeutics, 232
Sunset Designs, 8, 9
SuperGen, 64–65
Syk, 56
Syk inhibitor drug, 76

Tagrisso (osimertinib), 219
Tang, Kevin, 208–9
Telios Pharma, 235
texaphryns, 17, 18, 28–29
Thomson Corporation, 51
Tiger Global Management, 133
Topper, James, 171–72
translational science, 52–53
Travolta, John, 119
Trout Group, 102
Trout group, 48
tumor cells, radiation and, 17
Turalski, Thomas, 48, 49, 51, 54, 59–60,
 98, 114, 126–27, 133–34, 135, 169
tyrosine kinase inhibitors, 20, 24, 215.
 See also BTK inhibitors
tyrosine kinases, 129, 233
tyrosine-protein kinase transmembrane
 receptor, 126–27

UCLA, 7–8
Ulrich, Roger, 166
University of California–Santa Barbara, 6,
 7, 11, 65–66, 214–15
University of California–Santa Barbara
 Foundation, 11, 214
University of Oxford, 228
US Patent and Trademark Office, 40